Paul Robeson

Revolutionary Lives

Series Editors: Sarah Irving, University of Edinburgh;
Professor Paul Le Blanc, La Roche College, Pittsburgh

Revolutionary Lives is a series of short, critical biographies of radical figures from throughout history. The books are sympathetic but not sycophantic, and the intention is to present a balanced and, where necessary, critical evaluation of the individual's place in their political field, putting their actions and achievements in context and exploring issues raised by their lives, such as the use or rejection of violence, nationalism, or gender in political activism. While individuals are the subject of the books, their personal lives are dealt with lightly except insofar as they mesh with political concerns. The focus is on the contribution these revolutionaries made to history, an examination of how far they achieved their aims in improving the lives of the oppressed and exploited, and how they can continue to be an inspiration for many today.

Also available:

Salvador Allende:
Revolutionary Democrat
Victor Figueroa Clark

Hugo Chávez:
Socialist for the Twenty-first Century
Mike Gonzalez

Frantz Fanon
Philosopher of the Barricades
Peter Hudis

Leila Khaled:
Icon of Palestinian Liberation
Sarah Irvin

Jean Paul Marat:
Tribune of the French Revolution
Clifford D. Conner

Sylvia Pankhurst:
Suffragette, Socialist and Scourge of Empire
Katherine Connelly

Percy Bysshe Shelley:
Poet and Revolutionary
Jacqueline Mulhallen

Ellen Wilkinson:
From Red Suffragist to Government Minister
Paula Bartley

Gerrard Winstanley:
The Digger's Life and Legacy
John Gurney

www.revolutionarylives.co.uk

Paul Robeson

The Artist as Revolutionary

Gerald Horne

PlutoPress
www.plutobooks.com

First published 2016 by Pluto Press
345 Archway Road, London N6 5AA

www.plutobooks.com

Copyright © Gerald Horne 2016

The right of Gerald Horne to be identified as the author of this work has been
asserted by him in accordance with the Copyright, Designs and Patents Act 1988.

British Library Cataloguing in Publication Data
A catalogue record for this book is available from the British Library

ISBN	978 0 7453 3531 5	Hardback
ISBN	978 0 7453 3532 2	Paperback
ISBN	978 1 7837 1755 2	PDF eBook
ISBN	978 1 7837 1757 6	Kindle eBook
ISBN	978 1 7837 1756 9	EPUB eBook

This book is printed on paper suitable for recycling and made from fully managed
and sustained forest sources. Logging, pulping and manufacturing processes are
expected to conform to the environmental standards of the country of origin.

Typeset by Stanford DTP Services, Northampton, England

Simultaneously printed in the European Union and United States of America

Contents

1

"The Best Known American in the World"

Paul Robeson—activist, artist, athlete—experienced a dramatic rise and fall, perhaps unparalleled in U.S. history. From consorting with the elite of London society and Hollywood in the 1930s, by the time he died in 1976, he was a virtual recluse in a plain abode in a working-class neighborhood of Philadelphia.

What helps to explicate this tragic arc of his life is a fateful decision he made when fascism was rising: he threw in his lot with those battling for socialism and decided to sacrifice his thriving artistic career on behalf of the struggle against Jim Crow—or U.S. apartheid.

He was a forerunner of the likes of Malcolm X and Dr. Martin Luther King, Jr. In fact, one cannot begin to understand the lives and trajectories of those two men without considering Robeson. Like Malcolm, he was a militant: a turning point in his dramatic fall was when he confronted President Harry S. Truman face-to-face in the White House, berating him because of the lynching of African-Americans and Washington's lassitude in confronting same. However, because Robeson was multilingual and lived abroad for years, he was able to develop a global appeal that dwarfed what the Muslim Minister only sought to accomplish in the final months of his life. Like Dr. King he had a mass appeal among African-Americans. But, unlike this Nobel Laureate, Robeson was not only an artist whose performances stirred emotions and fealty worldwide, he was also allied with a then rising socialist left and allied trade unions (both of which too had global ties), providing this performer with a reach that even Dr. King at his height found difficult to match.

The argument of this book is that you cannot fully appreciate how the Jim Crow system came to an end without an understanding of the life of Paul Robeson. Robeson pioneered the struggle against Jim Crow throughout the 1930s and 1940s. It was only with Robeson's fall that King and Malcolm could emerge as they did; the undermining of Robeson created a vacuum that these two leaders filled.

* * *

It was early 1952 and legions from Nelson Mandela's African National Congress were on the march in Johannesburg. But what struck the journalist covering this anti-apartheid demonstration was the singing voice pouring forth from loudspeakers, as thousands strode forcefully: it was Paul Robeson's.[1] This was an act of defiance in that the authorities there had banned his recordings as early as 1949.[2] "They sing their songs of protest," chortled Robeson then, "including some of mine, may I modestly add."[3]

The novelist Howard Fast wrote with accuracy during this era that "there is no child in Eastern Europe who cannot sing you one of the favorite songs of Paul Robeson . . . ."[4] Yet another journalist striding through Jerusalem a few years later was struck to hear Robeson's voice emerging from the window of a sidewalk abode.[5] In 1957, Robeson's wife commented that "his records are played regularly by popular demand over [the BBC] . . . over national networks and in public places in Europe, the Soviet Union, China, in Asia and Africa. A friend told us only a few days ago that he had been in a supermarket in Mexico recently and heard Paul singing 'Ol' Man River.'"[6] Two years later, Nobel Laureate Pablo Neruda ecstatically told Robeson that "the whole people of Chile love you" but his homeland was not alone since "Peru, Argentina, Bolivia, Brazil" were of a like mind. "Everywhere you are admired," he insisted.[7]

Less than a decade later in 1968 Robeson's birthday was celebrated widely in China and, it was said, deemed to be "an event of major international significance," not simply because of his socialist beliefs but because his artistry ranked him alongside "Caruso and Chaliapin as a singer . . . ."[8]

Born in 1898, Paul Leroy Robeson, a descendant of enslaved Africans in the U.S., was globally renowned—not just as a singer but as an actor and athlete and political activist. As a singer and actor, he was as celebrated as Michael Jackson and Denzil Washington would be; as an athlete, he was as illustrious as Mario Balotelli; as an activist, he carried the moral weight of Nelson Mandela.

He was "probably the most famous living Negro" said the tribune of the U.S. elite, *TIME* magazine in 1943.[9] No, said an admiring reporter in 1964, upping the ante, as he termed him "the best known American in the world."[10] The more reserved Nobel Laureate, Linus Pauling, called him simply "one of the greatest men of the twentieth century . . . ."[11] The more reserved *New Statesman* said in 1936: "he is one of the most impressive actors alive."[12] Coretta Scott King, the widow of Dr. Martin Luther King, Jr., was among those acclaiming him upon his death in 1976, calling him "one of the finest artists, most brilliant minds and greatest champions of human rights that has lived in this century."[13] The Trinidadian intellectual, C.L.R. James, who collaborated with him on a remarkable play in London about the Haitian Revolution, asserted in 1983, "I do not believe that any human being in the twentieth century . . . achieved the world-wide fame and recognition that Paul Robeson did."[14]

The top [American] football coach, Lou Little, said of Robeson, "there has never been a greater player in the history of football . . . ."[15] Robeson's skills on the gridiron were so advanced and involving, as it did, hand-to-hand combat and fancy footwork, that he was seriously approached to fight then heavyweight boxing champion, Jack Dempsey.[16] An acquaintance of Gene Tunney, the man who had bested Dempsey in the ring, recalled his saying that the next heavyweight boxing champion of the world could be, "if he wanted it, a young man named Paul Robeson."[17]

The razor-sharp reflexes of the burly 6ft 3ins Robeson, whose weight was well above 230 pounds, convinced boxing promoters that he would have acquitted himself well in the ring. Similar qualities he possessed—cat-like quickness combined with muscular brute force—also allowed Robeson to state credibly and modestly, "I was pretty good at basketball."[18]

Yet, it was left to Robeson's comrade—the Father of Pan-Africanism, W.E.B. Du Bois—who in the 1950s, called Robeson "without doubt" the "best known American on earth" in that "his voice is known in Europe, Asia and Africa, in the West Indies and South America and in the islands of the seas. Children on the streets of Peking and Moscow, Calcutta and Jakarta greet him and send him their love." Yet, with all this, there was a reigning anomaly: "only in his native land is he without honor and rights."[19]

The reason was simple: after U.S.–USSR relations plummeted post-1945, Robeson refused to join the consensus. His view was that just as the two powers collaborated against the ultra-right from 1941–45, this engagement should continue thereafter in pursuit of the apartheid backers at home and abroad and the colonialists too, while Washington did not agree.

But Robeson was part of a larger African-American consensus. His nineteenth-century African-American predecessor as a pre-eminent tragedian and interpreter of Shakespeare—Ira Aldridge (who fled the U.S. and became a British subject)[20]—also felt more comfortable in Russia: it was his "second homeland", says his biographer, probably because like Eastern Europe generally, where he too spent a considerable amount of time, there "they were not interested in perpetuating the vestiges of [African] slavery",[21] the normalized pattern in the U.S.

The intersection of U.S. "Jim Crow laws"—or apartheid—with Robeson's globetrotting, which introduced him to sharply diverging realities, also played a role in his persecution. "Typical of American artists," he observed in 1963, "I had to go abroad to really make it on the 'big time'" and it was abroad that he encountered a new world. "I found little color prejudice in Spain, in the Scandinavian countries and none at all in the Soviet Union. Naturally this freedom from color consciousness attracted me and still does," but this attraction infuriated many in his homeland where finding anything positive to say about Moscow was seen as being not only improper and immoral but, perhaps, a sign of mental derangement.[22]

Moreover, Robeson refused to cut his views to fit prevailing fashion. "I'm a Marxist," he told a New Zealand journalist in 1960.[23] "I'm a convinced socialist," he informed an Australian questioner during that same year.[24] "I am a radical," he said earlier, "and I am going to stay one until my people get free to walk the earth."[25] More to the point, his close comrade, William Patterson,[26] declared, "Paul Robeson was a revolutionary,"[27] determined to deploy his immense talent on behalf of constructing a socialist commonwealth—not just in the U.S. but worldwide.

The problem for Robeson was that his homeland was at the tip of the spear during the Cold War and felt compelled to repress vigorously those like Robeson who refused to accede. Nobel Laureate and long-time Londoner Doris Lessing observed that "even the worst time of the Cold War" in Britain was "mild compared to the United States . . . no British Communist was ever treated with the harshness the American government used towards Paul Robeson and some other American Communists."[28] Pete Seeger, the famed folksinger who too was persecuted in the U.S., told Robeson directly that "you have been the most blacklisted performer in America . . . ."[29]

Like many African-American artists—before and since—Robeson attained widespread popularity in Europe, then leveraged this lionizing back home, and then worldwide. "Negro artists have always gained a fine [and] welcome an appreciation in Europe," said the Jamaican writer Claude McKay, "and especially England" rather "than the United States . . . ."[30] What catapulted Robeson to prominence, first as an artist, then as a politico, was a lengthy sojourn in London, which began in the 1920s and may have lasted to his dying days but for the onset of war in 1939 (though he visited frequently thereafter). It was in 1960 that he informed an inquiring New Zealander that "so, for any views I have, Britain must take the responsibility. Not America and not Russia."[31]

Robeson was alluding to the fact that a turning point in his life occurred in London in 1928 when he met—and was influenced by—Shapurji Saklatvala, a Parsi born in Bombay [Mumbai], and one of the first Communists to be elected to Parliament.[32] He learned about socialism not from Maxim Gorky, the famous Soviet writer, but George Bernard Shaw, the famous British writer. "My whole social and political development," he confided in 1958, "was in England and I became as much a part of English life as I now am of American."[33] "You'll have to blame Britain for my political views," he reminded an interviewer in Melbourne, since it was there that "I became an advocate of socialism."[34] He learned about the devastation of colonialism in London too, from similarly impeccable sources as he and his spouse befriended the leaders of the liberation movement of British India. It was in 1931 that Eslanda Robeson conferred with M.K. Gandhi; "he said he felt the Negro and the Indian had a lot in common,"[35] was her apt summary.[36]

What was true for Robeson was similarly true for many of his U.S. counterparts. That is, in a dialectical fashion Britain had become a leading colonizer and imperialist nation and simultaneously produced some of the sterner critics of these systems of exploitation. It was in 1936 in Manhattan when Robeson's close comrade, the black Communist Ben Davis—who was to be elected subsequently to the New York City Council representing Harlem—encountered his good friend: Robeson was splayed across the bed reading a foundational work by the British Communist intellectual, Emile Burns.[37] It was true that he read Marx and Lenin in German and Russian and that he was impressed with a Soviet Constitution that pledged anti-racism[38] but the fact is that Robeson (and a good deal of the U.S. left) were heavily dependent upon the insight and research of their U.K. counterparts, including Rajani Palme Dutt,[39] whom Robeson deemed to be "one of Britain's leading Marxist thinkers . . . ."[40] This lengthy list also included Maurice Dobb,[41] Maurice Cornforth,[42] J.D. Bernal,[43] J.B.S. Haldane,[44] Christopher Caudwell,[45] Christopher Hill,[46] Harry Pollitt,[47] et.al. This is not to mention premier intellectuals from British colonies, e.g. Eric Williams of Trinidad,[48] nor the British who migrated to the U.S. and became leaders of the left, e.g. the "Dangerous Scot," John Williamson.[49] Indeed, though Robeson denied more than once that he was a member of the U.S. Communist Party, his closeness to London comrades raises questions—rarely asked, hardly answered definitively—as to whether he was ever a member of the party in Great Britain, more of a likelihood than U.S. membership.

"I 'discovered' Africa in London," said Robeson, which "profoundly influenced my life," referring to his subsequent political commitments and his meeting there such leading figures as Kwame Nkrumah of Ghana, Jomo Kenyatta of Kenya and Nnamdi Azikiwe of Nigeria. "I spent many hours talking with them" and "studied" the languages of these nations, including "Yoruba, Efik," and "Ashanti." It was in London that he discussed Africa "with men like H.G. Wells and [Harold] Laski and [Jawaharlal] Nehru." His interest was so intense that "British Intelligence came one day to caution me about the political meanings of my activities . . . ."[50]

But tellingly, his "discovery" of Africa in London was tied inexorably to his other preoccupation: socialism. "It was an African" in London, he noted later, "who directed my interest in Africa to something he had noted in the Soviet Union. On a visit to that country he had travelled east and had seen the Yakuts, a people who had been classed as a 'backwards race' by the Czars," in a manner not unlike what had befallen Africans in e.g. North America. "He had been struck by the resemblance between the tribal life of the Yakuts and his own people of East Africa," leading Robeson to think that socialism too could uplift Africa; "so," concluded Robeson, "through Africa I found the Soviet Union . . . ."[51]

Robeson and Nehru met in London in the 1930s and the Indian leader was so moved by his presence that he penned an ode to him, informing readers that "you have been the voice of man . . . the song of germinating earth/and the movement of nature." This homage was a reflection of the fact that Robeson's signature song, "Ol' Man River" was adapted into several South Asian languages with often the Mississippi River transmuted to the Ganges.[52]

The British-Barbadian observer, Peter Blackman, was agog in describing the rapturous reception of Robeson before his forced departure in 1939: he

> has always been popular in England. In 1939 I attended a meeting in a working-class district of London at which he sang; the crowds in the streets, an inspector of police told me, were bigger than any that used to turn out to see Edward VIII when that monarch was at the height of his popularity as Prince of Wales . . . Cabinet members bid discreetly for interviews, members of Parliament and hall porters [alike] jostle one another to shake his hand,

while "the bulk of the audiences [he entertains] are middle and working class folk"; yet "even with halls packed, thousands are turned away . . . ."[53] After the U.S. in the 1950s rejected his right to travel and sought to ruin his livelihood, Robeson fought an ultimately successful battle that led him to tell British readers in 1960, "it was largely due to pressure from this country that I eventually got my passport. That's why I make my temporary home here."[54]

There was a mutual love affair between Robeson and Britain, to the point where at one juncture he considered relinquishing his U.S. citizenship and adopting British nationality instead,[55] a path chosen earlier by Ira Aldridge and numerous other African-Americans in previous centuries and decades. As one analyst put it, "Robeson was adored in Britain. No other country in the world did so much to keep Robeson in the public eye during his long containment" by the U.S. authorities and "no other country did as much to protest his treatment."[56] In 1973, at a time when solidarity with Robeson was designed to bring a rebuke from Washington, Labour Party stalwarts who saluted him included Harold Wilson, Denis Healey, Tony Benn, Jim Callaghan and Roy Jenkins.[57]

Robeson was popular in Britain—the springboard for his global acclaim—not least because he was deeply knowledgeable about British culture. Gaelic was among the many languages he studied. As early as 1938, *The Scotsman* reported that he had a "working knowledge of Gaelic."[58] But what made Robeson unique was that he strived to connect national streams of culture to an all-encompassing global culture. "When I was in Scotland," said Robeson, "I was reminded of how near the Gaelic folk songs are [close] to our own. When I sing them I feel that they express the same soulful quality that I know in Negro music. Indeed, they contributed no small part to the development of our music and the Gaelic speaking Negro was not uncommon in the Southern States two centuries ago . . . ." Likewise, Robeson found a "close kinship between the Negro music" and "the music of Ireland . . . ."[59] Thus, when interviewed by the *Glasgow Herald* in 1960, he sought to discuss the affinity between Hebridean songs and the Chinese, African and Hungarian folk songs, all of which were part of the "pentatonic mode."[60]

Robeson found a "great likeness of many of the African languages in mono-syllabic base, in use of tone, to the Chinese-Tibetan languages; the similarity in structure of many of the East African languages to the Hungarian-Finnish-Turkish-Japanese family of languages; also the likenesses of philosophical concepts, of concrete ways of thought, and in many cases, similar art esthetic" between and among diverse language groups. He compared the "curve form of the Ashanti with those of the Chinese—and the basic aesthetic similarity . . . ." He had the "pleasure and privilege to sing many of these lovely melodies in Scotland, in Glasgow, Edinburgh, Aberdeen, Dundee, Perth, etc." and was taken by the "likeness of the Hebridean chants and folk songs to Afro-American music—lovely Hebridean melodies such as 'Kishmul's Galley', the 'Skye Boat Song', 'Briskay Love Lilt'," all exemplary of the "mutual influences of different musics upon the other,"[61] which demonstrated the essential unity of the human race. For Robeson, language was not just a tool of communication, but also a way to forge a deeper connection with social—and political—consequence. The U.S. Embassy in Paris took note when in 1958 he informed a Communist journalist of the "singer's belief that the different musical expressions of all countries are but so many inseparable links in the same chain—and he demonstrates this relationship vocally to 'L'Humanite's' correspondent by comparing a Negro spiritual with a selection from Boris Godunov."[62]

"The film I was most proud to make," he told the BBC in 1960, "was 'Proud Valley', the story of a Welsh mining village. Much of it was made in the Rhondda Valley and the Director was Pen Tennyson, a direct descendant of the great poet."[63] "I was brought up on English ballads", not Negro "spirituals" as was thought; "it was English ballads I used to sing," initially: "I knew dozens of them . . . they earned me my first recognition as a singer . . . ."[64]

Decades of attention to the so-called "special relationship" between London and Washington notwithstanding, Robeson had tapped into a longstanding current of sympathy between African-Americans and Britain that stretched back to the founding of the U.S., when the enslaved generally sided with the redcoats, not least because of the gathering abolitionism in the U.K. and the slaveholding status of the victorious rebels.[65] This trend continued in the nineteenth century when leading U.S. abolitionists, e.g. Frederick Douglass, were frequently to be found in London, Dublin, Cardiff, and Edinburgh.[66] Robeson exemplified this trend when in 1958 he acknowledged openly that the "relentless, powerful, compelling [factor] is the pressure of world opinion against racism in the United States"; it was "beyond the shadow of a doubt," he thundered, "that the United States cannot afford to ignore the pressure that comes from abroad."[67]

It was in 1937 that the then affluent Robeson funded the Council on African Affairs (CAA), a U.S. based grouping that crusaded for decolonization of Africa and the Caribbean with the belief in large part that as this beleaguered continent and region were liberated, citizens there could then pressure Washington to liberate African-Americans in turn.[68] Repeatedly over the years, Robeson—according to his close friend and biographer, Lloyd Brown—adjudged the CAA "the one organizational interest among many with which he was identified and that was *closest to his heart* . . . "[69] [emphasis in original]. Robeson exemplified these bold words when in 1950 he collaborated with Patterson in filing a petition with the United Nations charging Washington with "genocide" against African-Americans.[70]

Part of what made Robeson a revolutionary was his rejection of narrow nationalism and his uplifting of a radical international-ism and it was this—as much as anything else—that caused the tremendous persecution of him by the U.S. authorities since he was effectively eroding Washington's sovereignty in pursuit of racial equality domestically and the socialist commonwealth globally that would guarantee it. Seamlessly, Robeson argued that as reflected in their art and culture and music particularly, humanity was one which undergirded why, he thought, humankind was destined for a unified socialist commonwealth. He paid a steep price as a result: His income dwindled from a hefty $104,000 in 1947 to $2,000 or so a year shortly thereafter,[71] as the Red Scare deepened.

* * *

Paul Robeson was born on 9 April 1898 in New Jersey. A mere 48 hours after his birth, the U.S. moved to declare war on Spain and Cuba; Puerto Rico and the Philippines were seized from Madrid, and the Hawaii Kingdom was overthrown during this same period. This evolution of U.S. imperialism, this bringing under U.S. rule so many described as "colored", exacerbated the white supremacy whose slaying became a preoccupation of the mature Robeson. His father, the Reverend William D. Robeson, was born in North

Carolina in 1845, but in 1860 escaped from enslavement and then attended Lincoln University in Pennsylvania. In 1878 he married Mary Louisa Bustill, whose family traced their ancestry as far back as 1608. Princeton where the couple settled and where Paul was born was "spiritually located in Dixie," Robeson recalled later with the "decaying smell of the plantation Big House": it was a "Jim Crow"— meaning apartheid—town: "the grade school that I attended was segregated and Negroes were not admitted in any high school"; of course they were barred from Princeton University,[72] whose president, Woodrow Wilson, went on to occupy the same position in Washington where he heightened the apartheid practice there—and nationwide—over which he had presided in New Jersey as governor.

Robeson was a feisty child, a trait displayed not long after he was born. Decades later, one visitor to his home back then recounted to him a "rather vivid recollection of you as you were then. For while asleep on the couch in the living room, you marched up to it and yanked my hair to awake me. Your mother had placed me there because I had a headache," which hardly ceased after this abrupt end to her resting.[73]

Robeson's parents produced six progeny[74]—five sons and a daughter—but the turning point for young Paul came in 1904 when his mother, a near invalid was fatally burned in a household accident, leaving an emotional void for this now motherless child. The beset family moved from Princeton in 1907 and wound up in neighboring Somerville. This change in environment accentuated his always close relationship with his surviving parent, whose example left a deep and lasting impression upon him. As with the son, Robeson described his father as having "the greatest speaking voice [I] have ever heard," a "deep sonorous basso, richly melodic and refined, vibrant with the love and compassion which filled him."[75]

Another turning point for young Robeson came in 1908 when he disobeyed his father, who then chased him, fell and, as the still startled son described years later, "knocked out one of his most needed teeth. I shall never forget my feeling," he recalled. "It has remained ever present . . . never in all my life afterwards . . . did he have to admonish me again. This respect became a source of tremendous self-discipline which has lasted until this day," he said as he approached the age of 60. "What would 'Pop' think?" This became his mantra, his command, his guiding light.[76]

Robeson later told the vast BBC audience that the Christmas holidays "in my childhood were not so happy because I usually spent them with neighbors or cousins while my father had to go to other towns to preach. I used to feel that I was an outsider—never quite one of a family—my mother died when I was six. But I remember one Christmas morning going into church and a certain song made a deep impression on me and cheered me up quite a bit"; the song was "Get on Board Little Children."[77]

This positive paternal influence proved to be exceedingly helpful for—as he stated bluntly—"I grew up in extreme poverty . . . ." At the tender age of twelve he was working in Rhode Island, in posh, racially segregated hotels. He was scrubbing floors.[78] Nevertheless, such drudgery was not the trademark of his youth. "I was brought up," he stressed, in a "*vocal* household" in that "my father was the finest public speaker I have ever heard"; thus, "in my home, all through childhood, we 'orated', recited, debated or just 'spoke'—for fun. With the single exception of my sister . . . we all belonged to debating teams in grade school, high school and college . . . ." As Robeson saw it, "Negroes have what I call *melodic speech*. This is particularly true of Negro preachers. They chant, intone, orate, sing, talk—moving naturally and freely from one plane to another," just as Robeson did from singing to declaiming to acting and this upbringing shaped his talent. "Some playwrights have been interested in melodic speech," particularly "Shakespeare and Eugene O'Neill. If you change around the words of their lines you will often lose the music, the rhythm, the 'color' and the impact of the line . . . ." Robeson, who began appearing before audiences at the age of eight—"in Sunday school, in my father's church, on debating teams and in glee clubs"— had multiple opportunities to exercise his supple vocal cords.[79] It was in 1914 as a student that he first performed the lead role in *Othello*, the first of many triumphs in this tragedy.[80]

Still, at the age of 17, in his final year of high school, he had no vocation in mind. But then—in 1915—he won a statewide oratorical contest, adumbrating his future by speaking eloquently of the great founding father of Haiti: Toussaint L'Ouverture. Citing the immortal words of the abolitionist, Wendell Phillips, Robeson declaimed in words that were to define his future, "when I want to find the vanguard of the people, I look to the uneasy dreams of an aristocracy and find what they dread most."[81]

Apparently, studying held no dread for Robeson for he was admitted as a scholarship student to Rutgers University in New Brunswick, New Jersey—a leading institution. Until 1915 only two African-Americans had ever attended this school—even though it was supported by taxpayer dollars, a good deal of which were contributed by African-Americans. As it turned out, he was the only "Negro" there during his 1915–19 tenure.[82]

The resonant speaking voice he had developed—which became his hallmark as a singer and actor—developed further at Rutgers. Subsequently, he described to the BBC that during his time there he would bicycle to Somerville, about 15 miles away, where his father had a pastorate. At times the Reverend Robeson would invite a so-called "Revivalist Minister" to address the congregation, who was known for his impassioned declamation. "One Sunday," said Robeson, "I was in the church talking about the relative positions of science and religion. I prided myself on being pretty level-headed," he confided "but a Revivalist Minister who was in the church looked at me and came and stood over me" menacingly. "Before you knew it," continued the budding materialist, "I'm on my knees praying and within half an hour I'm walking down the aisle, just as you've seen them at Billy Graham's meetings," speaking of the notorious evangelist. But that is not all he took away from his close contact with religionists for, he said, "as the son of a minister, I heard a great deal of Bach's music in my youth" and "as I grew up I learned to love his music . . . ."[83]

It was his father who, in a "moving experience," said Robeson, who chose to "teach me in Hebrew" from the Bible. It was in college that he embarked on his "abiding" preoccupation: languages, beginning with Greek and Latin.[84] "In my college days," said Robeson later, "Latin and Greek" and "language study" generally became his constant companion. "I was quite a Greek scholar," he said. "I enjoyed learning languages."[85] And this intellectual interest dovetailed with a political imperative. "I believe," he said in 1963, "that there was, way back, one language, one music, one people" and what made Robeson such a unifying global—and revolutionary—figure was that this profundity he articulated was embodied in his own person.[86]

However, he not only displayed facility with foreign languages. During the height of his popularity, the Californian Communist leader, Dorothy Healey, escorted him to an all-Negro party and was surprised to find that upon arrival he "immediately began using Black English colloquialisms in this crowd in a way he never had when I was with him in a group of whites."[87] Those attending a gathering in Los Angeles of the left-leaning Progressive Party—which Robeson chaired—were taken aback when he spoke for ten minutes in fluent Spanish to those of Mexican origin in attendance.[88] The versatile Robeson reputedly had a better reading understanding of Chinese, than he did of Spanish.[89]

Besides music and language, the youthful Robeson also developed a keen interest in sports. During his first year in college, he sought to join the [American] football team, which brought a sharp introduction to racist violence. "One boy slugged me in the face and smashed my nose, just smashed it," he said with equal amounts of wonder and anger. The injury delivered provided "trouble to me as a singer everyday since," he lamented. "And then when I was down, flat on my back, another boy got me with his knee and fell on me. He managed to dislocate my shoulder." But in an early lesson that buoyed him throughout life, his sainted father convinced him not to quit since he should see himself as not just an individual—but also as a representative of "All Negroes." "So I stayed," said Robeson.

> I had ten days in bed, a few days at the training and then out for another scrimmage. I made a tackle and was on the ground, my right hand palm down on the ground. A boy came over and stepped hard, on my hand. He meant to break the bones. The bones held but his cleats took every single one of the finger nails off my right hand!

"That's when I knew rage," he added with lingering vehemence and it was that rage that he converted into doggedness that propelled him into one of the best athletes ever to compete in this blood-sport.

Thus, on the next play, it seemed as if the whole team "came at me. I swept out my arms" and "the three men running interference," sought to block him but instead "went down" because of a legal blow administered by the now enraged Robeson. "I wanted to kill" he said triumphantly and "I meant to kill", said this proponent of self-defense. But the coach intervened.

This display of aggression was at a practice session, directed at teammates—yet even this exhibition of violence hardly prepared him for actual games against opponents. After one brutal match in 1918, Samuel Rosen, who came to know Robeson, lingered near the entrance to the stadium and soon everyone but Robeson had departed. "He walked along down the long corridor toward the exit," said the distressed observer. "Not a soul with him. He was completely abandoned by his teammates"; the touched Rosen concluded, "it was the first time that I really understood what it meant to be black."[90]

Then there was the game with Washington and Lee University, a Virginia school named after two pre-eminent slaveholders. Naturally, their team not only had no black players but also refused to play any team that did. So, the coach benched the angered Robeson and the team suffered, unable to prevail. Yet, of the sports he played—including basketball, baseball and track and field, in all of which he excelled superbly—he confessed that [American] football was his favorite.[91] Perhaps it was because of the roughhouse tactics which toughened him helpfully for future battles that endeared him—though in basketball too, a reporter noticed that "every time he was near the basket, at least two of the opposing players were on top of him," and, inexorably, "he was knocked down."[92] Robeson's sterling success on athletic battlefields unsettled the rudiments of white cum male supremacy, paving the way for desegregation.[93]

What steeled Robeson for future battles was not only his preparation on athletic battlefields but, as well, the shock of the death of his father on 17 May 1918. Robeson was heartbroken; according to his future spouse, he became "quieter, more thoughtful, lonely."[94]

Fortunately, his college years were not consumed by racist violence and personal setbacks. His professor in English literature was an authority on Shakespeare. "He became my dearest friend among the professors," said Robeson. "It was he who brought me to New

York to see my first Shakespearean play." Robeson was impressed: "I remember to this day," he said years later, "the clarity of their diction" which then compelled him to take "courses in phonetics at London University . . . ." This interest in Shakespeare merged effortlessly with his interest in music and his acculturation in the church. "Get some of the records of the divine Mahalia Jackson," he counseled later, "or listen to the poetic bard-like songs of Ledbetter [Lead Belly] or Sonny Terry. This bardic tradition," he advised, "goes back to the land of our African forebears. Today in any of our churches one can hear the preacher (leader) and chorus (congregation) creating a kind of modal antiphonal or polyphonic, contrapuntal singing—reminiscent of an African chant. These bard-like songs and chants are similar to those of the Scotch Hebridean bards" and "the Welsh bards of Druid tradition" and the "Irish bards who inspired Sean O'Casey" and "the unknown singers of the old Russian Bylina, the bards of Icelandic and Finnish sagas, the ancient singers of American Indian lore, the bards of the Veddic hymns of the India of the East, of the Chinese singer-poets, the Hassidim," et al.

The essence of Robeson's lifework—and the heart of his socialist credo—was his fervent belief that humanity was one, all marching—albeit at different speeds—to the same goal.[95] The seeds of this cultural expansiveness were sown in college.

His intellectualism was reflected in his grades, receiving an "A"—or excellent—in Public Speaking and the History of Art.[96] He graduated from Rutgers with honors—inducted into the prestigious Phi Beta Kappa, a fraternity of the academic elite—and signaling his future course, gave an address in Brooklyn on the "New Idealism."[97] His senior thesis, an adroit examination of U.S. constitutional law calling for "equal protection under the law", prefigured his subsequent admission to the law school at Manhattan's Columbia University,[98] where his tuition was paid in no small measure by his laboring part-time as a professional [American] football player.

On a hill overlooking Harlem—which had recently witnessed an influx of migrants from Jamaica, Barbados and the region once known as the British West Indies, —this Ivy League school both was influenced by and stood apart from its teeming neighborhood. For decades to come, Robeson would be shaped by the urban nodes that were London and New York and it was the latter that first left a deep impression upon him. "Harlem has been the scene both of wonderful moments of happiness and achievement and some of the bitterest experiences of my life," he later recounted.

I can remember walking along Seventh Av[enue] in an old army overcoat, wondering if I would ever be able to afford to clothe myself respectably. I have been broke in Harlem, gone without food in Harlem, and looked for work in Harlem. It was at the Polo Grounds that I played my first football games and each time I pass 155 St[reet] and Edgecombe Av[enue] [where it had been sited], a lump comes in my throat . . . .

It was in Harlem "in the early hours of the morning I listened awestruck to the deep laughter and wit of Bert Williams," the comic actor of Bahamian origin. It was that "great master", when Robeson

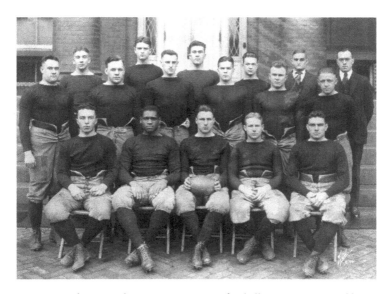

Figure 1 Robeson with Rutgers University football teammates: In addition to being an outstanding artist, Robeson was also a star athlete. (Daily Worker and Daily World Photographs Collection, Tamiment Library/Robert F. Wagner Labor Archives, New York University, New York City)

was still toying with becoming an attorney, who gave him a "pat on the shoulder" and "words of encouragement", steering a "bewildered young actor" to fame and fortune.

"I can still remember humming the last strains of 'Little Gal' that lovely song of Rosamond Johnson's set to the words of Paul Laurence Dunbar," the Poet Laureate of black America "and then rushing from the old Plantation Room into the subway train at 50[th Street] and Broadway. There just across the aisle was dear Florence Mills, the simple, nightingale-voiced star, and how proud I was when she too gave me a nod and a smile of recognition. I recall with profound respect and admiration the evenings with James Weldon Johnson reading his fervent poems," a reference to the acclaimed diplomat, human rights leader and lyricist. An indelible impression was made on Robeson by a "short, never-to-be-forgotten chat with that great scholar and tireless fighter, W.E.B. Du Bois."[99]

While a student at Columbia, Robeson would stroll northward to Lewisohn Stadium during hot summer nights; there he could hear the New York Philharmonic at reasonable prices—and be influenced by their superb musicianship.[100] Harlem was to remain dear to Robeson to his dying days; it was where his funeral was held in 1976. But the kind of encouragement he received from other stellar figures there served to ensure that he would reciprocate, befriending other up-and-coming artists, when he too reached this elevated stage, which was to occur rather shortly.

2

Rising Star

As Paul Robeson was leaving Rutgers in 1919, African-Americans were being subjected to ghastly pogroms, as soldiers having risked their lives in Europe during the Great War were at times slain in their uniforms, a reminder that they should not think that their blood sacrifice would bring rights.[1] There was fear that the relative equality experienced by these young men in Europe—particularly France—would embolden them upon their return and they must be compelled to abandon this course.

Such burdensome thoughts hung ominously in the air as Robeson entered Columbia Law School, a prestigious institution that sat uneasily adjacent to Harlem, an iconic community that had attracted in recent years a large black population, particularly from Jamaica, Barbados, and Trinidad. Also to be found in this vicinity was Eslanda Goode, a young woman of African and Spanish Jewish background who had become attracted to him. Part of this circle was Raymond Pace Alexander, who later became one of the leading jurists in black Philadelphia. He and Robeson met as early as 1918, at a track-meet in Pennsylvania and the skilled attorney said they "became fast friends. We had several classes together" at Columbia, he recalled, and in 1921 the future Ms. Robeson was his "guest at a picnic at one of the famous steamers of the Hudson River Line on which occasion I introduced Essie to Paul."[2]

Robeson and Eslanda were smitten and in August 1921 decided to wed[3] and—despite rockiness—they were to remain married until her death in 1965. They were a kind of odd couple: he was tall, well over six feet high, and over the years carried a fluctuating weight that at times tipped the scales at 250 pounds. She was much shorter and—not a minor detail in a color obsessed U.S.—she was much lighter than her darker skinned husband, which at times allowed her access where he was barred. Exuding confidence, she described herself in 1942 definitively:

> I am 45 years old . . . weigh[ing] 125–135 pounds; am 5 feet 4½ inches tall [and] on the sturdy side with powerful shoulders and chest (I was a swimmer and still am); am muscular . . . olive colored with very black hair . . . speak a little French, some German, a very leetle [sic] Russian . . . .[4]

To earn income Robeson played professional [American] football for the Milwaukee Badgers, where he excelled on the field, as he had done at Rutgers.[5] His son, Paul, Jr., observed that Robeson was "billed by the media as the greatest defensive end in the history of football," an opinion confirmed by the premier analyst of the sport, Walter Camp.[6]

Their first home was established in Harlem—321 West 138th Street—a rather small, incommodious abode on the top floor of a private home. The responsibility of marriage and the felt necessity for added income had led him back to the football field and, also, to unlimber his performing talent, this time as an actor in New York City. As with so many of his capacious ventures, he was encouraged— if not pushed—in this direction by his ambitious spouse.[7] "Our early married life was a struggle," said Robeson subsequently, and added pointedly that if his spouse had not "gently propelled" him, he would not have gone as far.[8]

"When I was working my way through law school," he told the BBC subsequently, the couple "suffered from [a] lack of cash. So, we'd arrange summer concerts and get in an audience at a shilling a head. That helped to pay the rent and the grocery bills."[9] At this juncture, Robeson hardly realized that he could make a decent living as a fulltime performer. By his own admission, he was

> mighty worried about paying my way. I've done a couple of amateur plays but I know nothing about acting. Then a guy comes along and tells me that Mary Hoyt Wyborg has written a play called "Taboo" and they're looking for a Negro actor. He was to play opposite the

famous English actress, Margaret Wycherly. Well, I happened to know her dresser and—I got the part.

It was "this play," he informed the BBC, "re-named 'Voodoo' which brought me to England" for when he began "the rehearsals in New York I knew nothing of the stage—but an elderly Negro coached me in every line and in every movement. Without him by my side," he revealed, "I would never have made the grade—and his name was Alex Rogers," who also happened to be a talented lyricist.[10] This may have been a case of false modesty, a trait for which Robeson could be accused, since a Manhattan newspaper echoed the sentiments of many when it asserted that Robeson "dominates the play."[11] But as so often happened for Robeson and other African-American artists, it was when this play debuted in London that his career accelerated.[12]

For as with academia and singing and sports, Robeson also excelled in acting to the point that he attracted the increased attention of London impresarios and by 1922 he was sailing eastward from New York.

"I shall never forget," said Robeson, "arriving in Southampton . . . I thought I had never seen any land as beautiful—green and companionable. I longed to fling myself flat upon my face and hug the cool earth . . . . I've always felt that way," he confessed, "about the South of England . . . ." This was his "first welcome to [the] land where I was to spend so many happy years," and it did not disappoint, as "the people were so kind . . . I sensed none of the prejudice I had left . . . ."[13] It was during this sojourn that Robeson developed a taste for football ("soccer" in the U.S.) Subsequently he was asked in Edinburgh, "do you ever go to football matches in Britain?" He responded with eagerness, "as often as possible. The first big game I ever saw over here was Celtic v. Hibs at Glasgow in 1922."

Britain made a lasting impression on him—and vice versa—as his acting attracted favorable notice. This visit sharpened his understanding of Jim Crow—apartheid—in the U.S., as it deepened his appreciation of Britain. Later, while visiting Edinburgh he was asked, "have you ever been refused rooms in hotels in the U.S.A. because of your colour?" His answer was unequivocal: "often." Then he was asked, "have you ever been refused rooms in British hotels because of your colour?" The answer was similarly unsparing: "No, but it has happened to other coloured people less well known than I am."[14]

He was able to dine in many of London's leading restaurants but while starring in theater in downtown New York, he found it hard to find a decent meal, despite the profusion of eateries there. There were restaurants and other establishments from which he was barred, just as a traveler he could not secure suitable seats on trains because of Jim Crow laws.[15]

But then it was London that was the primary focus of his emerging career. Reminiscing later, Robeson observed that "the first song I sang in England" was "'Go Down Moses'", which was "way back in 1922." Noting the "off-beat play in New York called 'Voodoo'" that had brought him to the east bank of the Atlantic, he derided it, saying it "wasn't much of a play and I wasn't much of an actor," which was all too self-deprecating. "During the play I was supposed to fall asleep and dream; while I was dreaming, I hummed 'Go Down Moses' to myself" and the producer said, "'sing it'. I did." Then he was told, "'Sing another' and by the time the play closed I was singing several spirituals" and thus was launched the singing career of a man who became notorious because of his powerful voice. Arguably, it was London that opened the doors wide for his talent to emerge, for it is questionable if he would have been able to flourish on the west bank. That led to a tour where "we stayed in digs and I made many friends with many people in all walks of life. Thus began what [I] feel has been a lifelong friendship with the British people. I love their music, their tradition[s] and folk songs" since "the Scottish, Welsh and Irish songs appeal to me very deeply and I love to sing them." That this mutual attraction emerged almost accidentally was serendipitous for all sides.[16] Later on, Robeson added more texture to how his singing career began: "when I was a young man in Harlem," he told the BBC, "I sang for a short time with a group of singers led by a youngster from Portuguese East Africa," meaning Mozambique. "He studied at Columbia University and married an American girl."[17]

He graduated from Columbia in 1923—then worked for a law firm but curtly departed after a secretary (in a racist slight) refused to type his letters.[18] Perhaps if he had not endured such slights, he would have considered a legal career—but such was not to be.

His budding stardom as an actor at once shielded him to a degree from racism in Britain but was insufficiently blinding to obscure the reason why. This was the more impressive since, in many ways, Robeson's global popularity began in Britain. He was also pushed in that direction by his unfortunate experiences at home. Whatever the case it did not take long for him to attract the attention of the heralded playwright Eugene O'Neill. In early 1923 the Irish-American writer was told that Robeson was "desirous to meet you in regard to a part in your new play." Further, O'Neill was told, "if you have a Negro part to cast you will find that Mr. Robeson has in my opinion very unusual and extraordinary ability as an actor and most admirable qualities as a student and a man,"[19] all of which proved to be true. Indeed, Eslanda Robeson concluded that the Provincetown Players, a U.S. theater troupe closely associated with the Nobel Laureate, "were really responsible for Paul's choice of the stage as a career." For upon their meeting the boozy, somewhat irascible O'Neill and the younger thespian would talk for hours on end, "for days, for weeks," said Ms. Robeson.[20] For the favorable reviews in London led to his breakthrough appearance in O'Neill's *The Emperor Jones* in New York in 1923 and London thereafter.[21]

This play was not embraced warmly by all; assuredly, it was denounced by the organ of the then rising Jamaican activist, Marcus Garvey, who sought to build a global alliance of Africans and African descendants. It was a depiction of a fictional Caribbean isle and, said the *Negro World*, was a "travesty on the Negro race."[22] The popular, U.S. Negro columnist, J.A. Rogers, told his many readers that the play was "written for morons," while the filmed version made him "feel like making a dive for the garbage can after seeking it."[23] Robeson, who played the eponymous leading character on stage and screen, was to see this work repeatedly flayed[24] and, ultimately, his difficulty in finding roles that matched his developing political consciousness, led him to stray from cinema particularly.

If Robeson had been able to skim O'Neill's innermost thoughts, he may have given more credence to some of Garvey's more astringent evaluations. For in private correspondence, the playwright confessed after hearing Robeson sing, "I'm about fed up with Negro spirituals" then went on to discuss the now prominent performer acting in one

Figure 2 Robeson's breakthrough performance in 1923 in Nobel Laureate Eugene O'Neill's *The Emperor Jones* propelled him to stardom. (Daily Worker and Daily World Photographs Collection, Tamiment Library/Robert F. Wagner Labor Archives, New York University, New York City)

of his plays with a constructed "face (white)" that "could be designed for him and his face built up to fit it. White folks make up to play Negroes and there's no reason why the reverse shouldn't be practiced. He's the only actor who can do the laughter, that's the important point. It would be good showmanship, too—no end to the publicity it would attract."[25]

Yet, again, Garvey's journal was countered by what was becoming one of Robeson's chief defenders. London's *New Statesman* advised about this controversial play, "you ought to see it because of Mr.

Paul Robeson in the leading part. I have nothing but admiration for his performance," said their critic, John Shand, since where he was "good, he was magnificent"; his "voice, intelligence, physique and sense of the stage immediately made me want to see him in 'Othello'," the play that catapulted Robeson into the theatrical stratosphere.[26]

As so often happened with African-American artists, these favorable British reviews were leveraged for gain in the U.S. itself; in this instance, *Opportunity*, the organ of the National Urban League, which catered to the millions of African-Americans then fleeing the terror of the former Slave South for points northward; their critic hailed Robeson's "fine and impressive acting" while quoting at length from nine equally favorable British reviews.[27] Strikingly, the mainstream U.S. periodical, the *Saturday Review*, said that Robeson in this play "has many moments that are superb and one rarely sees so fine a physique upon the stage" and, besides, Robeson "can act with the whole of his magnificent frame."[28]

The play was made into a movie, though—interestingly—the positive reviews of his performance applied mostly to the former rather than the latter. For at least cinematically, the critique of *The Emperor Jones* was understandable. Robeson's character is depicted as cunning, intelligent, and resourceful. As a Pullman porter—a segregated post generally reserved for Negro men—he is exposed to stock market tips and other inside information which he exploits for personal gain. The denouement occurs in the jungle, where the Robeson character perishes after a rebellion of his black subjects. The work was seen as powerful and plausible and the box office concurred, as the film did well in Harlem and elsewhere—though contemporary audiences might wonder what the fuss was about, given the stodginess of the acting and plotting.[29]

Robeson, too, was unhappy with the cinematic version of O'Neill's play. It was a "failure" on many levels he opined. Why? "Partly because scenes in it were changed around from the proper psychological order of the play"; moreover, the "director had some fool notion that Negroes had moods and could only play when they were in the proper mood . . . ." Such sour experiences were to drive Robeson away from cinema. But he left reluctantly for at least two reasons: film (along with recordings) allowed him to reach into every nook and cranny globally and, besides, it was quite lucrative, a factor which was to grow in importance as he began to subsidize various political causes.[30]

Robeson's spouse lauded the theatrical version of this work, confiding to her diary after the Manhattan opening that "Paul was superb. Applause and stomping and whistling [was] deafening after final curtain. Paul got 5 curtain calls . . . ." The leading Negro actor, Charles Gilpin, was among the celebrities present, poised to welcome Robeson to their ranks; Gilpin and O'Neill "quartered down in [the] dressing room after [the] play," doubtlessly dissecting Robeson's performance and his bright future prospects. "O'Neill and Mrs. O'Neill [both] seemed thrilled with Paul's performance," as did others who were poised to propel him to stardom.[31]

But working with O'Neill inadvertently opened another door for Robeson, through which he strode boldly. The script of the play called for him to whistle in the forest "to keep up my courage," he recalled later, "and since I cannot whistle I had to sing instead," an accidental performance that stunned those assembled, contributing to yet another career as a singer.[32] Still, any hearing Robeson's resonant baritone voice could easily have suggested that he should pursue a career as a concert singer.

But Robeson's dilemma was captured when another O'Neill play in which he starred—*All God's Chillun Got Wings*—which touched upon the ultra-sensitive issue of so-called "mixed race" liaisons, also met with protest: Robeson played the spouse of an abusive white woman. The Ku Klux Klan—the terrorist and racist gang which held sway in a number of state capitals—was fiercely outraged because of the explosive theme.[33] The atmosphere for this work was not ideal. Robeson recalled later how the "New York theatre was picketed because a lot of angry citizens felt it was wrong to present a play in which a white woman was married to a Negro." This rattled Robeson: "I was never sure I wouldn't be beaten up when I came out of the subway on my way to the theatre." What unnerved Robeson was his perception of his own inadequacies. "Now, I'm not an actor, you know. Oh no, I'm not," he insisted. And to "work with "Flora [Robson]," a standout of the British stage, "was a revelation" since she "had all the technique of the great actress, but it was quite unobtrusive. It was so flowing that one wasn't conscious of it as technique," which is one definition of great acting. "I'll never forget," he continued, "the opening night. After all, we'd been rehearsing for some time and I should have been prepared but I hadn't realized that [she] had something in reserve. We came to that scene where [she] stand[s] behind me with the dagger and spits out that one, terrible, obscene, word—'Nigger!'" And "on the opening night [she] did it with such intensity that I nearly shot out of my skin. I was really frightened . . . ." But, as was typical of his BBC interviewers, keen to draw distinctions between Britain and the U.S., he was asked, "was it different here in London?" Yes, responded Robeson, it was "very different," in terms of a dearth of tension and a lesser amount of unease about miscegenation, not to mention an absence of picketing.[34]

Soon the young actor was huddling with other bright lights from the theater, as recounted by his spouse. "Paul had a most interesting visit with Koiranksy, the Russian critic and collaborator with the famous Stanislavsky. He is to give Paul a 'lesson' regularly in the art of acting. Says he thinks Paul is a great artist and just needs a little technique"; and, thus, "they will go over 'Othello' together," soon to be Robeson's stellar stage role. "We are stunned by the good fortune," she said.[35]

Their fortune improved even more dramatically when the couple— she was effectively his manager—"concluded arrangements with Oscar Micheaux," the prolific African-American auteur and producer, "for Paul's film. Made satisfactory contract for 3% gross after the first $40, 000 the picture brings in. Salary $100 for three weeks."[36]

Robeson did work with Micheaux, but then a major film studio in Southern California called, promising the moon: "we have a fine chance of putting through a big picture deal for you," he was told. "Paul, this new . . . film will give you a tremendous opening if your first picture makes a hit," so "do try to see that your first picture is sound commercially. An 'artistic failure' may be all right on the stage but it helps no one in pictures . . . ."[37] (As things turned out, Robeson's record in movies was mixed, with his critically panned first sound film, *The Emperor Jones*, being typical of his cinematic reception.)

Nevertheless, ever more lucrative offers continued deluging the Robesons—as shall be detailed below—many of which were accepted. One manager, Ms. Robeson noted, "made a most attractive proposition to me" in that he "wants to take over Paul for exclusive management for two years, with an option," and to sweeten the pot he would "advance $10,000 cash to Paul"; she was bedazzled by this offer, terming it a "huge attraction".[38]

With such laudatory reviews and collaborations, Robeson and his wife quickly became virtual commuters from New York to London and in the latter city, most notably and strikingly, they were quickly ensnared by a glittering array of luminaries. Still in New York they met George Gershwin, the famed composer: "quite young and nice," said Ms. Robeson. "He played his 'Rhapsody in Blue'" providing a "wonderful time."[39] The now heralded couple attended the farewell concert of the esteemed Feodor Chaliapin, who—Ms. Robeson pointed out proudly—"remembered Paul and recognized him, shook his hands very cordially" and, it could have been added, passed the torch of politically committed singing to him.[40]

Another command performance was provided by the mystical Negro writer, Jean Toomer, whom she found "fascinating. I had enjoyed reading his 'Cane' so much. Is very tall and fine looking and you literally *see* his mind work," since he was so "clear and logical", she stressed with the drama in writing that rivaled her spouse's work on the stage.[41] It was unclear if Ms. Robeson reflected the view of her husband when she said of the writer, Zora Neale Hurston, "I like [her] less and less the more I see of her."[42]

Communing with the literati—and glitterati—the Robesons were increasingly to be found in the swankest of soirees. On 17 January 1925, Robeson, at the behest of the tastemaker Carl Van Vechten, sang at the latter's Manhattan home before a crowd of 150 that included the influential publisher, Alfred Knopf: it created a sensation.[43] Then, on 19 April 1925, even the typically effervescent Ms. Robeson was floridly ecstatic. "Today is one of the most significant times in our lives," she began. "The All-Negro concert by Paul" and his accompanist "Larry [Brown] took place at the Greenwich Village Theatre tonight. The house was sold out yesterday and at 8:15 P.M. when the theatre doors opened, the lobby, sidewalk and vicinity was [sic] packed" and "hundreds were turned away. The audience was very high class. When the boys appeared, there was thunderous applause, lasting three minutes" and "they were both very nervous"; yet, "after each number, the applause was deafening" with "curtain call after curtain call . . . ."[44] What drove the overwhelmingly positive reception to this concert was the startling fact that he was—as Robeson put it— the "first Negro to give an all-Negro" presentation of "music on the formal concert stage."[45]

One U.S. Negro periodical saluted the "versatile" performance by Robeson in his command of "Negro spirituals and secular songs" elevated by the "gorgeous beauty of Robeson's voice"; an indication of the quality of his performance was the fact that "fully as many were turned away as the little theatre could accommodate and the venture has made necessary a second revival."[46] Robeson's spouse did not exaggerate when she spoke enthusiastically of the "huge crowd filling the lobby and the sidewalk in front of the theatre"; nor did she engage in puffery when she wrote that "all the seats and all the standing room had been sold" and that "at the end of the programme the entire audience remained seated, clamouring for more," and their enthusiasm was rewarded with "many encores."[47]

The April 1925 concert also marked the intensifying warmth of Robeson's tie to Walter White of the National Association for the Advancement of Colored People (NAACP), the premier organization battling for equality. White, a talented writer in his own right, was as fair-skinned as Robeson's spouse and used this phenotype to investigate lynchings of African-Americans undetected. "I have known [Robeson] for nearly ten years," said White in 1927, a man he found to be "one of the most talented individuals I have ever met in this or any other country."[48] "You can always count on me to the limit," said White with enthusiasm in April 1925.[49] Robeson was impressed with his novel about this barbarous practice. It was in August 1925 that Ms. Robeson "came home from breakfast and found Paul crying and cursing over Walter's book. This is a supreme compliment for Paul never cries except when deeply [moved]." It was suggested that the book be converted for the stage, that it would "make a marvelous play" and "Paul would be the ideal man to cast as the hero. Things look interesting!"[50] she concluded beamingly.

Ms. Robeson recalled fondly how White in turn "worked untiringly for the success of the concert"; he was "one of those rare beings," she exulted, who was a "loyal and consistent friend"; it was "through Walter that Paul met Carl [Van Vechten], Heywood [Broun], Konrad Bercovici . . ." the "Spingarns [Joel and Arthur]," and a number of others who could make, and break, careers. In fact, after the onset of the Red Scare when Robeson became the leading target, White and Arthur Spingarn turned against him vociferously.[51]

Robeson went to Philadelphia and "had a nice visit with Roland Hayes," his peer as a singer, she said.[52] Buoyed by the applause still ringing in their ears, the now affluent couple headed eastward once more for England and at sea they were importuned by Senator Joseph Frelinghuysen of New Jersey, a member of the U.S. elite, who, Ms. Robeson commented pointedly, "came and sat down and had a long talk with Paul" and gave "him a personal letter" to deliver to the U.S. Ambassador in London and, further, sought to "arrange for Paul to sing for [President Calvin] Coolidge on our return. He was perfectly lovely," she cooed, a reflection of the rising popularity of Robeson.[53]

By the early summer of 1925 he and his spouse were residing in London and enjoying every moment. "He loved England," she said. "The calm, homely beauty and comfort of London" was appealing to both. "He felt even more at home in London than he had in America," she concluded. "There were few inconveniences for him as a Negro in London. He did not have to live in a segregated district, he leased a charming flat in Chelsea . . . ." In Manhattan he faced restriction and outside this charmed zone, life for him was even more difficult. "At hotels outside of New York," said Ms. Robeson, it was almost impossible for him to secure accommodation . . . ." As for Robeson, he was captivated by London: "I think I'd like to live here," he said—"some day I will,"[54] he proclaimed, confidently and accurately.

By late August 1925 the peripatetic couple were ensconced in London, residing at 18 Milton Chambers, 128 Cheyne Road, a decided upgrade from their first residence in Harlem. "Our front rooms overlook the Thames," chortled Ms. Robeson, "we are between Albert and Battersea Bridges, near Whistler Bend in the heart of Chelsea."[55]

Though the Robesons were lodged in one of the more affluent sections of town, when house-hunting they were appalled to find "lovely places with [a] toilet in the backyard!" and "so many lovely places have no baths at all . . . ." The site they doted on in Chelsea was "beautiful" with such amenities as "bath, electricity, phone, etc.," all for "four guineas."[56] Not far away in Hampstead—it was "beautiful"— said Ms. Robeson, they encountered Emma Goldman, who had made her mark as an anarchist in the U.S.: this activist admired the man she called "dear Paul" and pledged to "come behind the stage after the performance," adding, "I wish with all my heart that Paul's inter-pretation of the Emperor [Jones] should make the cold blooded Englishman realize his greatness."[57] She shared intelligence about the Irish writer, James Joyce, and provided Robeson with contacts in Germany.[58]

Ms. Robeson was taken with Goldman, "a middle aged Jewess—with a fine mind—but starved for love", who she "enjoyed" thoroughly.[59] Still, it was with Goldman, who was becoming a militant opponent of the recently proclaimed Soviet Union, with whom Robeson discussed this controversial nation, as his experience with Jim Crow and the welcome he received in London by way of contrast, was forcing him to clearer political realizations.

In October 1925 the Robesons headed for the French Riviera. They chose Villefranche-sur-Mer, a tiny French town, midway between Nice and Monte Carlo, a lovely quiet village nestling at the foot of the southern Alps. There the couple sat in the nude. There they bumped into Claude McKay, the radical Jamaican writer who had spent time in Moscow, who introduced them to the similarly radical Max Eastman. "Paul listened eagerly to the talk about Russia and Socialism," said his spouse. He also dined with Rex Ingram, an African-American actor, who was able to brief him about opportunities opening in Hollywood.[60]

Carl Van Vechten was a godfather of the then ongoing "Harlem Renaissance," a spicy potpourri of arts, centered in the uptown community that Robeson had called home but with tentacles reaching deeper into the African Diaspora and the continent itself. It has been insufficiently recognized to what extent Robeson was not only an exemplar of this heralded "Renaissance" but, it is likely, also its most public and popular personality. This was known to Van Vechten who seized the occasion of the April 1925 concert to praise Robeson's "natural bass [sic]voice," which possessed an "exceptionally pleasing quality" and was "of considerable range" besides. Before his appearance in O'Neill's plays he had for a period substituted for the bass singer with the Four Harmony Kings in *Shuffle Along*, the well-attended musical. Like others, Van Vechten too thought that Robeson "in the poignant simplicity of his art" resembled Chaliapin.[61]

In 1925, the stormy applause in New York was mirrored by a similar outburst in London. "Paul and Larry gave a concert at the Drury Lane," said Ms. Robeson and managed to "pack that vast theatre. The audience stomps and cheers approval and the press is enthusiastic"; then "the Prince of Wales commands them to sing for him and the King of Spain; the Duke and Duchess of York request them to sing; Lord Beaverbrook, Baroness Ravensdale" and other royals and nobility too numerous to note "do likewise . . . ."[62] On behalf of the Prince of Wales, Brigadier General G.F. Trotter, writing from St. James's Palace, instructed Robeson that a "party" was being given "here" and all "would be pleased if you could come and sing to His guests," one of many such invitations Robeson was to receive in coming years.[63]

With this, Robeson's career took off like a gyrating Roman candle. He had vindicated the weighty words of Czech musician, Antonin Dvorak, who as early as 1893 had become "convinced that the future music" of the U.S. "must be built on the foundations of the songs which are called Negro melodies. They must become the basis of a serious and original school of composition which should be established in the U.S.A."[64] Robeson's adaptation of Dvorak may not have been accidental in that he admitted that "during my younger days it was my privilege to study with Harvey Loomis, who was a student of Dvorak's" and, "most importantly" the actor's "dear friend" was "Harry T. Burleigh," a leading figure in his own right and "often Burleigh" too "spoke of Dvorak . . . ."[65]

Robeson, with a twist, took this insight and applied it worldwide, as he sang—initially a range of spiritual and secular songs grounded in the Negro experience—before record audiences, twice in King Albert Hall in London, and for the British Royal Family, the Prince of Wales, Winston Churchill, et al. He toured Ireland, Scotland, Wales, and Scandinavia.[66]

What had become a part-time preoccupation—performing—became his occupation, a decision made all the easier since it could be pursued beyond the narrow confines of North America, particularly in Britain and Ireland, which had become two of his favorite nations. Later, speaking to the BBC, he recollected about visiting "Ireland many times. I've kissed the blarney," was his insider conclusion, "and known many great Irishmen. The great playwright Eugene O'Neill was a friend of mine. I knew James Stevens and [James] Joyce—a lot of his material makes sense to me," he said in a pre-emptive move deflecting points about the latter's alleged elliptical writing style. "But whenever I used to go to Ireland," he continued, "I was always carried away by a sense of fantasy." Indeed, he continued,

> one day I found myself on a train not far from Cork. Looking out of the window I saw mists covering the tops of the hills. They looked mysterious and inviting and quite suddenly, I had a mad urge to stop the train. I wanted to get out and walk up to the top of those hills, right up there into the clouds. I actually had to stop myself [and] in that moment I realized that it is the Irish countryside itself that opens the doors of the mind to the strange and compelling world of fantasy which is so much a part of the tradition of Ireland.[67]

His notoriety was not limited to Ireland. He recounted to the BBC his early performances in Wales, singing "Negro spirituals." He managed to sing "in "Welsh with a wonderful Welsh choir that made the spiritual sound very near to heavenly music" in that, irrespective of language—Robeson's overarching theme—the message was transmitted. "[T]he Negro's easy approach to death," was an attitude adopted creatively given the atrocious conditions faced: in other words death, was "something which comes even as a comfort, a reward—not something to be afraid of."

The rapturous reception he received in Wales contributed to his being tapped to star in *Showboat*, a musical featuring what became his signature song, "Ol' Man River", whose lyrics he adapted creatively over the years, as his own consciousness deepened, converting it from a baleful lament into his trademark: a song of struggle. Ultimately, Robeson was to perform this song countless times, including a memorable performance in Harlem in 1947 when he was under siege. This was, said Robeson then, a "song which has for me a meaning that is both sentimental and social, I changed some of the words. Instead of the words, 'I gets weary and sick of trying', a'm tired of livin' and scared of dyin',' I sang, 'I keep laughin', instead of crying. I must keep fighting until I'm dyin' . . . ." It was this transmutation that symbolized how Robeson the artist became a revolutionary force.[68]

Showboat ushered onto the global stage a new age for the musical in which songs became integral to the narrative and character development, rather than gratuitous routines.[69] However, like *The Emperor Jones*, it was not greeted with equanimity by all critics. J.A. Rogers, the prominent U.S. Negro columnist, declared that this work was a "deliberate attempt on the part of the White American to carry his anti-Negro propaganda into Europe."[70] In assessing Robeson's early theatrical career, it is neither easy nor simple to find examples of work that stand the test of time—or even of the era in which it was produced.

There were many turning points in Robeson's dazzling career but this musical was one, as he described it later. This musical, he said, "not only saved my life, it saved Larry's too," referring to his accompanist. "You see, back in 1927 we were two very hungry characters," for with his added income came added expenses and another hallmark of Robeson's life was that he was not an expert manager of money. "I might say we were starving," he continued. "Then I was booked to sing in Paris where they gave me a very big build-up. After that I was supposed to go on a tour of Europe." But upon arriving in France, "it was October and I caught influenza. What did I do? I sang—and this was one of the failures of my life. The house"—as was typically the case—"was packed with famous people" but he gave

> not much more than a croak, and they couldn't hear that more than three rows back from the front of the stalls. Two weeks later, I'd gotten over my influenza and I sang again, but nobody came to listen and the grand tour was off. My son, Pauli, was on the way at that time and my wife, Essie, needed me. So, I left poor Larry, flat broke, in Paris and with all the cash we had between us, I went home. Then a friend got me a job in "Showboat" in London. That was my turning point.

Such was his historical assessment. "Three weeks later, Larry was with me and we were well known enough to do a Sunday concert on the stage at Drury Lane. A week after that we packed the Royal Albert Hall" and, he concluded triumphantly, "that's what 'Showboat' did for us and now you can understand why I'm always happy to sing the great song from the show—yes, 'Ol' Man River.'" He knew the composer, George Gershwin, from their stay in New York and "in my early days he often played for me at parties" and also attended his other turning point—the April 1925 concert in New York, where "his first idea for his opera, 'Porgy and Bess' sprang from listening to our music."[71] *Showboat*, a story featuring Dixie treachery, was a wild success and led directly to the Robesons settling in Hampstead by 1929, the London neighborhood they had looked upon longingly for some time. Their residence, as Ms. Robeson put it, was "overlooking the famous Heath."[72]

Paris marked a departure for another reason, for it was from here that he raised searching questions about his singing, that were to lead him down a fruitful intellectual and cultural path: learning more languages so he could communicate more effectively with diverse audiences. "As for my singing," he said, "I'm convinced that in order to attain very substantial success financially I'll need other songs— some in the language of the country in classics that they know. They'll come & rave over our program once or twice—but they really don't get the words—the songs are simple . . . ." He pointed out that Roland "Hayes went to Italy for concerts & lost money. He had to cancel his Russian trip . . . ." But, given his escalating expenses, "we must have money" and, thus, "I must be the complete artist"; for "with our debts and responsibilities", there was no alternative. Of course, if he returned home this language dilemma would evaporate, which is why, "the money is [at] home" while "Europe should be visited for work only alternate years. These are my firm convictions"—but as things turned out, this was not true.[73] For Robeson instead began to deepen his knowledge of languages. This introduced him to the unity of humankind and thus dovetailed with his developing socialist beliefs, which too reflected a universal yearning.

Robeson may have had more than one "turning point" because, like a rocket propelled into the cosmos, there were various boost phases as he shot higher and higher. Surely, his meritorious reputation as an artist appeared to be boundless as early as the late 1920s, as his renown in Europe served to boost further his recognition in his homeland. Intermittently, from 1926–28 he was touring Europe in concert, which led to equally rapturous receptions during yet another episodic tour of the continent from 1931–33.[74] That year of his complaint, 1927, was also the year in which he and Lawrence Brown appeared at a now fabled benefit for the Harlem Museum of African Art.[75] Within months the Robesons were hosting parties at their London flat, with guests like Fred Astaire, Alberta Hunter, and Lord Beaverbrook making appearances.[76] Sir Philip Sassoon also had become part of their circle.[77] Soon, Robeson was a favored guest at the House of Commons where he was spotted by an eagle-eyed journalist chatting "earnestly" with the Prime Minister, Ramsey MacDonald.[78] To cap it off, in November 1927 Robeson became a father, when his only son, Paul, Jr., was born.[79]

Sooner still, he was to hear that the bon vivant, Harold Jackman, "came back to Paris with glowing reports of your London success...."[80] While back in Paris, the alumni magazine of Rutgers was now proud to claim their most talented alumnus, telling one and all that Robeson was the "present reigning favorite of the Parisian amusement world," as "many notable Parisians" and "a host of celebrities" were to be "seen" at his over-subscribed concerts.[81]

Robeson was flying high, indulging the luxury of philosophical musings. ("Art is creation or rather re-creation of beauty. Artists see what others omit. He brings it to others . . . .")[82] Yet, he was sufficiently grounded to be capable of filling Manhattan's Carnegie Hall, the Mecca of musical artists, named after a fabulously wealthy Scottish-American steel baron. "Had no trouble at all in filling it with my voice," he said in 1929; "over 1000 people were turned away. The attendants at the Hall said that no one had ever filled the hall twice in 5 days"—which he accomplished easily.[83]

Robeson remained bi-continental, for by 1928, along with his spouse, their newly born son, Paul Jr. or "Pauli", and his mother-in-law were all occupying a large, late-Victorian abode in St. John's Wood in London, replete—in Van Vechten's words—with "servants" with "Cockney accents" and, in the fashion of the day, a "dining room," featuring "large oil paintings of Turks. Elsewhere whatnots, porcelain glass & various knick-knacks." Van Vechten had arrived there for a party, which was "lovely. There was a great deal of food & much champagne. All the distinguished Negroes in London were there. [Turner] Layton and [Clarence] Johnstone," a well-known vocal and piano duo, "who sang" and "Leslie Hutchinson" came too, who happened to be one of the biggest cabaret stars of that era. Then there was the usual assortment of elite Londoners—Lady Ravensdale (Lord Curzon's daughter), Hugh Walpole, and most of the stars of the English theatre. Robeson sang too, helping to make the event "a great success." Van Vechten told Gertrude Stein, "I think you should come to London to go to a party at Paul's and I'm sure he would give one for you."[84] Robeson was the toast of London with the wittily, droll novelist Evelyn Waugh, penning a portrait of him in one of his best-known novels, *Decline and Fall*.[85]

Before adoring audiences in crowded venues, he was singing in Vienna, Prague, and Budapest, with the enraptured assembled often including U.S. ambassadors and potentates; it was not deemed unusual when they came backstage to congratulate him or offered to entertain him at their residences, something they would be loath to do back home.[86] The press had gotten hold of accounts of his income. The *Philadelphia Tribune*, an African-American journal, initially reported that Robeson had "sung before English royalty" and the supposedly related point that he now had an "attitude that it would be beneath his dignity to appear in a colored review." But then it added that that he had signed for the princely sum of $500 "up front", which would also be his "weekly salary", plus 5 percent of the gross in amounts ranging up to $20, 000 and 10 percent for sums thereafter, to sign to appear on stage.[87] (In inflation-adjusted terms, $500 in 1928 would amount to roughly $6,500 today and $20,000 about $260,000.)

It was during this period that he made the acquaintance of His Royal Highness, the future King George VI; he recalled "Down the Lover's Lane" written by Will Marion Cook with words by Paul Laurence Dunbar, both acclaimed African-American artists; this work, said Robeson, was a "great favourite of George the Sixth from the moment when we first had the privilege of playing it to him when he was Duke of York, way back in 1929."[88]

Yet with all the hosannas of praise that greeted his most quotidian of utterances, Robeson remained dissatisfied. Just before his Carnegie Hall triumph, he had ventured to the theater and left, as he observed, "upset about American audiences" as they were "so terribly crude," present only "for entertainment not because of love of Theatre" and certainly not for enlightenment. "Very strange feeling for me to be sitting in balcony," since—though he was financially capable—"I am almost afraid to purchase orchestra seats for fear of insult" and, by way of sharp contrast, "when in England my being in theatre is almost an event", certainly not a cause for insult. In New York, close by where he was born in New Jersey, there was "no sense of peace-calm-freedom as in London. I feel so oppressed and weighted down," he wailed. Then there was the standing offer to take the lead role in the play that was to define his legacy: "I am very alarmed about [the] chances of 'Othello'," he moaned, thinking of the inter-racial love scenes. "Don't see how American audience will accept play. Of course the liberal group [would]—but [the] mass of theatre goers—never . . ."[89] (During this era, U.S. producers often steered clear of this tragedy, or made sure the lead actors were all white, with the Moor played in "blackface," i.e. with their face covered in ebony dye of some sort.)

Robeson was twisting in agony, able to escape the normalized ravages that had beset so many Africans in North America but knowing full well that a sorry plight continued to bedevil too many others. And even in London, which he had constructed as an idyll, there were serpents in the garden. For near the same time he was unleashing his torment in his diary about the U.S., an executive at London's swank Savoy hotel was apologizing. After consulting with the manager of the Grill Room there, Philip Cox informed "Dear Paul and Essie" that those in charge there, "so far as he is aware," did not know of any who "referred to a colour bar or to any restriction whatever" that had been raised in order to exclude the couple. "Their policy is to attract people of all nations," even those who at first glance seemed to hail from the slums of the British Empire, colonized Africa. "They say that the very fact that you went there so often in the past proves what their policy has been—and it is still the same," he

Figure 3 Robeson, who lived in London for a good deal of the 1920s and 1930s, not only moved decisively to the left during his residence there but as a result of his association with African and Caribbean students and intellectuals such as Jomo Kenyatta of Kenya and C.L.R. James of Trinidad, also developed an astute Pan-African awareness. (Daily Worker and Daily World Photographs Collection, Tamiment Library/Robert F. Wagner Labor Archives, New York University, New York City)

assured. Attached was a "night cable" detailing that the "question of the Colour Bar against the Negroes in England is being raised for the first time in acute form" by the Robesons and "several public bodies have protested . . . ."

Robeson would not have been surprised by the designation of the true culprit: "the annual invasion of American tourists is blamed by many persons for the exclusion of Negroes from some restaurants and hotels recently," for, as was their wont, these interlopers insisted on the global export of their peculiar folkways.[90] Cox admitted that a "sensation was caused" by "the receipt of a letter from the celebrated American Negro singer and actor, Paul Robeson, stating that he and his wife had recently been refused admittance to the dining hall and Grill Room of a leading London Hotel . . . ."[91]

At this juncture, Robeson was better known as an artist but since he was already well on his way to becoming the best-known U.S. Negro, i.e. a member of a dispossessed group in a potent nation, he was beginning to be looked towards as a tribune by others similarly situated. This included Herbert Murray of Victoria, Australia, of the "Australia Aboriginal Progressive League," who informed Robeson that "we are having a hard time fighting with the white folk," referring to "we people who are a despised race, a race who has been denied really the right to live . . . ." Imploringly, he beseeched Robeson, "you should visit Australia," since "we have a met a lot of your people who have performed on different stages here . . . ."[92] Robeson was not able to comply for decades.

Though the Robesons had climbed the slippery pole of success, they had chosen not to shroud their objections to a "colour bar" that they might have been able to personally evade but which would entangle others not as well situated. Ultimately, Robeson was to conclude that intermittent objections to noxiousness were not enough: there had to be a root and branch overhaul of society, a process that involved construction of a socialist commonwealth.

3

Rising Revolutionary

When Robeson played the lead role in *Othello* in London in 1930, box-office records were set and the tragedy ran for six weeks.[1] Reportedly, it garnered a hefty £22,000 in the first few weeks of production.[2] It was not unusual for early performances to be greeted by 20 or more curtain calls.[3] His already skyrocketing reputation ascended further for this production struck a chord in the populace. This was not unlike what had happened in the nineteenth century, when Robeson's predecessor as premier tragedian, Ira Aldridge, was also catapulted into further prominence when performing this same role in Europe.[4] This suggested that the plot involving a "Moor," in a contradictory relationship with the state, tapped into unresolved dilemmas about racism and the "colour bar," which Robeson had confronted only recently in London in a blaze of publicity.

The inter-racial scenes in this play also resonated, for just as Robeson was entering the stage in London, a worldwide cause célèbre was erupting in Scottsboro, Alabama,[5] when nine black youths were falsely accused of sexual molestation of two white women. They were headed for execution, like so many African-Americans previously— but, then, the International Labor Defense [ILD], initiated by the Communist Party, launched a global campaign in league with Moscow. This campaign saved the lives of the accused and led to significant reforms of the criminal justice system in the U.S. This effort, which led to raucous demonstrations at U.S. legations across the globe, converted Jim Crow into an international concern—not unlike that which befell South African apartheid a few decades later. The ILD was led by Robeson's good friend from Harlem, William Patterson,[6] also an attorney who had strayed from the path of wealth accumulation and had become a leading U.S. Communist; it was their conversations in Europe that compelled Robeson to make a more decisive turn to the left and socialism. The concatenation of *Othello*, combined with Scottsboro, was a catalyst for Robeson's transformation. And the glowing reviews he received in London redounded to his advantage in his homeland, for the NAACP (National Association for the Advancement of Colored People)—which had within its leadership one of his biggest fans, Walter White—began to beat the drum of publicity on his behalf, flooding the news media with press releases about his triumphs.[7] But it was not just White: according to one source the pre-eminent intellectuals Rebecca West and Aldus Huxley argued that "they never saw better Shakespearean acting in all their lives . . . ."[8]

Robeson was not so moved by his handiwork, for as he subsequently told the *New Statesman*, "for the first two weeks in every scene I played with Desdemona"—the love interest of Robeson's Othello—"that girl couldn't get near me. I was backing away from her all the time like a plantation hand in the parlour."[9] In other words, Robeson knew that a major taboo of U.S. life, the violation of which could lead to lynching, was heterosexual mixing across the color line, and even when engaged in a fiction on stage, this taboo haunted his performance, giving it added resonance.

Speaking of his tempestuous scenes with Desdemona, Robeson said, "I wouldn't care to play those scenes in some parts of the United States. The audience would get rough; in fact, might become very dangerous," with outraged audience members charging the stage with mayhem in mind, possible if not likely.[10] Robeson well knew that in 1930 not only could he not perform *Othello* in the U.S. in the way he did so in London but, most likely, a production in his homeland was highly improbable then. After all, he and Desdemona had to kiss and embrace several times, in violation of basic norms in the republic, while, said Robeson, "the English don't mind."[11]

His previous well-known roles in *The Emperor Jones* and *All God's Chillun*, especially the latter, presented like issues, but, said Robeson, "presented no problem of understanding"; that is, in "approaching a role," as an actor he had to grasp "the understanding of the character, his background, his language and the portrayal of the character in terms of theatre technique . . . ." But these two O'Neill creations, treading as they did familiar U.S. ground, were easier for Robeson to grasp—the question of a "Moor" in Europe centuries earlier was quite different. "The milieu of the play was not my own familiar background," he conceded. "The characters were not people I had always known or known about . . . ." The "one familiar and for me saving fact was that 'Othello' to me was an African Negro (not a Moor)," and "I played him as a Negro . . . ." In sum, "'Othello' was another matter." But when performing this character decades later in London, "I decided to get into Othello from the inside—from his point of view," a new interpretation founded on a deeper understanding of Shakespeare, based on extensive study; thus, he said, "I have come to think of Othello not so much as a Negro but rather as a foreigner and alien who finds himself in a strange country, society and culture . . . ." This deeper understanding, too, was part of Robeson's own political maturation, driven by his turn to the left, generated by Scottsboro and his personal friendship with Patterson.[12]

Robeson's groping as an actor in his attempt to grasp the lineaments of Othello was of a piece with his groping as a black man seeking to grasp the lineaments of capitalism, colonialism, and white supremacy. As for the former, he confessed later, "I didn't know what the hell I was doing" as an actor in *Othello* though "I was praised to the skies as a natural genius"; but in 1930, "I had more false pride than today and wouldn't admit I was like a child stumbling in the dark."[13] Playing Othello provided Robeson with a profounder understanding of white supremacy; to that extent, it was art that helped to drive him to revolutionary understanding. Performing this role, he said, "has taken away from me all kinds of fears, all sense of limitation"—quite simply, "it has made me free."[14]

Seemingly, the confidence he gained from the generous praise heaped on his stage depictions reverberated to the benefit of his concert appearances. His acting heightened his public profile making many more willing to pay to hear him sing. "Paul's tour is going splendidly," said his spouse with brio in 1930: "everywhere he has phenomenal houses in these days of unsuccessful concerts."[15] The sterner critic might also have described Robeson's relationship with his spouse similarly as "unsuccessful." Robeson was constantly in the public eye and was praised lavishly for his handsome good looks and, according to Eslanda, was not opposed to taking advantage of this sensitive situation. Another U.S. national, Anita Reynolds, was in London during this time and, she tittered, stories of the Robesons' fraught relationship "were making the rounds" there. He was "rumored to be having an affair with a woman who was very close to the royal family. His Rolls-Royce could be seen parked within walking distance of her home. Mrs. Robeson chased all over London looking for the car and trying to catch him . . . ."[16]

As with so many other couples, these "stories" would have remained safely tucked away in the vapor of rumors—except they were confirmed by Ms. Robeson in her revealing book about her husband. In these remarkable pages, she unveiled the shakiness of their relationship, confirming the stories about what many saw as Robeson's wandering eye for other women, leaving her with bruised feelings. Needless to say, Robeson was displeased with this part of her otherwise arresting biography. The allegations to this end led Martha Greuning to seek an "injunction to restrain" publication of this biography, leading to dueling thrusts from opposing counsels.[17] "Clever move to have your book appear on the day after Paul's opening night in 'Othello'," mused Emma Goldman; she went on to note that "Paul is doing strenuous work, singing so often and traveling about the provinces. It is fortunate that he has such splendid physic, adding, "he will be [the] most handsome Othello I have ever seen . . . ."[18]

These random assertions—his traveling (or "carousing" as Ms. Robeson might have said), his "splendid physic," or physique, and how he was "most handsome" was also the message delivered in the book, albeit more directly and explicitly. During this time a controversy erupted when a Philadelphia exhibition banned a life-size nude sculpture of Robeson; though this was on racist—not salacious—grounds, one observer was among many moved to note that Robeson's "figure is almost an exact replica of Adonis." Another commentator made it clear that "lack of clothing is not reason for the rejection," though this absence was what attracted so much attention in the first place, suggestive of the obviousness of the physical attractiveness of Robeson.[19]

Too much can be made of this since, after all, any extra-marital liaisons of Robeson were designed to be surreptitious. For example, the press targeted the British heiress, Nancy Cunard, as a Robeson paramour and rival of Ms. Robeson, but she was dumbfounded by this allegation, remarking perplexedly, "I met him once in Paris in 1926,"[20] and that provided hardly enough time to consummate a romance. Still, the press continued to vibrate with stories of his assumed liaison with Cunard, forcing Robeson to deny ever more bizarre stories of their relationship. "The article is absolutely absurd," he told one periodical of one assumed exposé since "Miss Cunard has never been in a studio in which I was broadcasting and consequently could not have been ejected at my suggestion"; hence, he rejected these "dreadful attacks,"[21] but they kept coming since, as a celebrity, Robeson was fair game, a recipient of poison-tipped arrows and a target for a public with an apparent ceaseless interest in his personal life.

Moreover, and strikingly, the presumed object of Robeson's romantic attention in coming years, according to his spouse, was Nina Mae McKinney, an actor of note who happened to be African-American. "Don't start listening to Harlem gossip," she warned her mother, "except to be amused by it" since "[I] am not influenced by any of it, in the slightest" for "I graduated from that years ago . . . . I'm much too busy doing things which interest and satisfy me to stop for that junk. It all may or may not be true as the stuff Nina Mae said about Paul being her man" since "she may even believe it herself . . . .")[22] In short, some stories about Robeson's affairs seemed either fanciful or of small concern to his spouse. As so often happens with celebrated figures, there were those who claimed ties to Robeson—or projected ties upon him—that were not real.

Still, this could not obscure equally real problems in their relationship. From the onset, Eslanda had invested quite a bit of her life in building her husband's career at the expense of her own. It was in 1924 that she revealed in her diary, "start my month's vacation from Presbyterian Hospital today. Am sick to death of the Lab, and do hope that I won't ever have to go back."[23]

By 1931 she was commenting, "discussed divorce with Paul and we are both quite happy and pleased over the prospect of our freedom"; just before that she observed, "Paul urges me to stay here [meaning Switzerland—a frequent haunt for the couple and the site, as shall be seen, of one of his more intriguing films] so he can carry on with Peggy," his presumed lover, "I suppose. It would be inconvenient having me in London and trying to meet her [there]."[24]

The Robesons shared many commonalities—a similar political trajectory particularly—which is why they were married for decades but, as so often happens, there were differences between the two: She had her own complaints. Their "permanent break" was "inevitable" since

we have never had the same tastes in people, places, things. His education was literary, classical, mine was entirely scientific, as a chemist; his temperament was artistic, mine strictly practical; he is vague, I am definite . . . he likes late hours, I am an early bird . . . he is not ambitious, although once having undertaken a thing [e.g. language study] he is never content until he accomplishes it as perfectly as possible; I am essentially and aggressively ambitious [in contrast].[25]

She could have added that while he had found his métier as an artist, she was still stumbling and would not find her footing for some time as a journalist.

Then there was her ambition for him, which drove him to ever greater heights and in which she reveled. "[I] a member of one of the 'socially elect' Negro families" in Washington, D.C., she said of her elite status in the U.S., which was true. "I have met and in many cases become friends with many world class celebrities, and I have learned to find my way about in Paris, Berlin, Prague, Vienna, Budapest and Bucharest"—all true too. "I know personally nearly every Negro of interest and importance both at home and abroad"— equally accurate. "I have acted as 'guide' in Harlem to many people from Count Hermann Keyserling, the eminent German philosopher to Mr. Noel Coward,"[26] the noted British playwright. The problem was that her spouse was not as impressed with such "accomplishments" as she was.

In informing the singer and actress, Etta Moten, about financial arrangements, Ms. Robeson said with pride that "our own [agents] are the finest in the business but are straight musical agents and handle"—she added proudly—"only the world known musicians, such as . . . Rachmaninoff [and] Horowitz" and Robeson.[27] In other words, Robeson was in the ionosphere of artists—a perch that did not include Moten—and such heights were pleasingly important to Ms. Robeson, not as much to her spouse.

Though she was directing his career, she was not a good manager of money either, leaving the couple to borrow thousands of pounds to liquidate debts at a time when his income was climbing steadily.[28] "Financially of course I'm still struggling," said Robeson, at a time when he had attained a measure of fame and the income that goes along with it.[29] Robeson, who was loath to write (this was of a piece with the reclusiveness that gripped the last years of his life and his preference for reading, studying and learning), let alone write of his social conquests (unlike Eslanda) was then evolving to the point where learning languages—a pre-eminent solitary pursuit—was his defining habit, and, thus, was growing apart from his spouse. From all appearances, he was not as concerned with the world of celebrity fame, which seemed to captivate Ms. Robeson.

As so often happens, financial pressures were exacerbating the everyday pressures of marriage. Resolving this tension—which is what the couple did—was to save their marriage. "I don't make enough money here to warrant all the fuss," Robeson warned his wife. "Really when straight tax and super tax is added I make nothing. And living expenses are terrible . . . ." He was pondering seeking a tax haven, in Kitsbuhel, Austria, also a skiing haven in the Alps. If not there, perhaps Salzburg, or maybe "outside Paris. It will be much cheaper & I can come over to England to fulfill engagements," a site of his most lucrative opportunities. "I certainly need different audiences for my work," he counseled, a necessity driven by his growing interest in performing in different languages, a path initially driven by commerce but which was to lead, ironically, to socialism. "People who are interested in us," he advised, "will have to see us mainly on the Continent . . . ."[30]

"Your letter upset us very much indeed," was the response of Van Vechten to their impending split: "we cannot quite imagine you and Paul apart."[31] But that was precisely what was on the cards, in the wake of Robeson's triumph as Othello.

The couple came to see that wife and manager involved different roles that could easily conflict, inducing rifts. Of course, these roles could be mutually reinforcing. "Noel Coward has been marvelous to me," she enthused, and "had come often to the flat to talk with me, dine with me, and I had been out with him . . . ."[32] "I am so glad we are friends," said the British writer, "& thank you for being so sweet to me . . . "[33] "Will be delighted to have dinner," he added as her marital problems reached a new crescendo: "looking forward to seeing you then . . . ."[34] It did not hurt the career of Robeson, the actor, for his spouse and manager to be friendly with a leading playwright.

The marital tension exacted a toll.[35] "Paul is ill again," wrote Eslanda, "a very bad cold, perhaps a mild attack of influenza."[36] "I hear on all sides that he is very depressed," she informed Van Vechten; "so unsettled mentally" besides "he doesn't know his own mind. When he gets his divorce, he may get himself together," she added with a scoff. "I hate the idea of him being unhappy and disorganized," his present state.[37]

"Terribly ill with nerves," reported Ms. Robeson, of herself in late 1930; "a nervous breakdown that went into paralysis and lost the use of the whole left side of my face. I was a sight" and "tho[ught] I would be permanently paralyzed." Thus, she moaned, "I'm not coming to America with him this time mainly because he doesn't want me. He's fallen in love with another girl" and, thus, "his life is rather complicated"; i.e. "he has not only strayed but gone on a hike."[38] Her husband, she said, needed a "good rest"—but an objective observer could have made the same prescription for her.[39]

Marital conflicts led to others: the London press reported that whereas Robeson was sympathetic to Marcus Garvey, the Jamaican organizer, his spouse was not.[40] She was enthusiastic, for example, about the play by Wallace Thurman, entitled *Jeremiah the Magnificent*, which she described as detailing the life of "Garvey, the famous West Indian Rascal."[41]

Yet—and as often happens with couples—they overcame this rough patch and once again it seemed that the question of racism was a factor, in that his presumed paramour was not black and there was concern how an inter-racial couple would fare in the U.S. The same question was a factor when Robeson's comrade, William Patterson, left his Russian spouse behind in the Soviet Union when he returned to the U.S.[42] The personal was merging with the political, all of which was driving him toward deeper political understandings. Robeson's extra-marital liaisons were disproportionately with "white" women but it was this kind of relationship that would not be easy to eventuate in marriage: this difficulty helped to lead him back to his "black" wife. Moreover, though the record is not clear, it is probably not coincidental that his reconciliation with his spouse coincided with his deeper political engagement (in that a "white" wife would have complicated his ability to become a leader of African-Americans) and also coincided with his increasingly close relationship to Patterson, who was impelled to make a similar racial choice.

With a kind of martial stability emerging after months of rockiness, Robeson was able to turn his attention more fully to his art and what was becoming its close complement: the study of languages. The world had not stood still as the Robesons bickered. The Scottsboro case—a racist frame-up of nine black youths in Alabama based on a spuriously explosive charge of inter-racial rape—was delivering a dose of adrenalin to America's bloodstream, as millions marched worldwide, serving to augment membership in the Communist parties that had arisen concomitant with the Russian Revolution of 1917. At the same time, in direct reaction, fascism was increasing too, first in Italy, then in Germany.

Now resident in continental Europe, the Robesons had a ringside seat as this tumult unfolded. "We are here en route to Bucharest from Vienna," said Ms. Robeson, speaking of Budapest, "then into Yugoslavia."[43] They were traveling regularly to Berlin, "where Paul will do 3 special performances of 'The Emperor Jones' in English."[44] Then in the midst of their marital woes they managed to star in *Borderline*, filmed in Switzerland. "Paul and I had great fun making a film in Switzerland a few weeks ago," Ms. Robeson asserted and on the way there they "enjoyed Berlin enormously,"[45] which was not their opinion most decidedly when they visited the German capital a few years later, after Hitler's rise. It was an "experimental movie" she said correctly about a film that was a cinematic breakthrough and, as well, helped to solder a marriage that seemed on the point of disintegration.

It was a silent film with English inter-titles that involved a fraught matter that Scottsboro and *Othello* and, not coincidentally, their own lives confronted: inter-racial relationships. It was avant-garde in execution, influenced by the Soviet cineaste Sergei Eisenstein, with whom the couple would soon become acquainted in Moscow. It was groundbreaking too, dealing with race and sexuality at a time when such issues were hardly the staple of cinema. It may have been reconciling too, in that it offered an acting opportunity to Ms. Robeson, providing her with a career option and allowing her to participate more directly in the art that was becoming the preoccupation of her husband. It was also significant that this film was made in Europe, not Hollywood, a site where such cinematic daring, least of all involving the benighted "Negro", was not on the agenda. With rich and imaginative cutting, or "montage", and riveting foci, the story is told of two Negroes who drift in and out of a small town poisoned by petty jealousies, vicious malice and gossip. Throughout the film, those who are defined as "white" are presented negatively, as—according to one critic—a picture of "sordid calculation and unbridled jealousy," of corruption and decadence, while the blacks symbolize what is pure and natural. Daringly, there is a glimpse of a white man being lynched for his attention to a Negro woman.[46]

After the artistic success of this Swiss film, the artistically energized Robeson returned to London and, said his spouse, began "trying out a new stunt. He took the Savoy Theatre for a week and offered his own program," which turned out to be "such a success." This "took him on the road of a 10 week tour" as audiences were enthralled by his "group of spirituals, one group of folk songs, 1 group of secular songs" and "the last scene from 'The Emperor Jones.'"[47]

Robeson also found time to embark on a course that would simultaneously influence his language study, his art and his politics. It was in 1920s and especially 1930s London that Robeson "discovered" Africa or, more precisely, met countless African exiles who shaped him inexorably. This growing list included Joshua Nkomo, a founder of the movement that helped to lead Zimbabwe (then Rhodesia) to independence.[48] He also collaborated with the League of Coloured People in London, which too included a modicum of individuals of African origin.[49] He had begun to take courses to that end at the

School of Oriental and African Studies at the University of London.⁵⁰ "That discovery," he said, "profoundly influenced my life." Robeson "came to know many Africans," including future presidents and prime ministers, such as "Azikiwe and Nkrumah and Kenyatta." A number of these "Africans were students and I spent many hours talking with them and taking part in their activities at the West African Students Union Building," said Robeson. "Somehow they came to think of me as one of them; they took pride in my successes," of which there were many then; "and they made Mrs. Robeson and me honorary members of the Union." He "also came to know another class of Africans—the seamen in the ports of London, Liverpool and Cardiff . . . ." So inspired, "I studied [their] languages—as I do to this day," he recalled in 1953; this study included "Yoruba, Efik, Benin, Ashanti and the others" and it was then that he "came to know of the remarkable kinship between African and Chinese culture[s]," which contributed to his advocating closer cooperation between the two, notably after the triumph of the Chinese Revolution. He pored over relevant British publications, e.g. the *New Statesman*. "I argued and discussed the subject [Africa] with men like H.G. Wells and [Harold] Laski and Nehru . . . ." He became so passionate about the topic that "British Intelligence came one day to caution me about the political meanings of my activities . . . ."⁵¹

Whitehall—and British intelligence services too—may have known that he subsidized the budget of the West African Student Union, which included numerous presumed radicals. When he spoke to them, auditoriums were jammed routinely. At one effusive gathering in the 1930s, attendance was at a record high, as loud cheers greeted his pledge that anti-colonialism would become his life cause and visiting the continent would become a priority to that end.⁵²

This visit by intelligence officials may also have been driven by Robeson's own words, for example when he informed an inquisitive Manchester journalist, that for "three or four months of every year I'm going to live in Africa among my own people." In fact, said Robeson, "I shall make my headquarters in Africa," a seemingly likely prospect, since by that point he had "already learned two African [languages]." If that were not enough to cause consternation among the colonialists, he also was "contemplating singing in Java, Malay,

China and Japan." Why not? "I am studying their folk songs," said Robeson,[53] in their own languages and desired an outlet for his virtuosity. A contemporaneous account asserted that he was on his way to Cape Town—a venture that did not materialize—but this too may too have peaked interest among intelligence operatives.[54]

It was in the 1930s that he arrived at a realization that was to take on significant import in coming decades: "I am one of the very few," he said, "who persists in suggesting that the African cultural form is in many respects similar to the old Archaic Chinese (Pre-Confucius, Pre-Lau-tse)." As Ethiopia was on the verge of being torn by an epochal Italian invasion and China was reeling from sharp lances from Japan, Robeson was sufficiently prescient to observe, "I am as interested in the problem which confronts the Chinese people, as well as in those which concern, for example, Abyssinia. To me," he said with typical profundity, "the time seems long past when people can afford to think exclusively in terms of national units . . . ."[55]

As Robeson came to know more about Africa, it had multiple effects: it enhanced his understanding of his own people—African-Americans—and increased his desire to participate more fully in their uphill battle. It led him to Moscow, in that the Soviet Union was one of the few nations which took a strident anti-colonial position. It not only led him to study more languages but it also influenced his acting choices, particularly in cinema.

And this language study, inspired in no small part by Africa, increased his popularity as an artist—since he would sing in songs of various nations—creating more lucrative appearances, (frequent concerts ultimately paid more handsomely than infrequent, and often demeaning, films); his concerts were particularly popular in Europe, but that in turn was bringing him face-to-face with the rise of fascism, a development that ultimately radicalized him. Surely the virtuous circle created allowed him to reside comfortably in London, a fact discovered by the visiting African-American journalist Shirley Graham[56]—who was to become later the wife of W.E.B. Du Bois,[57] Robeson's friend and comrade during numerous Red Scare battles in the U.S. Graham was struck by the "vine covered brick house in Hampstead, one of the most beautiful and exclusive suburbs of London," she informed her mostly black—and no doubt impressed—

audience: "facing the famous Heath with grounds sloping down from the back to a lovely park" and "swept by cool breezes from the Channel," it also featured an "old fashioned English garden." A "solemn faced French butler"—apparently the Robesons had replaced their aides with "Cockney" accents—"will conduct you up the winding stairways to the big library-sitting room on the second floor. Books, books, books!" were all about. There were "solid big chairs" and "lovely rugs," and, readers were assured, contrary to press accounts, an "utterly happy wife." Adjoining the library was a room for Robeson's use and, it was added with similar reassurance: "large, high-ceiling" and "wholly masculine as befits a big man . . . ." Yes, she rejoiced, "he has genius, he has brains, and he has a *wife*" [emphasis original].[58]

Of course, this was partially propaganda—though not in the pejorative sense—in that her African-American audience, under perpetual assault for its alleged intellectual deficiency, could jubilate in her portrait of a brainy Robeson, just as this same community told constantly about its supposed family breakdown, could jubilate about the drawn role of Ms. Robeson. It was precisely this kind of press coverage that was converting Robeson into a folk hero among blacks, an attraction that would lure him back home once war erupted in Europe and the tug of his people's desperate struggles could no longer be ignored.

But it was not just star-struck visiting Negro journalists who were seduced by the radiance emitted by the wattage of the Robesons. Alexander Woollcott was at the apex of the reporting profession in Manhattan and had little incentive to portray Robeson in flattering terms. But that he did, depicting the artist simply as "the world's most famous Negro." Woollcott was stunned to hear Robeson speak Russian without an accent, all the more remarkable since this skill was developed without residing for any length of time in the Soviet Union. Robeson, said the impressed journalist, "has such extraordinary powers of concentration that he can sit rapt at Linguaphone [language tapes] twelve hours a day, leaving it only long enough to go to the icebox for an occasional glass of milk but never leaving it at all to answer the persistent telephone . . . ." As Woollcott saw Robeson, he strayed from language study "only when word comes from Mrs.

Robeson that the rent is due," and then and only then "does the man emerge and sing or [act] for a week or two"; then "back he goes into the luxurious seclusion of the work . . . ."[59]

Once he was asked about his study of languages, asking how many could he speak, a simple query for mere mortals. But Robeson found "it hard to answer" in a "few words." "The learning of languages" was "not only fun, but a game with rich rewards." "I have learned French, German, Spanish, Chinese, Efik (an African language) and Yiddish. I can read the literature in these languages, can sing songs in them with such impeccable pronunciation, accent and even inflection and 'color' that people to whom these languages are native will not believe that I am not fluent"—and, he added, "I would probably be able to do a play in any of these languages with a little help . . . ." He doubted his fluency in these languages while confirming "I can follow and take part in some not too specialized conversation in them. After I have lived in those countries for three months, I am confident I could be fluent." He was then polishing his "Hebrew, Norwegian, Czech, Modern Greek, Ancient Latin and Portuguese"— yet, with all that, he conceded openly in 1950, when such assertions brought no premium, "Russian is the only foreign language I can say I read and speak fluently," that is, "I can sing songs in Russian with ease and confidence . . . ." For "in the learning of languages, I work at catching the essential spirit of the language" and "I think I speak Russian more than any other foreign language because I like it better . . . ." In fact, "I would probably be able to do plays better in Russian than in modern English because I find the language richer, warmer, more fully expressive, more colorful than modern English . . . ." He went further to assert that "the Russian language today is comparable to Shakespearean English—young, forceful and rich."[60]

Yet, it was not Russian and African languages alone that had attracted Robeson. During the summer of 1932 he told his spouse that "my French is coming fine . . . and I'm also working on German and Spanish . . . ." The latter language was becoming the de facto second official language of his homeland, while the former exposed him to a catalog of songs and well-paying concerts. Of course, he added, "my Russian is unbelievable," which apparently was infecting his personality: "I do remain so *esoteric* at times. Very Russian I guess" [emphasis original].[61]

His knowledge of Russian was propelled by budding interest in the Bolshevik Revolution and tireless labor, both of which were becoming hallmarks of his life. This knowledge required countless hours of study and it became difficult for some journalists to accept that a man thought of as an actor, a singer, a celebrity, would spend so much time in this fashion. So one reporter noted, "I happen to speak it too and I tried him out on it! We chatted for a while in the language and he told me that having mastered it and French and German, he was now turning his attention to Hebrew . . . ." So, there sat an impressed reporter and the then garrulous Robeson: "we sat and smoke and drank incredible quantities of lemon tea," as they discussed Dostoevsky and Pushkin. The latter two, readers were told, were "his favorite Russian authors whom he reads for hours at night when he can't sleep or 'when I'm not over fond of the world'" or when he couldn't perform because of problems of central heating in London "which dries his voice up so that he can't sing . . . ."[62]

Robeson's voice was sufficiently suitable for Du Bose Heyward and George Gershwin to press him to star in their newly created *Porgy and Bess*. "This particular combination," said Heyward, "you, George and myself . . . stood to produce something at least memorable, perhaps almost great"; though it was understandable why Robeson turned him down in light of his admission that he was "gathering authentic ideas and themes from the primitive Negroes in the back country" of Carolina.[63] Ms. Robeson made it clear that her spouse was "enthusiastic" about playing the leader of a Carolina slave revolt, Denmark Vesey, rather than the saccharine character that was Porgy.[64] Heyward's spouse was happy that "you are enthusiastic in the idea of a Vesey play," though he conceded that it had "very little" of the all-important "man-woman interest. The theme is solely Vesey's devotion to and work for his cause," with "no song and very little laughter . . . ."[65] Heyward found it to be a "personal disappointment" that "we are not going to be together"[66]—but if he had paid attention to Robeson's trajectory, he would not have been surprised by this rejection.

With the attention delivered by his star turn in *Othello*, his "discovery" of Africa, the urgency of the Scottsboro case, directed by his old friend from Harlem, William Patterson, the concomitant growing influence of Communist parties, particularly in London and Moscow, and the rise of fascism, Robeson was at a crossroads. His personal triumphs seemed to wane in comparison to the problems encountered by other Africans, including his own family. "I can come in" to exalted and luxurious inner sanctums, he told a British journal, "but my own brother, my own father, cannot come in behind me."[67] This recognition helped to impel Robeson toward firmer political commitment.

The brief summary in the preceding paragraph hardly does justice to the depth and importance of the journey that Robeson took, in terms of both kilometers and ideological distance. For it was a transformative trip to Germany, then the Soviet Union—the two nations whose confrontation in the early 1940s shaped the contours of the planet—that changed Robeson radically for all time. On the verge of this journey, the Robesons were residing comfortably at 19 Buckingham Street—"off the Strand", as their friend, Marie Seton put it. Though perceived as a comedown from Hampstead, this London home may have been more in line with the Robesons' growing political engagement. "The old stairs creaked" when "mounted to the top floor flats. One flat was too small for the Robeson family, so Essie's mother, 'Mama', lived with Pauli in another, just across the landing. The flat occupied by Paul and Essie had one bedroom, a living room and a study, kitchen and bathroom." Befitting a man who spent a good deal of his waking hours immersed in language study and philology, the flat "looked very much like the home of a London university professor," as it was "lined with packed bookshelves."

But also as befits so many university professors, he was swimming in his studies, only occasionally emerging from this reasonably tranquil pool to engage in other matters. But it was not just that the press of events was sufficiently intense to drive Robeson to deepen his already sprouting political commitments but a number of personal encounters solidified this emerging trend. For at that moment, Jewish refugees were flooding into London, escaping the early ravages of fascism's spread on the continent. He was asked to perform at benefits for them but, according to Seton, his terse response was "I'm an artist . . . I don't understand politics . . . ." But then he relented and his life was transformed as a partial result of these face-to-face encounters.[68]

It was also during this time, he recalled reflectively, "when I was speaking at a meeting of intellectuals in London about the winter of 1933 or 34" and then a "Negro man got up in the back of the hall and said, 'why don't you stop all this nonsense, you intellectuals and princes' sons. Don't you understand that the basic problem is the problem of the working class of Africa," that is, "the ones who are exploited"; so "why don't you go [to] Africa, especially why don't you follow what's going on in the Soviet Union?'" Never to shrink and shuffle away in such a situation, Robeson said, "I accepted the challenge" and "a couple of weeks later I found myself in Moscow," where he bumped into Patterson.[69]

It was just before Christmas in 1934 that the Robesons, accompanied by Marie Seton, headed for Moscow, with an intermediate stop in Germany. His German was fluent, which came in handy when he was menaced by storm troopers at a train station.[70] This German fluency evidently influenced his four-year-old son who, according to his proud mother, often "rattled along in beautiful German";[71] indeed, the younger Robeson "prefers to express himself in German."[72]

But German fluency did not seem to bring a sanctuary for these beset travelers. Robeson and his companions were standing on the platform when the authorities accosted him in particular. This "run-in" he proclaimed, "certainly would have meant my life" if he had been unable to retain his composure. "I remember getting ready for possible attack and determined to take some of the storm troopers with me,"[73] when cooler heads prevailed.

It was a close call. It was a "nightmare" according to Ms. Robeson. "Paul said he felt the atmosphere and the uniforms" reminded him of a "pack of wolves, waiting and hoping to be unleashed and released . . . ." Like her husband, this journey was too spurring a heightening of her own political consciousness, which in turn complemented and strengthened that of her better known husband: "I suddenly understand for the first time," she confided to her diary, "what the feeling must be of a black in Mississippi," i.e. "terror, fear, horror, tension, nerves strained to breaking point".[74] Such realizations were catalytic in driving the now politically engaged couple back across the Atlantic to their bedeviled homeland.

"I encountered trouble that might have well have meant my life," Robeson detailed later in speaking of a tense Berlin. Then it was on to the Soviet Union and after that visit, he returned to London renewed. "I saw the suffering about me with different eyes," he declared. "I realized that the suffering of my own people was related to the sufferings of equally oppressed minorities. Later I saw Austria in the dark days, Norway and Denmark on the edge of destruction"[75] and these enervating experiences led to the political thrust that would define him to his dying days: opposition to fascism at all costs and alignment with the force that seemed most disposed to confronting the same: Communist parties.

As his fluent Russian language skills suggested, Robeson's interest in the Land of Lenin was not new. He had first become interested in visiting Russia during the late 1920s when conversations with friends while on vacation on the Riviera had provided him with an initial vicarious exposure to the Soviet Union. That his invitation was tendered by the internationally acclaimed filmmaker Sergei Eisenstein only increased his interest. Actually, said his friend and biographer, Marie Seton, it was this acclaimed Soviet cineaste who made a "personal request" for Robeson to appear in Moscow for intense discussions about a proposed movie about the Haitian Revolution. He had "discussed this film with me," said Seton, "shortly after" returning from Mexico and "I transmitted an account of the project to Mr. Robeson."[76] That his visit in Berlin was diametrically opposite from what he had encountered in Moscow—including a tense conversation in the former metropolis with a Jewish friend[77]—only served to concretize his commitment to anti-fascism and solidarity with those of a similar outlook.

4

From Moscow to Madrid

R obeson had arrived in Moscow in the mid-1930s at a fraught
moment. "I was there during the purges," he recounted
later, and discussed this grave matter with Sergei Eisenstein,
particularly the tragic fate that befell Soviet leader Nikolai Bukharin.
This was an acknowledgment of the massive human rights violations
then unfolding but which Communists—and their sympathizers—
tended to rationalize as an unfortunate but necessary measure needed
to brace effectively for the fascist onslaught which was to cost tens of
millions of lives in the Soviet Union. Some on the left, alternatively,
blamed these violations on provocations engineered by these very
same fascists designed to ignite a bloodily massive over-reaction in
Moscow. Generally, Robeson leaned toward both viewpoints and this
opinion became part of the bill of indictment laid at his doorstep. He
provided these critics with more ammunition when, on a subsequent
visit to Moscow, he attended the Bolshoi Ballet with his young son.
Also there was Stalin: upon spotting him the audience with Robeson
included began to applaud spontaneously. He was moved to speak of
this leader's "wonderful sense of kindliness . . . here was one who was
wise and good," he exulted: "I lifted high my boy, Pauli—to wave to
this world leader."[1]

Being able to speak Russian and practice this language on a mass
basis for the first time seemed to strengthen Robeson's accelerating
fondness for Moscow. His dedicated focus was noticed by his spouse:
"it will be thrilling to see how [his] Russian turns out," she said.
"He's so keen. He feels that he can become an official and important
interpreter of Russian music and literature. He feels he understands
it, and is close to it, and he loves the language."[2] This love dovetailed
with his simultaneous growing fascination with the socialist
experiment, which mutually reinforced both.

Eslanda, in sum, was similarly impressed and it appeared that her ability to evolve in his political direction, or, perhaps, adjust accordingly, strengthened what had been a fraying marital tie. "Everywhere we have had marvelous audiences," she enthused; all were "wildly appreciative . . . ." Their son, she said, was "now in Russia Model School in Moscow. School No. 25. Stalin's daughter & [another top Soviet leader, Vyachseslav] Molotov's son, are his schoolmates." Both she and her husband expressed "astonishment at the complete lack of color consciousness" they witnessed and encountered, which drove them to educate their son in the Soviet Union. Since both were born in a color-obsessed U.S., this perceived dearth of color consciousness was bound to have maximum impact on the two, seeming to be other-worldly and ratifying the idea that socialism meant a new deal for Africans and African-Americans; it was this perception that had driven numerous Negroes—including Patterson and Robeson's other good friend, Ben Davis, into the ranks of the U.S. Communist Party.

There was a "New Year's reunion in Moscow" in early January 1935 with members of her family; a "high old time" was had by all, she said with satisfaction. "I am still full of vodka, caviar, champagne & Russian cigarette smoke . . . ." The "USSR is marvelous now," she rhapsodized, with "thousands of well stocked shops everywhere" and "everyone well fed & warmly dressed. Books everywhere," said the budding writer: "marvelous, cheap, everyone reads . . . ."[3]

They were residing at the National Hotel in Moscow and it was from there that she informed Van Vechten that "Paul's Russian is even more practical than he had hoped and everyone is astounded and delighted when he speaks . . . ." So motivated, Ms. Robeson intended "to learn Russian the moment I get home. We have spent days and nights with Sergei Eisenstein who has shown us all his films. Also [Vsevolod] Pudovkin" and other Soviet artists were part of this grouping. "We have been a great deal in the theater but prefer the films here, by far," a harbinger of Robeson's renewed interest in cinema upon his return. "We both love it here and profoundly interested in what they are doing," though it was "33 below zero and even the Russians hold their noses in the streets . . . ." They were hoping to "leave for Leningrad" soon, just "in time for Marian Anderson's first concert there. She <u>will</u>

be surprised,"[4] chuckled Eslanda but she and Robeson were to be even more surprised when this noted contralto chose not to follow the politicized couple to the left, which had been the chosen path for so many Negro artists and intellectuals to that point.

Ms. Robeson was as ecstatic as her husband about this trip, which served to drive them closer together. "Sergei [Eisenstein] introduced Paul to the packed audience and they applauded for a full two minutes," creating a "real storm. Paul spoke about how at home he felt" there. "They were astonished with his Russian, his accent and adored him. He gave the whole, short speech in Russian," she said, apparently as dumbstruck as those assembled. "Then he sang quite a lot of songs, which they loved"—in Russian, of course.[5]

In terms of his artistry, in the long run, Robeson's renewed dedication to moviemaking may have been the most important aspect of this visit. "Films are the medium of the future," said Eslanda, "more so in Russia than in any other place . . . ." To that end, "we spent a lot of time with Sergei Eisenstein" who was now "thinking over a [project] for Paul"; the seriousness of this effort was signaled when the three, "talked for days and days on end about it . . . ." Filmmaking is notorious for giving rise to abortive projects and this had occurred to Ms. Robeson, who noted with astringency that what was being discussed "may or may not" pan out. But since "Paul was on the front page every day,[6] this suggested that this film project would become reality.

Serendipitously, also in Moscow at that time was William L. Patterson, a fellow African-American attorney and friend of the couple, who had joined the U.S. Communist Party a few years earlier. Patterson was essential to their radicalization process as the couple saw him "three times for long separate visits while we were in Russia," while "all the government officials begged [Robeson] to go everywhere and see everybody"; this meant [Patterson] "was very pleased and flattered," not least since it assisted immeasurably his ongoing effort to recruit Robeson to the Communists' cause.[7] "Paul went over for a very long talk with [Patterson]", she said on 28 December 1934[8]— and such long talks left an indelible impression upon the artist who was becoming a revolutionary: in fact, those looking for a single day in which one can pinpoint when Robeson decisively turned to revolution, it would be this day in late December 1934.

But the Moscow experience, too, left an indelible impression. As Eslanda recalled it, her husband captivated Moscow. As they ambled along the often snowy streets, ordinary Muscovites approached them and urged the couple not to leave but to make their home there. The fact that he spoke fluent Russian was essential to his popularity in the Soviet Union. This popularity led the couple to consider abandoning both Britain and the U.S. for permanent exile in the Soviet Union. He was "an instant success," said a delighted Ms. Robeson. "He has conquered them with his Russian, his pure accent and fluency, and of course, they simply pass out when they hear him sing," a tendency she thought "will sweep the country. It will settle us once and for all, with the place, and we will always have entrée here. Living is cheap and I mean [to] always have a flat here . . . ."[9]

Eslanda was not exaggerating. For Robeson's friend, Herbert Marshall, also encountered him in Moscow during this journey and left with a similar impression. The universality of socialism began to dovetail with Robeson's attempt to universalize his repertoire to the point that Marshall who "greeted Paul and his wife Essie as they first set foot in Moscow", found that his songs in concert "became more international than any other singers in history . . . ." Then he sought to extend this trend to the stage as he "wanted to play Othello in Russian with a Russian company and to sing 'Boris Gudonov' . . . ."[10]

With his Russian language aptitude burnished, Robeson and his accompanists departed Moscow on 6 January 1935, after intensive conferences with Eisenstein and Patterson. It was then that Patterson pressed him to return to the U.S. to join the struggle against Jim Crow, a request that led to an initial demurral—but an ultimate acceptance. But at that juncture, Robeson was unconvinced. "I found in London," he said later, "a congenial and stimulating intellectual atmosphere in which I felt at home" to the point where "I thought that I was settled for life."[11]

Upon returning to London, he was to be found more frequently at sites such as the Royal Institute of International Affairs and Chatham House, speaking about the problems of Africa, alongside the Prince of Wales, the foremost Tory politician, Stanley Baldwin, and other leaders from Australia, Canada, South Africa, and New Zealand.[12] In early 1935 he was visiting Ireland for a second time and drawing parallels between the music there and that of his homeland,[13] and reflecting upon the history and reality of the land that had been denoted as London's first colony. Such comparisons were nothing new for Robeson, who now seemed to be more enmeshed in studying than performing. "The Negro spiritual and the Hebrew chant have the same plaintive note," was the message delivered to a Jewish publication. "Both of our peoples have known oppression and I feel at home singing in Hebrew," a language he had heard at the knee of his late father. "Perhaps," he continued, "that's why I feel so close to the Jews—that and the fact that in London and New York, both my best friends are Russian Jews . . . ."[14]

From Dundee, Scotland, he waxed at length about his affinity with the Hebrides. "I am convinced," said this bona fide linguist, "I shall be able to learn Gaelic, much more easily than French or German. I learned to speak Russia in six months" and thought this feat could be duplicated in learning Gaelic.[15] Slowly but surely, Robeson was developing a theory of music that would then merge with his theory of politics. That is, music showed that humanity was one and the diverse struggles of humanity likewise demonstrated that the socialist commonwealth was the one common goal to which all were advancing and, indeed, that this was the universal resolution of these struggles. "Countries as far apart as Scotland and China" had music that used the "universal pentatonic scale," he said, and it could also be found in the music of African-Americans "and the songs of India and the ancient Hebraic chants."[16]

The Moscow visit had not crushed his intense interest in languages but, instead, had accelerated this trend, for his growing fascination with the philosophical universalism of socialism underscored his strengthening belief of the unity of all humankind. Eslanda thought "in due time" that Robeson would "take a Ph.D in philology. He adores languages and is now doing comparative work in African languages . . . ."[17]

His study of languages often took place in the comfortable Robeson flat on Buckingham Street, near the Strand, close to the Thames, convenient transportation nodes, theatres, and so on. Nonetheless, despite their increasing global profile, the couple seemed to face a perpetual household deficit. Days after returning from Moscow, Ms. Robeson was groaning about how it would be "hard going for the next few months, as I have all these bills to settle," rattling off "Harrods" and "Jaeger", two stores popular with fashion devotees. Being in the public eye, in the crosshairs of gossip columnists, and being part of an industry that placed a premium on glamour,[18] the Robesons had to be fashionably attired—which came at a steep cost.

But as their politics evolved—a process compelled by the rise of fascism and its antipode: anti-fascism—the Robesons' view of consumption evolved accordingly. The conversations with Patterson taking place in a Moscow convulsed with change, left a deep imprint upon Robeson particularly. Robeson began to rail against crass materialism upon his return from Moscow, the sort that "places the acquisition of property above all else," that "makes possession of material comforts an end in itself . . . ."[19]

Hence, despite these financial pressures, upon his return to London a renewed Robeson turned his attention to what may have been the least lucrative of his artistic pursuits: the stage. By April he was starring in a play about an African chief trying valiantly to keep rapacious Europeans away from the gold imbedded in his nation.[20] Peter Garland penned a part specifically for him with an African related theme.[21] By May 1935, he was receiving rave reviews for his performance as a stevedore,[22] an emblem of his developing socialist ideology which saw such proletarians as being in the vanguard of a revolutionary upsurge. The theme of this work was that the persistence of racism was due not least to its deliberate incitement by bosses in order to make for a more pliable Negro workforce. As millions marched globally for the Scottsboro defendants, this play provided a withering indictment of Jim Crow.[23] His friend and biographer, Marie Seton, was effusive, proclaiming that with this production "for the first time in the theatre Negroes were shown fighting for their rights and lives, with white workers joining them in their resistance to a racist mob."[24] A few years later he took this portrayal of working-class militancy on the stage to a new level with his role in *Plant in the Sun*, which centered on a sit-down strike in a U.S. candy factory.[25]

This play made a strongly dramatic appeal, a call to arms, to organize unions, a signature theme for Robeson in the coming years. The moral for workers was simple: stick together or the boss will beat you all down.[26] Reflecting his growing egalitarianism, instead of occupying the star's dressing room at the Theatre Royal, Drury Lane, he shared one room with the whole company. Possibly, the atmosphere of ease thereby created among the cast contributed to the play becoming a sensation, drawing the likes of Jawaharlal Nehru and Krishna Menon, creating a lifelong bond with Indian stalwarts.[27] (Refusing to exercise class privilege, Robeson even insisted on sweeping the theater.)[28] It was then that Robeson began to donate heavily to the cause of Indian independence; this was significant for although he received £500 per concert, he appeared in *Plant in the Sun* for almost nothing.[29]

His depiction of Toussaint L'Ouverture, hero of the Haitian Revolution, in the eponymous play written by the Trinidadian intellectual C.L.R. James, prompted the *New Statesman* to term him "one of the most impressive actors alive".[30] Robeson—said the *New York Times* with enthusiasm—"naturally outshone the large cast."[31] It was staged at the 730-seat Westminster Theatre, on the fringes of London's West End, and its modest circumstances notwithstanding, received a thunderous reception. Robeson was singled out with a stormy ovation at the final curtain with one contemporary critic claiming that that play "must surely stand as the most outstanding anti-imperialist play ever to make it onto London's West End during the interwar period."[32] Though he was offered fabulous salaries to star elsewhere, he preferred less remunerative but more meaningful roles.

Yet, as his huddling with Eisenstein in Moscow suggested, Robeson had hardly turned his back on movies but, unlike the stage, here his best efforts were subject to the deviousness of film editing and the misdirection (or simple expediency) of shooting films out of sequence. This was the backdrop to the production of perhaps his most controversial and damaging artistic creation: his role in *Sanders of the River*, a drama about Africa that, somehow, he thought would be anti-colonial. This production was wracked with difficulty from day one. "I do not yet . . . quite understand how the picture came to finality," said Alex Waugh, the interior designer, later, "what with money troubles" for the producers "and the difficulty of shooting Africa in England . . . ."[33] In this movie, Robeson portrays a literate and well-educated African leader, who is in alliance with British colonialism. The pro-colonial theme of this movie was evident and the depiction of Africans was similarly objectionable. Certainly, all viewers were not displeased with this production. One correspondent in Los Angeles breathlessly told the Robesons that "audiences . . . 'ate it up'" for "not once but at least five times in the eight showings of 'Sanders' I witnessed the audience burst into applause."[34] In Jerusalem, where, Robeson was told, the "building up of a Jewish national home seems to be going forward at a very lively pace," Maier Richard Harris was equally elated. He saw it in Tel Aviv, "the 100% Jewish city", and "it made an outstanding success, being held over for an entire week." The "Hebrew papers had the highest praise for the picture" and "I personally," he stressed, "thought *you* were excellent".[35] As late as 1960, Kathleen Ross felt compelled to inform Robeson that "like many other white children I was always threatened with ['] if you don't be good the black man will take you away['] & I was really scared"—but then she saw 'Sanders' and "started reading everything I could" about Africa, "& I thought how stupid I had been to be scared."[36]

There was a similarly enthusiastic response to his star turn in the filmed version of *Showboat*, with one Hollywood executive claiming that it was a "sensational success . . . you knocked 'em cold." James Whale of Universal Pictures claimed rarely at "any preview or showing of any picture," had he witnessed "such overwhelming enthusiasm. After the singing of 'Ol' Man River'," he bellowed, "the house went just crazy"; the "spine chilling effect of that one song I shall never forget . . . ."[37] Such adulation paved the way for Robeson's journey to Egypt where he starred in *Jericho*.[38] "The British Ambassador came along," he told the BBC later, doubtlessly attracted by the opportunity to rub shoulders with stardom.[39] They were in North Africa for "two months," said Ms. Robeson; it was "most interesting" though "certainly strenuous."[40] The former reference may have been a veiled allusion to allegations spread by the U.S. authorities that it was in North Africa that Robeson and Lady Mountbatten were enmeshed in a love affair.[41]

Unfortunately, fervent endorsement of Robeson's cinematic handiwork was not the opinion of his comrades or progressives generally. All told, Robeson acted in about a dozen films and other than *Proud Valley*, which was filmed in Wales among coal miners, he was generally dissatisfied with his cinematic efforts. This dissatisfaction led him to abandon movies as early as the 1940s, though his concert and theatre performances continued unabated. The years in which Robeson appeared on screen (roughly from the 1920s to the early 1940s) also marked a period when all but the most comic and jesting Negro figures were driven from Hollywood. This formidable barrier helped to drive him to London, but, as *Sanders of the River* suggested, this European capital of cinema proved to be hardly different. One critic concluded that "British film differs from American pictures in that it depicts [the] Negro in [a] heroic light,"[42] but Robeson's career did not altogether confirm this thesis.

Perhaps being overly generous, Robeson argued that it was sly editing that sabotaged this film—from his viewpoint. Evidently Robeson was unduly impressed with the African dancing on which the producers expended thousands of feet of celluloid and which too moved many audiences.[43] A chastened Robeson admitted that the film "resolved itself into a piece of flag-waving in which I wasn't interested," amounting to a "total loss. But I didn't realize how seriously people might take the film until I went back to New York" and was confronted by angry critics, such as his friend and comrade, Ben Davis. "There I was met by a deputation who wanted to know how the hell I had come to play in a film which stood for everything they rightly thought I opposed. That deputation," he noted tellingly, "began to make me see things more clearly,"[44] a gross understatement in that this experience both drove him away from filmdom and toward deeper political engagement.

At the film's premier, Robeson seethed. By one account, he stormed out.[45]

Another report asserted that he refused to rise and either speak or sing for the audience. Instead, he departed angrily with his fury[46] matching the vehemence of his sturdiest critics.[47] His ire was not assuaged by the fact that the premier in London raised a hefty 20, 000 pounds, a "record for all time" for the "Newspaper Press Fund," he was told. Nor was the pain eased by a London film executive informing his spouse that her husband's "perfect figure—probably the finest of all contemporary males"—was shown to good effect on the screen, i.e. "that his being practically nude is not nearly so noticeable as it would be if he had a bad figure . . . ." He was hardly comforted by the allegation that "the picture, as you know, is a tremendous success."[48] When *Sanders of the River* premiered, the London press reported that in Leicester Square there were police cordons and appearances by the Queen of Spain, the U.S. Ambassador and assorted peerages—while Robeson himself was "mobbed by excited women."[49] This was followed by Robeson in concert—according to another bewitched reporter, holding "6000 spellbound" at the Royal Albert Hall.[50]

Robeson's good friend, Ben Davis—like Patterson, an African-American attorney who turned his back on potential wealth for the uncertainty of becoming a professional revolutionary, a full-time Communist—denounced *Sanders of the River* as a "slanderous attack" on Africans, a declaration with which Robeson asserted his agreement.[51] Another friend, the heiress, Nancy Cunard, was irate, calling the movie "nothing else than one more intense effort at a justification of imperialistic exploitation."[52] The journal of Marcus Garvey, though admitting that Robeson was a "Negro of genius," reprimanded him for the movie roles he felt compelled to perform.[53] Nigerians studying at Cambridge University were irate; in this they were simply following the lead of anti-colonial leader, and Robeson friend, Nnamdi Azikiwe.[54] In Palestine, one Robeson correspondent thought the "story was weak and propaganda for British imperialism. You really deserve more worthy vehicles in which to express yourself," a thought that had occurred to Robeson too. "How are [you] getting on with your Hebrew?" he asked, as if a vehicle in that language might be next and more suitable.[55]

It was not easy to reject filmdom since the pay was quite gainful and, unlike concerts or plays, allowed him to extend his influence into the four corners of the globe. As early as 1932, Universal Pictures in Hollywood offered him $100,000 to appear in four films, all to be completed within a year. With the appeal delivered by film, Maxwell House Coffee then offered him $60,000 for a year's contract—30 minutes of his time once a week for a year would be his commitment.[56]

Writing to the Robesons—in 1938 at their residence on Highgate Road in London (the family having moved), John Corfield of British National Films was considering a "cash payment of . . . 5000 [pounds]" for one film appearance, plus a "percentage", a "generous one," he added enticingly. Though perhaps seen as generous in retrospect, Corfeld was apologetic, scraping and bowing because he was not able to offer more; "the present state of the industry," he observed, "with steadily falling receipts and with the majority of film production companies in this country either idle through lack of funds or actually in the hands of a Receiver" made it difficult to offer more.[57]

Robeson had options beyond London and Hollywood, for it was then that Sergei Eisenstein in the Soviet Union wrote "Dear Essie and Paul!" with evident excitement. "I am extremely pleased," he said, "to inform you that all my troubles are over," a vague reference to the political instability in Moscow that had led to purges and executions. "New people are running the film business, everything is changed and I'm working full-speed on one of the most important pictures to be made this year." He was referring to *Alexander Nevsky*, a cinematic landmark, which, said the filmmaker, "deals with the great victory we Russians had in the XIIIth century over the German invasion," an obvious harbinger of what was to come. "How modern the theme is," he added, "and how close to everything happening in Spain and Austria," noting "the final defeat of the Germans in 1242 I hope to become prophetic"[58]—which was bloodily prescient.

Robeson's friendship with Eisenstein—and Moscow—proved to be beneficial. It was in 1937 that an executive from Universal Pictures contacted Robeson from Moscow, reporting that he was finding a favorable reception as he screened "the print of our 'Showboat'," which the Soviet authorities "have just been looking at with the view of purchasing same for this country," since "the main interest centers around you and your popularity in Russia . . . ."[59]

Robeson was noticeably interested in working with Eisenstein, though, alas, they were unable to collaborate. It was in 1938 that he informed a curious interviewer that, hitherto, the dramatists he had been working with—mostly British and Euro-American—"usually go wrong when they try to write a part for a Negro character. Not unnaturally they tend to see him as a specialized person. This distorts the importance given to the character and makes him unrepresentative." He distinguished the character he played in *Plant in the Sun*, which was "written by the author as an Irishman," an indicator that, he argued, writers should "write about a character they know in their own experience . . . then let me play the part and give it [a] special not unrepresentative Negro flavour." In any case, even this admonition did not necessarily boost his fondness for filmmaking, since that industry represented the clearest example of the workings of capitalism—slumps, booms, speculation, over-production, etc.

Of Robeson's three artistic outlets—concerts, theater and cinema—the latter two (particularly moviemaking) involved significant capital outlays by investors, most of whom were not politically progressive, which led inexorably to often damaging compromises on Robeson's part. Capital investors were not necessarily interested in anti-capitalist and anti-imperialist productions. Concert singing, on the other hand (with the lucrative complement of recordings providing global reach), was not so compromising and, inevitably, this is where Robeson turned as his revolutionary leanings deepened, for this outlet allowed not only for the expression of anti-capitalist and anti-imperialist sentiments, but anti-racist sentiments as well.

Yet, signaling the restiveness that was soon to make Hollywood a byword for radicalism, necessitating—in the eyes of conservatives—a decisive and transformative purge and shakeup that would ensnare Robeson,[60] he stressed that in the movie industry, as he told the interviewer Sidney Cole

the workers in the studios have the power and they ought to realize it. During one of my films I was struck by this very forcibly. There was everybody on the set, lights burning, director waiting, head of the company had just come on to the set with some big financial backer to see how things were going—and what happened? Everything stopped. Why? Because the electricians had decided it was time to go and eat as they just put out the lights and went off and ate. That's my moral to your readers.[61]

The moral to Robeson was that he had landed in a market—moviemaking—which turned out to be a major export earner for the U.S. and, besides, massaged consciousness globally at the same time. He then donated his income, and time, to building working-class and revolutionary movements that placed the power and wealth of movie moguls in the bulls-eye. Their response in turn was to isolate Robeson politically, denude him of wealth and make him radioactive politically.[62]

Thus, despite this leverage, he had to give up film acting because of the problem of finding adequate scripts. This he regretted since, he thought that film was his true medium, i.e. in the intimacy of working close to the camera—close-up shots in short—he could express his personality more sympathetically and with less strain, especially compared to the projection and, at times, histrionics, required for concerts and the stage.

Though it was not detailed by Eisenstein in their correspondence, Robeson was eager to bring to the screen a reworked reprise of the London stage drama featuring the Haitian Revolution. When he travelled to Moscow in late 1934, a central purpose was to confer with Eisenstein about a Haitian project. His trip, said Marie Seton, was "at the personal request" of the great Soviet moviemaker and intense discussions ensued immediately after he landed at the airport. "I transmitted an account of the project to Ms. Robeson," said Seton, but as so often happens with capital-intensive film projects, this one too was stillborn.[63]

The skilled U.S. writer Waldo Frank thanked Ms. Robeson for providing a copy of the book on the topic by C.L.R. James (*The Black Jacobins*), which inspired him to draft "very roughly the idea I had for a truly great [work] about Toussaint." He intended it "for Paul", though it "depends on him." Frank was also communicating with "two lovely young Negro writers", one of whom was Richard Wright, who emerged from the same political milieu as Robeson and who went on to write a novel, *Native Son*, making him as prominent in literature as Robeson was on the stage. But what might have captured Eslanda's eye was his concluding dig: "you two don't know what you're missing spending your life in a stagnant eddy (swiftly turning into a sewer) like England . . . Let Paul read this, please," he insisted.[64] But "Paul" did not have to read this jab from Frank in order to realize that there were stirrings back home, driven by anti-fascist ripples from abroad, the impending alliance with Moscow and the concomitant surge of the anti-Jim Crow movement that was to impel the Robesons to cross the Atlantic—but this time for a longer, more permanent period.

Robeson's frustration with movies helped to fuel his revolutionary fervor, as he came to recognize that the status quo could not contain his more capacious ambitions. "I want to make a film about Samuel Coleridge-Taylor," he said in the 1930s, referring to the turn-of-the-century British composer, routinely referred to as the "African Mahler"; and "Joe Louis" too (the heavyweight boxing champion otherwise known as the "Brown Bomber", a contemporary of Robeson). "But the Hollywood companies would not let me do the latter"—nor was the former actionable either. "They say it would never do for a coloured man to be shown knocking out a white boxer . . . ."[65]

These reluctant executives may have noticed interviews he was now giving to the U.S. Communist Party daily newspaper. In one he was open about his affection for the Soviet Union. "I intend to live there," he declared. "It's the only country in the world where I feel at home." When asked the question that would bedevil him for years to come, he said that he wasn't a member of the Communist Party. "I'm a member of the Friends of the Soviet Union," he confessed.[66]

Robeson did not rest supine while Hollywood moguls blocked his best efforts. To the contrary, his response was to escalate his growing activism. His disappointment with *Sanders of the River* was countered by his growing ties with the West African Students Union in London; for example, there was a notably festive dinner dance at 62 Camden Road with Robeson as the special guest, but also featuring a star-studded lineup of future anti-colonial leaders including Jomo Kenyatta of Kenya and Z.K. Matthews of South Africa. For the occasion, the Robesons were attired in "Yoruba"—or Nigerian—dress,[67] a symbolic statement of where their interests were headed and an implicit refutation of a recent era when they felt compelled to expend their income on the latest fashion from Harrods. Attendance at these students' event broke all previous records and Robeson's presence may have been a factor. There he informed the assembled that from this point forward he would devote his life to the cause of a liberated Africa and, thus, intended to tour the continent soon. "Loud cheers" greeted his declaration that he was funding the group—and intended to continue doing so.[68]

This ovation was more than complemented by surging opinion on the continent itself. The future Nobel Laureate and United Nations leader Ralph Bunche was travelling in East Africa during this era and noticed echoes of home: "Paul," he wrote, "you surely are an idol of the Bantu [sic]"; in other words, "when one mentions American Negroes they all chorus 'Paul Robeson' and Joe Louis . . . the rumor still persists that you are coming down to the Union [of South Africa] soon; if you do the black folk will mob you with enthusiasm."[69]

A signal of Robeson's growing commitment to the liberation of Africa from colonialism, which endeared him to so many Africans, was indicated in 1937 when he provided a then hefty $1,500 to launch what became the most important U.S. grouping in this contested realm: the Council on African Affairs. This subsidy was considered "splendid" by one of the group's early leaders, Max Yergan, who was to turn on Robeson viciously as the Cold War heated up. It made ironic his final comment: "I hope Essie and you are rather securely cut off from the great horde of people who are always trying to get at you . . . ."[70]

The funding of various causes had become Robeson's trademark and, said a U.S. Negro journal, meant that he was "to London what Bill Robinson is to Harlem," a reference to "Bojangles", a famed dancer, performer and Hollywood star, also known for handing out money. "Paul is made a regular sucker by all the touch artists of America and Africa who work with him in pictures and in plays," including the "tea room leftists who hold him up as a sort of God."[71]

In any event, this increasing Robeson identification with Africa and the left apparently did not damage a similarly growing affection for Britain for it was then that he was importuned to stand for election for the Lord Rectorship of Edinburgh University.[72] To that end, he was regarded by a local periodical as "Aberdeen's favourite singer."[73]

Robeson's soaring popularity was inseparable from his ascending role as a prominent anti-fascist. A visiting journalist reached this conclusion after interviewing him in 1937. "The artist and social thinker in Paul Robeson have fought their last battle for mastery," said Louise Morgan not without cause, "and the social thinker has won." She was sitting in his London flat and it was there he informed her why the "present commercial theater and films no longer interest him." As he was to insist to his dying days, "Personal success is not enough." For what was animating Robeson as they spoke were "events in Abyssinia and China," which had led him "beyond the racial problem to the world problem of which it is a part." Robeson was at a crossroads once more, toying with the idea of becoming a writer, which would have surprised many of the correspondents who often despaired of ever receiving a letter from him. "At the moment," said Morgan, "he is reading three novels by American Negro writers with a view to making dramatic versions of them. The theatre he feels is at this time his most important medium." Robeson's muse was also rising: "I should like to do a chain gang sequence," he asserted, "and the story of a Moroccan who, fighting in Spain becomes conscious of the real issue and joins the Government side."[74]

But as this latter comment suggested, what transformed Robeson in a manner not unlike his journey to Moscow was his travelling to war-torn Spain to perform on behalf of a government then under siege by rightists backed by German and Italian fascists in a haunting presentiment of the world war that was to shortly unfold.[75] There he sang defiant songs in Spanish that boomed over loudspeakers so that they could reach the ears of both loyalists and those seeking to destabilize the duly constituted regime.[76] By early 1938 he remained with the British activist Charlotte Haldane, still on the frontlines in Spain, soothing the seriously wounded with his singing.[77]

Speaking on the Spanish Civil War at the Albert Hall in London, Robeson made the statement that was to define the rest of his life and was to inspire artists and cultural workers for generations to come: "Every artist, every scientist must decide NOW where he stands. He has no alternative. There is no standing above the conflict on Olympian heights," since "the artist must take sides. He must elect to fight for freedom or slavery. I have made my choice. I had no alternative." Why? One reason was, he said, because "the history of the capitalist era is characterized by the degradation of my people," a recognition of the central role of the African slave trade. He had flown to London to speak, after first considering making this address from Moscow but changing course after Berlin pledged to jam any radio broadcast from there.[78]

Figure 4   Robeson traveled to Spain during its epochal civil war during the 1930s where at great personal risk he performed on the frontlines. The anti-fascism he honed there was at the heart of his political philosophy. (Daily Worker and Daily World Photographs Collection, Tamiment Library/Robert F. Wagner Labor Archives, New York University, New York City)

Spain held pride of place in Robeson's rich storehouse of memories. "I remember," he said later, "speaking on a platform" with such British eminences as Sir Richard Stafford Cripps, future Prime Minister Clement Attlee and former Prime Minister David Lloyd George, all united in defense of Spain. "I helped the Labour Party," with which he had developed a close relationship, particularly with its left-wing, "raise fifty thousand pounds" for the besieged of Spain. He then travelled there with Attlee.[79] It was then that he may have had the opportunity to confer with Attlee about the recent rebellion in Jamaica: Robeson was the main speaker when the Negro Welfare Association in London rallied in defense of the rebels.[80]

He also found time to appear alongside John Gollan, a leader of the Young Communist League in London at a "great youth rally" at "Empress Hall, Earl's Court" that not only highlighted the tragic events in Spain but similarly unsettling developments in China and Czechoslovakia—depredations signaled and perpetrated by militarist Japan and Nazi Germany respectively.[81] His star wattage also infused the "Negro Committee to Aid Spain," a U.S.-based grouping that included numerous leaders, including Ferdinand Smith (of Jamaican origin, and the most powerful black trade union leader in the republic); the writer Langston Hughes; and many more.[82] A generous gift from Robeson served to jumpstart "the Negro People's Ambulance for Loyalist Spain", an effort that was prompted by Patterson—as the alliance of the two attorneys deepened further.[83]

Spain represented a hinge moment for Robeson. Meeting the volunteers from the U.S. in Spain—which included a complement of African-Americans who played roles in the military there that they could not play at home—and witnessing their sacrifice and grit, nudged him toward returning to his homeland. He had been going back for short visits periodically and by 1939, with the press of war on the continent, he made this decision permanent.[84]

After war arrived in Europe in 1939, Eslanda found London to be "pretty exciting" but it was tranquil compared to Spain. "Paul and I had our baptism in Madrid and Valencia," she said ruefully, "so we are very much hardened and are merely interested, instead of frightened. We are cautious but our stomachs don't turn over when we hear the sirens."[85]

This was not the only transformation the couple was enduring. Near that same time he found that "at my concerts [I] had noticed the most genuine and enthusiastic applause always came from the gallery" and "those were the people I wanted to sing to and play to . . . ." Thus, he concluded, "all my concerts in the future will have a five shilling top" admission fee, to facilitate working-class attendance, which was both an artistic and political choice. Their enthusiasm buoyed his performance and the audience generally, while enriching this constituency buoyed them as the anti-fascist struggle gained traction, mandating their enhanced participation.[86]

Surely, the English were attracted to him, such as when, in 1938, it was reported that a stunning "20,000 holidaymakers" mobbed him at Devon's Torquay Pavilion when he arrived for a recital.[87] They flocked to him because he was a star, because he was a symbol of an oppressed group—Africans—and their ability to fight back thereby lifting humanity generally. They flocked to him because he spoke their languages, English and increasingly, Gaelic (there were certain British leaders who were not as capable here).

When not performing, Robeson could be found either listening to records, as he sought to learn even more languages, or reading—novels, histories, books in various languages—a process that found him sporting horn-rimmed spectacles.[88] The knowledge and insight gained also meant that he was far more informed than the typical "celebrity," enhancing his popular appeal further.

Though he was to be found visiting the frontlines of Spain and stirring audiences in concert, Robeson's passion was learning: languages particularly. This was not an intellectual conceit, nor was it the pedantry of a dilettante, but a way to take the revolutionary cause to a higher level. When Robeson could speak and sing to the thousands who amassed to hear him in their language, it struck a deep chord, endearing him to those assembled and driving many more to his revolutionary banner. But the war clouds hanging over Europe would compel the Robesons to alter the comfortable status quo. Even before the pivotal year that was 1939, Eslanda was complaining about the "war threat" and the fact that she "had to seriously consider" if it made sense to risk leaving their son Pauli in Moscow, "with Moscow becoming rapidly more and more inaccessible, because of German activities in Poland, Czechoslovakia, Lithuania and Austria. With Spain and Russia on my passport," she sighed, "it is very difficult for me to [travel] through any German territory now and it is impossible to reach Moscow quickly, except thru German controlled territory. Even the Scandinavian air route has a stop in Hamburg"; then there was the related problem of the "additional difficulty of telephoning" her son in that "the lines are thru Berlin or alternatively thru Warsaw . . . ." The Robesons were in such a dilemma that there was the "possibility of our going to South America."[89]

Options were narrowing and the walls were closing in on them. As early as the fall of 1938, Ms. Robeson was told bluntly that "it looks as if it is going to be very unsafe in London, so you and your family had better get out quickly."[90]

It was 6 September 1939 and Ms. Robeson was at her garrulous best in London, chatting about her spouse "filming hard as ever, making 8 o'clock time in the mornings, which is much more revolutionary than war" for the notorious night owl. Their present abode—St. Albans Villas, Highgate Road in the Dartmouth Park area of Highgate—was chosen by her with "an eye for safety at the time. We have a grand shelter of our very own, right here in the house, with heavy thick walls all about . . . ." . . . .[91]

The onset of war in Europe led to the Robesons decision to abandon the continent, though neither he nor she could envision that this was a fatefully momentous decision. Though they were to visit London thereafter—including a lengthy stay in the late 1950s after his passport was returned—this sad and hasty adieu to London, where they thought they would reside indefinitely, delivered Robeson into the hands of his tormentors, a reality that became clear after the war that had forced them to leave in the first place came to a screeching halt in 1945.

5

"The Tallest Tree in our Forest"

P aul Robeson considered *Proud Valley*, filmed in the coalfields of Wales, just before his fateful return to the U.S., his proudest accomplishment in cinema. A production of Ealing Studios, it tells an affecting story of an African-American miner and singer and his relationship to the harsh reality of coalmining in Wales. The story mirrored Robeson's life in that like his character in the movie, he too won the hearts of the working class in Wales (and England, Ireland and Scotland besides). Viewed from the perspective of Hollywood, even today it is hard to find a film that better captures the life of a black working-class man. Providing the movie with the heft of verisimilitude was the fact that local Welsh from the impoverished Rhondda Valley performed admirably alongside Robeson.[1] "There have been many films dealing with Scotland, Ireland and England," said one critic in 1940, "but never (with the possible exception of 'The Citadel') has Wales been put on the screen . . . ." This film was Robeson's parting gift to the nation that he had come to admire.[2]

This cinematic triumph gave added sustenance to Robeson's heartfelt words to Britain's Communist newspaper on their anniversary, informing these radicals, "I have never been met with more warmth than here in Britain . . . I came here unshaped. Great parts of my working class roots are here," an indicator of his heartwarming experience in Wales. "The reception that I have had here," he insisted, "has passed all bounds . . . ."[3] "My whole social and political development was in England [sic]," he proclaimed in 1944, as he "became as much a part of English life as I am now of American."[4] For Robeson conceded freely, "I had planned to leave the United States for good and I was living in London, shuttling over to Russia every summer to see my boy. I thought I saw more tolerance for Negroes abroad than I did here," speaking of the U.S., which was an accurate perception.[5]

This decision to leave the continent was taken reluctantly, given the niche he had carved in London and Europe, a decision made all the more wrenching in light of his positive experience in Wales. "I would go down to Cardiff in Wales," he recalled fondly in 1965. "They have a wonderful opera in London," he reflected, "but the Welsh, they have their own language too, they felt that they wanted their own theatre. So somewhere among the miners, before you knew it, there was an opera house in Wales. The same way in Scotland," he said.[6]

Given his experience with *Sanders of the River*, Robeson was understandably wary about movies, even though the script for the film shot in Wales was appealing. It was a "good story," said Eslanda, "although heaven knows what it will be like when we get through shooting. You know what films are!"[7] This admonition reached a crescendo when shortly after returning to the U.S. Robeson had a small role in *Tales of Manhattan*, which he saw as offensive as *Sanders of the River*. A distraught Robeson admitted to the *New York Times* that, "I thought I could change the picture as we went along and I did make some headway," but his handsome paycheck could not compensate for the ugliness he witnessed on the silver screen: "it turned out to the same old thing," he said angrily, "the Negro solving his problem by singing his way to glory. This is very offensive to my people," he insisted. "It makes the Negro child-like and innocent and is in the old plantation tradition. But Hollywood says you can't make the Negro in any other role because it won't be box office [profitable] in the South. The South wants its Negroes in the old style." In this multiple-part movie, Robeson appears alongside Ethel Waters, as they depict a poor couple who stumble upon $40,000, with predictable stereotypes and buffoonery.[8]

Waters and Robeson "let us down" was the consensus expressed by the Harlem based *New York Amsterdam News*.[9] Under fire, Robeson denied that he had received a hefty $50,000 for his work in this debacle; it was 10 percent of this amount, he claimed and "by the time I paid my agents, travelling and living expenses, that amount had dwindled," he responded with an accuracy that simultaneously made it seem that he had sold out for a pittance.[10] He went further to endorse picketing of the film and considered joining the picketers himself.[11] Robeson made a pledge that the industry helped him to keep, promising to abandon Hollywood for good until the industry mended its ways in portrayals of Negroes.[12]

Later he castigated *Sanders of the River* fumingly: "that film is responsible for my present crusade as a defender of my people," he argued: "it was the turning point in my public career," since "I committed a faux pas which . . . convinced me that I had failed to weigh the problems of 150,000,000 native Africans . . . ." He cried, "I hate that picture [and] have tried to buy it [the rights] but because it is a tremendous money-maker, have not been able to do so. I have, however, given to charity every dollar earned from it," particularly funding "scholarships or loans" to African students.[13]

Robeson departed Europe on 30 September 1939 and was not to return again until August 1945, when the war on the continent had concluded, then returning to his beloved Britain during that same period.[14] Thus, the U.S. was on the brink of war and the ruling elite was as worried as ever about whether African-Americans would remain true to the republic in light of the hellish Jim Crow they endured and the repeated appeals made by Tokyo for this oppressed group to follow Japan, the self-proclaimed leader of the "colored races." Though Robeson's tie to Moscow is often derided, this is one-sided—akin to judging a boxing match while only focusing on one of the fighters— since it elides the point that (by far) African-Americans in their quest for global aid to combat Jim Crow were attracted to Japan. Even the faction heralded for bringing an end to Jim Crow—that led by Dr. Martin Luther King, Jr.—was patterned after and received sustenance from M.K. Gandhi and India.[15] The point is that Jim Crow had such a sizeable support base among Euro-Americans that external support was crucial in order to erode it and as the U.S. itself discovered from 1941–45, Moscow's support could be timely and effective.

As a consequence of Japan's appeal to African-Americans in particular, Robeson was recruited to make counter appeals via radio, urging patriotism and promising a better day if only he were heeded. Robeson's words were so moving that they were taken to the White House so that President Franklin D. Roosevelt and his activist spouse, Eleanor Roosevelt, could listen. "They were very generous in their approval," Robeson was told, as were others in the listening party including "Lord and Lady Mountbatten . . . ."[16] Ms. Roosevelt was appreciative, telling Robeson that "the President and I appreciate the tribute you pay to us and the valiant work you are doing in his behalf."[17]

Subsequently, Robeson and Eleanor Roosevelt were pictured clasping hands, a symbol of the "popular front" or the alliance that fascism had impelled, driving together liberals and radicals.[18] This was part of Robeson's continuing anti-fascism, which also took the form of publicizing Washington's effort to fund the war through bonds, a campaign of which he became a spokesman.[19]

This was also part of Robeson being welcomed and embraced by a nervous U.S. ruling elite, worried about the future in light of the challenges launched from Berlin and Tokyo. With the US in a military alliance with the Soviet Union, his solidarity with Moscow was not controversial but, to the contrary, was useful to the U.S. ruling elite which could embrace Robeson and at the same time muffle its own now compromising anti-communism. Just after the German attack on the Soviet Union, Robeson was addressing a youth congress in Philadelphia and one fan subsequently recalled proudly how the successful artist "with a few short sentences . . . made everyone understand what the Soviet Union means to progressive humanity" and "then you sang 'From Border to Border'." The mother of the writer Paul Levitan was pregnant with him and as she and the "audience left the hall, [she] turned to her friends" and said, "'if the baby will be a boy, we'll name him Paul.'" Such was the riveting potency of Robeson.[20]

Thus, Attorney General Francis Biddle—the nation's top law enforcement official—and his wife invited the Robesons to join them at a special concert, an invitation which was tendered the day before Germany's brutal invasion of the Soviet Union, which brought the war to a bloodier level.[21] Even Congressman William Dawson of Chicago—one of the few African-Americans to serve in that august body—was moved to tell Robeson, "I take pride in your reflected glory . . . ."[22]

But, as suggested by the aforementioned presence of Lord Mountbatten, Robeson did not neglect the British Empire during this tempestuous time, as evidenced by officialdom in Ottawa thanking him profusely for "giving our Officers and men the pleasure of hearing you sing for them,"[23] a thanks that was to become ironic a few years later when Canada barred him from entry at Washington's behest. Similarly, Jawaharlal Nehru of British India was keen to tell Ms. Robeson in 1939 that he had "been in mountains for the last ten days", as he was "trying to escape from the troubled politics of the plains below. It has been delightful,"[24] as was his friendship with the Robesons. Months later, Robeson was invited by Caribbean activists in Harlem—led by Jamaicans—to be their "honored guest" in a rally for "self-determination."[25]

Though initially settling in Harlem, in a charming apartment building overlooking the Bronx and Yankee Stadium at 555 Edgecombe Avenue,[26] along a bluff with a commanding view, by 1941, the Robeson family were residing in a well-appointed estate in Enfield, Connecticut, two hours' swift driving north of Manhattan, just outside of Hartford, capital of the Nutmeg State. It was a large Georgian-Colonial house featuring pillared stucco. Many fine old trees shaded the deftly manicured lawn. There were twelve rooms and three baths, with a tasteful living-room paneled in burnished mahogany, set off by a large and lushly marbled fireplace. There was a tennis court, a swimming pool, a bowling alley, a billiard room and a hall suitable for both concerts and dances. It was baronial splendor well befitting a singer and actor deemed to be at the height of his artistic powers.[27]

"We are all simply crazy about the country [rural area] and have settled down permanently to country life. The house is divine," said Eslanda Robeson "and exactly suits us and it is all much too good to be true"; it was "very lovely, with the low Berkshire hills at the back and a modest 2½ acres . . . ." Her husband "loves the quiet and low gear of the place and flies home for every moment he can spare when on tour."[28] It was "really a lovely house," she said rhapsodically, "and its only fault is that it looks a bit more impressive than it is. It is very simple, very sturdy and absolutely livable"[29]—which was all true but simultaneously a downplaying of the exceedingly comfortable lifestyle to which the couple had grown accustomed.

Robeson also resumed his touring as a concert artist, a necessity since he decided to turn his back on film and stage productions that were both profitable and positive, which in any case were hard to come by. A stunning assemblage of 150,000 heard him in Chicago's Grant Park in July 1940.[30] In September 1940 he joined in Harlem with the novelist Richard Wright and the musicians Hazel Scott and Andy Razaf—and 3,500 others—in a bold attempt to form the "Negro Playwrights, Inc.", an effort to produce high quality theatre for this increasingly distressed community.[31] In October of that year, he held his first recital at Carnegie Hall in five years.[32] By December he was singing a different tune, urging workers to join the United Auto Workers in Detroit, a union and a city that were to become emblems for militant solidarity.[33] Within months he had established a new box office mark in Philadelphia, attracting 7,500 patrons in an appearance with that city's celebrated orchestra.[34] It was then that he received a whopping $125,000 for a 51-city tour.[35]

Yet these recitals and concerts too provided no surcease since he had to confront the dilemma of whether he should perform before racially segregated audiences. In the midst of galvanizing African-Americans for a war that some viewed with skepticism, he was compelled in early 1942 to make a speech at his packed concert in Kansas City remonstrating angrily about Jim Crow seating. The agent that booked him there apologized almost tearfully, asserting that the uproar "caused me a great deal of distress" while pledging to "redouble my efforts to avoid situations of this sort for next season . . . ."[36] The editor of the local Negro newspaper congratulated Robeson "for the stand you took against segregation," since it "has spurred the Negro citizens here to wage a campaign against discrimination in our tax-supported buildings. You have given us a good start."[37] Robeson was a kind of Pied Piper of anti-Jim Crow, journeying from city to city inspiring fellow crusaders for it was thought if one as affluent as Robeson could protest and sacrifice, then surely others less endowed could.

Subsequently, Robeson reflected on this jarring episode. "In 1942 at the height of my success," he said in December 1963, "I stood before a packed and enthusiastic audience in Kansas City and said that I regretted having sung to them, because my Negro people were segregated in the audience" and "that I would never again perform before a segregated audience." And, he stressed, "I never have . . . ."[38]

Nonetheless, this was an uphill climb. Months later in Baltimore, Robeson was refused permission to sing at the Lyric Theater because of his insistence that the audience should be desegregated.[39] For despite the best efforts of this and other agents, the terrible spectacle of apartheid seating at his concerts was to bedevil Robeson for years to come, causing him unimaginable grief while causing him to redouble his own efforts to extirpate this pestilence. His bold effort to disrupt the status quo also labeled him as a radical, which then in turn caused the Daughters of the American Revolution to bar him from their concert hall.[40] Still, it was the future Negro millionaire, John H. Johnson—then in the infancy of a storied career that would lead him to fame—who saluted his "refusal to play 'Othello' in Jim Crow theatres," endorsing "the stand which you have taken,"[41] which hastened the day when this apartheid was to erode.

As a result, Robeson directed his formidable fundraising skill and immense personal magnetism toward anti-Jim Crow crusades. He joined with eight others in filing a pioneering lawsuit against Jim Crow seating at a San Francisco restaurant.[42]

This initiative included the harbinger of the youth armies of the 1960s that finally broke down the walls of legalized bigotry. The spring of 1942 found him in Tuskegee, Alabama—home of the late symbol of Negro capitulation, Booker T. Washington—but at a confab designed to contradict the latter's path. The Southern Negro Youth Congress was to be scorned after the war as just another "Communist front", a reflection of the unavoidable point that the Young Communist League played a pivotal role in bringing together a broad front tasked to tackle Jim Crow. But those who came to Robeson's concert for SNYC—including the NAACP's William Pickens and the pre-eminent U.S. military man, Benjamin O. Davis, and the head of the university Washington himself founded, Frederick Douglass Patterson—were then less concerned about the specter of red credentials as they were moved by the reality of anti-black bias.[43]

Yet at the same time Robeson was being wined and dined by the powerful and working tirelessly to ensure that the U.S. government survived a challenge from fascism, he was being monitored relentlessly by that very same government, nervous about his socialist beliefs. Somehow a functionary of the Federal Bureau of Investigation (FBI) office in Los Angeles got hold of a Robeson notebook with scribbling in Chinese and although the U.S. ostensibly was on the same side as the bulk of China's population then fighting Japanese militarism and imperialism, this discovery was viewed initially with grave suspicion, perhaps because of the rising Chinese Communist Party under the leadership of Mao Zedong. But then the bulldog of a director of the FBI, J. Edgar Hoover, had this document translated and found to his satisfaction that it was "clearly of no significance to anyone other than its owner."[44]

Figure 5 Robeson was a staunch defender of working-class activism and raised large sums of money for unions on both sides of the Atlantic. (Daily Worker and Daily World Photographs Collection, Tamiment Library/Robert F. Wagner Labor Archives, New York University, New York City)

Actually, a new softer stage in support of anti-communism had been reached because of the US's alliance with the Soviet Union against the Axis powers: still, there were signs that this was a false dawn at best. If Robeson had been paying closer attention to his personal relationships he might have detected this. Thus, Walter White and Carl Van Vechten had been instrumental in the remarkable rise of Robeson as an artist but by the time he was about to depart London, there were indicators that both had become disillusioned with him. "I see Paul has come out in favor of Russia against Finland," said Van Vechten, adding, "this is very bad business indeed . . . ."[45] Though Robeson had propelled Van Vechten up the social ladder, introducing him to Lord Beaverbrook, for example,[46] this New Yorker's friendship with the artist was now crumbling.

Even as Robeson was standing shoulder-to-shoulder with the U.S. in its death match with fascism, the U.S. authorities—specifically, the FBI—were eyeing him suspiciously. The same year that the FBI exonerated him for daring to scribble in Chinese, this same agency found that he "is a member of a number of communist front organizations," seen as a demerit—or worse. It was found questionable that at a fund-raiser in Manhattan for Spanish loyalists, he complained of the imprisoning of Earl Browder, the leader of the U.S. Communist Party. It was deemed troublesome that Robeson collaborated with "communist" filmmakers on a documentary film that "purportedly includes scenes that portray violations of civil liberties in the United States", along with "the struggle of the American pioneers with fascism, the struggle of labor unions against company spies and the gallant fight against Hitler." Though Moscow was then an ally, the FBI blanched when Robeson in concert sang songs in Russian.[47]

It was found alarming when a "Confidential Informant" asserted that Robeson "was a Communist party member and that he had joined the party after a professional tour in England." It was then that he met "Henry Pollet", a possible reference to British Communist leader Harry Pollitt, "who was believed to have converted Robeson to the party." Supposedly, Robeson donated "$300,000.00" to this organization.[48] Apparently, the FBI was unaware—but would have been keenly interested to know—that Robeson provided a subsidy of $100 per month for the respected U.S. Negro Communist leader, Harry Haywood, to finish a major study of "Negro Liberation."[49]

The FBI seemed particularly intrigued by the ties of Robeson that implicated global trends, particularly those involving Moscow—and this was the case even when the USSR was allied with the U.S.—and those involving the colonized. It was in 1943 that their agent reported anxiously that Ms. Robeson was a "personal friend" of Nehru and that she had "entertained" his nieces at her Connecticut estate.[50] Similarly, the FBI found it hard to ignore when Eslanda contacted Moscow's emissaries in Washington, inviting them also to her cozy—though far from abstemious—abode; it may have been indiscreet on her part to note that this residence was near "extremely important cities now in the defense industries". Still, she urged Maxim Litvinov and his wife, telling them affectionately, "we would love to have you stay with us," and making the two feel special by adding, "we ourselves never entertain", while adding "our very secret telephone number."[51]

The FBI would have been worried further if they had been able to read the correspondence between Ben Davis, Harlem's Communist chief, and Eslanda Robeson. "The Harlem Section of the Communist Party is beginning to break records," he exulted. "We have doubled our membership (securing 400 new members in three months)"—and "we've just begun."[52] Robeson and Davis were present at the creation of this tremendous upsurge in radicalism. "Ben and I first met here in Harlem some 35 years ago," said Robeson at Davis' funeral in 1964; "often passers-by on the avenue would be startled and amazed as Ben and I worked out some [American] football tactics on the sidewalk," as Davis too starred in this sport at Amherst College before graduating from Harvard Law School.[53]

Still, it was easy for Robeson to ignore the ominous clouds that were gathering for he was still being feted, still being courted by up and coming artists, a list that included the poet Countee Cullen, a leader in the field.[54] "I have a play which I wish you would consent to read", he told Ms. Robeson, since it "might interest Paul . . . ."[55] Ms. Robeson was dismissive of the entreaties made to the couple by the Harlem Bard, Langston Hughes; . . . Robeson had no such compunction about collaborating with Richard Wright and the musician Count Basie in working on a song hailing boxer Joe Louis.[56] "I know Joe," he said of the pulverizing pugilist and reigning hero of black America, "a warm, likeable fellow . . . ."[57]

"[Theodore] Dreiser would like very much to talk with you,"[58] was another missive Robeson received then, a reference to the premier U.S. novelist and journalist of the naturalist school. In that vein, Robeson was tabbed "guest of honor" at a dinner "in tribute to anti-fascist fighters" at the posh Biltmore Hotel in Manhattan that honored another famed writer, Dorothy Parker. Rubbing shoulders with him there were the novelist Thomas Mann; and the musicians Benny Goodman and Oscar Hammerstein.[59]

Like one hand washing the other, a status cemented in London helped to enhance Robeson's stature at home. It was a "pleasure to see you and Lombard Toledano last Wednesday,"[60] was the message passed to Robeson by Nobel Laureate Pearl Buck, in her reference to one of Mexico's most influential labor chiefs. "All good wishes for success against fascism, imperialism" and other ills was the then anodyne point delivered to Robeson by Jawaharlal Nehru in early 1942.[61] This was a turnabout for the recently jailed Indian politico, who earlier was complaining to Ms. Robeson after spending a "little over nine months in prison." Evidently, he assumed—correctly—that the Robesons' influence would be beneficial in convincing London to free him, just as the couple were to prevail upon him in the following decade to use his influence to ensure their U.S. passports would be returned. She had sent him books penned by Richard Wright, then he requested others by Upton Sinclair, so as to better expend his time in prison.[62]

This mutuality of literary interests stemmed from the time that Robeson and Nehru spent together in London, when to the Indian's astonishment, his interlocutor began to spontaneously recite poetry in Hindi in order to demonstrate the commonalities in speech patterns between those who spoke this language and those who spoke a language colloquially referred to in the U.S. as "Black English."[63]

The popularity of Robeson in South Asia also encompassed the tear-drop shaped island off India's southern coast, then known as Ceylon, now as Sri Lanka. East African soldiers stationed there celebrated Robeson's 47th birthday during the war.[64] Though organized by islanders, Robeson—described locally as "a legend in his own time"—was feted, fittingly, in a concert that featured music from both the Sinhalese and Swahili traditions.[65] This may shed light on why Eslanda Robeson was told subsequently that she might be "surprised to know to what extent the public here in Ceylon follow the career of both you and your famous husband."[66] Unsurprisingly, it was then that the formerly jailed leader, Nehru, asked Robeson plaintively, "Is there any chance of coming to India?"[67]

Robeson's prominence was being taken for granted. When a distinguished U.S. Negro journalist, P.L. Prattis, wrote in 1944 that Robeson "had been adjudged" to be "one of the 12 great intellects in the world today," this hardly caused a raised eyebrow or a ruffle of dissent;[68] perhaps this encomium was bestowed because of his linguistic ability, coupled with what was then seen positively as his friendship with Moscow—the latter being suggestive of political insight—both of which were indicative of intellectual capability.

As such, the alma mater of Dr. Martin Luther King, Jr.—Morehouse College in Atlanta—strained to extend an invitation to Robeson, requesting that he honor them by accepting their offer of an honorary degree.[69] This event in the late spring of 1943 was a festive occasion in this otherwise grim citadel of Jim Crow. Benjamin Mays, who was to serve as Dr. King's mentor, was effusive, terming Robeson's appearance "a great occasion. People were standing in large numbers and we erected a loudspeaker and put chairs on the campus for the people who could not get in. There were many outside." Dr. Mays proclaimed that Robeson "gave an excellent address and he received a grand ovation"; Robeson "sang and of course the house literally went wild with applause." Yes, he concluded with satisfaction, "those who have seen Morehouse commencements over a period of forty or fifty years declare this to be the best the college has had . . . ."[70] Scrambling to keep up, Howard University in Washington, D.C.— the self-proclaimed capstone of Negro higher education—then "unanimously voted to confer upon" Robeson an honorary degree.[71]

What Howard and Morehouse were recognizing was that Robeson's star continued to ascend, bringing eminence to these campuses when he arrived. This was particularly the case when he revived his signature role—depicting Othello—first in his hometown of Princeton then to the apex of theater that was Broadway, Manhattan. He had travelled a long way from his home on the corner of Green and Witherspoon streets in this university town. Bursting with pride, the town that once shunned him now boasted of his triumphs, particularly in London: "he twice filled [the] Albert Hall to its ten thousand capacity and gave a command performance at St. James Palace before the Prince of Wales", while "this past summer," it was said in August 1942, "he broke attendance records in Philadelphia" and "at Lewisohn Stadium" in Manhattan.[72]

One critic was disarmed by Robeson's appearance at the latter venue since "few concert stars" theretofore had "been able to pack Lewisohn Stadium" and "you could count on one hand the number of Negroes attending and still have three fingers left. But not so now" for "things have really changed" with the arrival of Robeson.[73] For he was able to attract diverse audiences, particularly African-Americans, introducing them to languages and cultures with which many were unfamiliar, internationalizing their consciousness and making it easier for them to join with less hesitancy and reluctance an anti-fascist crusade. There had been expressions of anti-Jewish fervor in Harlem, as an outgrowth of fascist influence but Robeson helped to undermine it, asserting "no Negro would dare be anti-Semitic in front of me."[74]

"Hebrew music moves me very deeply," he confided to the BBC. "One day I was mistaken for an Orthodox Jew" or one of the "Falashas" of Africa. "I grew a beard for 'Othello'" and as he hopped onto a subway train a chap with a beard began "talking to me in Hebrew" and Robeson replied accordingly. "Then suddenly his face breaks into a big grin and he says, 'You're not one of us, you're not one of the Falashas . . . you're Paul Robeson.'"[75]

Still, it was acting on Broadway in *Othello* that propelled Robeson to ever greater heights of popularity, making it less likely that he would be found on subways. *TIME* magazine, the arbiter of mainstream opinion, proclaimed in 1943 that Robeson was "probably the most famous living Negro." He "went to London, conquered it, he conquered half the cities of Europe"—probably an underestimate. As for Moscow—which this journal was to bludgeon repeatedly after the war ended—Robeson was cited as saying, "I felt I might have functioned there better than any place else in the world." He now received a handsome $1,500 per week performing in *Othello*, which was a "fraction of what he can earn singing at $2000 or $2500 a night. For 'Othello' he lost 35 pounds [and] now weighs [a svelte] 230 . . . ."[76]

Before departing London, it had occurred to Eslanda Robeson that reviving this role in the U.S. would catapult her spouse to the commanding heights of his craft. She eagerly made casting suggestions, observing that "a lot depends on the selection of the Desdemona" character in determining the play's success.[77]

Ms. Robeson proved to be prescient; the official premier was held in Philadelphia, with Robeson in brilliantly colored robes gliding across the stage. The future renowned jurist, Raymond Pace Alexander, was among those in attendance and he too—like the audience as a whole—leapt to his feet when the curtain descended, as all assembled erupted in a wild display of applause. The next day, an impressed Leopold Stokowski, the well-known conductor, met with Robeson, signing him to a quite substantial contract making him the first black person to appear as a concert artist before this eminent orchestra.[78]

Othello, the story of an African who had served the state valiantly but was traduced nonetheless, resonated because of the echoes it provided of Robeson's own life, campaigning for a government unwilling to confront the Jim Crow that bedeviled him. One of Hollywood's main moguls, Walter Wanger, was among the legions who expressed his "admiration and regard" for Robeson, adding "your accomplishments in and out of the theatre knows no bounds."[79] One fan of Robeson was among those who raved about his performance, terming it "one of the great Shakespearean productions of all time," noting how Robeson was able to draw upon the "rage you felt at the violent methods used by the white players to keep you off the football team and you found in it a model for the rage Othello must have felt."[80]

Yet, despite the enormous success, potential producers were frightened, fearing that a domestic audience would shun a tragedy involving an inter-racial love scene. Tension was in the air as a result, as Robeson had predicted when he performed the role in London years earlier.[81] "I make myself believe I am Othello and I act as he would act,"[82] was Robeson's simple explanation for the play's ground-breaking success and an indication of a style of "method" acting that would sweep through Hollywood in coming years.[83]

As evidenced by the aforementioned cities—Princeton, Philadelphia, Tuskegee, Washington, Atlanta, Kansas City—Robeson was engaged in a punishing travel regime, often traveling thousands of kilometers by train, a pattern that was to take a toll as his age advanced inexorably. By the time the U.S. entered the war, he was 43 years old. In 1942 alone his itinerary involved train travel from Manhattan to Dayton, Ohio to Chicago to Pasadena, California—a distance of 3,000 kilometers, all within days.[84] It was then that his good friend and better comrade, Ben Davis—about to be elected to the New York City Council as a Communist—bumped into Robeson and walked away worried. "He's well and I tried in the space of a few minutes," he told Eslanda Robeson, "to press upon him the necessity for rest. I have ways however of pressing harder," he added enigmatically.[85] Perhaps Davis could have persuaded Robeson to curb his consumption of what an astonished journalist termed "his one real weakness," i.e. his devouring of ice cream by the quart in one sitting.[86] Tellingly, it was reported in 1944 that "the moment" Robeson "sits down, [he] lights a cigarette," a habit not widely seen then as ultimately debilitating. "I work harder in one performance of 'Othello'," he said, "than I ever did in three concerts."[87]

Just before departing London, a worried Eslanda, was urging her spouse to adopt a new "diet and get his weight down." The once solid, broad-shouldered Adonis "gradually got so big, right before my eyes, that all semblance of that grand figure has long since disappeared under bulk"; Robeson "got bigger and I got madder and madder," an unsustainable predicament for both sides. On a visit to Manhattan, old friends who had not seen him of late, compared him to "an Ox," so "he got mad" and as was his tendency,[88] this anger fueled a prompt downsizing of his bulk. (As his success in competitive sports suggested, Robeson could ascend to great heights when challenged. Moreover, the fury he displayed in portraying Othello, was a partial product of being able to access an inner rage fueled by the indignity of Jim Crow.) But the question loomed: as domestic and global tensions rose and Robeson was targeted, would he be able to remain healthy?

Part of Robeson's regimen that could be exhausting was his continuing, almost maniacal, study. He was a prodigious reader, going through seven books a week. Studying Swahili and Yiddish were on his agenda in the early 1940s and, according to a bedazzled reporter, "he broke the back of Chinese in three months."[89]

"He started studying Norwegian at 8 o'clock one morning," said one amazed journalist, "and was writing it by 6 the same evening. He once turned down a 50 week radio engagement because he was in the throes of learning Chinese." He had embarked, it was announced in 1943, on the "formidable task of learning at least one example of every language group in the world" with "groups still to be tackled" including "Turkish, Mexican Indian, Hindustani and Georgian . . . ." To that end, he "usually wakes up at 7:30 A.M., reads or studies languages for half an hour and goes back to sleep again until about 10:30 as Othello is a strenuous part," then "he sleeps awhile in the afternoon too before his 5 P.M. dinner." His immense erudition did not extend to his diet since "his favorite meal is scrambled eggs, sausages and coffee. When he has a cold he drinks Scotch" and "between the acts of 'Othello', he needs a 'slight glass of champagne.'" Besides language study, he relaxed by indulging in the similarly complex game that is chess "and has a remarkable collection of chess books," though he never really mastered this complex game. He also enjoyed visiting "nightspots, [to] listen to the music, talk, relax and sometimes dance. He loves boogey-woogey, both to hear and sing himself."[90] In other words, Robeson's was a classic case of "burning his candle at both ends." There was the intense study of the would-be philologist and the sampling of earthly delights, then the hallmark of celebrated performers. How long could he maintain the intensity mandated by the demanding—though incongruent—realms of philologist and performer?

Upon showing up at his favorite watering hole, Robeson may have befuddled those assembled—according to a bemused journalist—by "absent-mindedly" having donned "two different socks" or, perhaps a "blue jacket and a black pair of trousers," considered a fashion faux pas. The affluent Robeson was "always forgetting to carry along money", inadvisable in some of the joints where the music he liked was played.[91]

Robeson was often to be found at Manhattan's Savoy, where revolutionary trends in music—subsequently denoted as "bebop"—were then being honed. Robeson was there "very often," as he recalled it, in order "to hear Count Basie, as I had often heard Chick Webb & Ella Fitzgerald." He was often "downtown" too, "to hear Don Shirley and Bach," then "up to Manhattan Casino to hear Charlie Parker," the godfather of the new music; there he would "get 'twisted around' trying to dance to those 'offbeat riffs'," then "down to the Apollo to hear Dizzy Gillespie take flight"; hearing the tinkling on the ivory keys of "Theolonius Monk really floored me," as did "the comparable Duke Ellington . . . ." As was his wont, Robeson sought to make linkages between and among his artistic pursuits, observing that the "Modern Jazz Quartet made a lasting pact with the Elizabethans and the Duke [Ellington] himself caught up with Shakespeare."[92]

Subsequently, he spoke glowingly of W.C. Handy, "a great character and a musician," the "Daddy of the Blues", adding: "I knew him well" for in his "'Joe Turner Blues' . . . as he said to me" the "original of the chorus is probably the prototype of all blues and it was sung all over the South." Robeson recounted how

> when I was a young man in Harlem, just round the corner from where I lived was a café. The musicians would go there after the night clubs closed around 2 A.M. I remember when I was in a show I'd go along and we'd have eggs and bacon. People would improvise on their instruments and sing, and many of the great songs were written that way. For me, it was spirituals on Sunday morning but on Saturday nights I rocked. Who rocked with me? Well, there was Fats Waller, Billie Holliday, Chick Webb, Louis Armstrong, Count Basie, Duke Ellington and many more—and among the youngsters who came along later was Lena Horne, Sammy Davis . . . I remember a young girl coming in one night. We couldn't see much of her through the tobacco smoke but when she sings—we stop and we listen. She sang "A Tisket, a Tasket" and the Count says to me, "Where's she from?" Her name was Ella Fitzgerald. She says, "I'm going to the Carnegie Hall."[93]

Later Robeson explained that "[Dizzy] Gillespie and [Charlie] Parker are not new names to me. I have heard them both play on several occasions and have been both stimulated by their imaginative creations and a little astounded by their incredible technique and

musicianship . . . ." Still, he sought to apply his critical intelligence
to this field, warning that the "Big Jazz Boom, which started around
1936" meant that "the music became Big Business." Thus, this musical
trend "deserves serious attention" and "perhaps in years to come
they [Gillespie and Parker] will be regarded somewhat as Debussy
and Stravinsky are now regarded by modern musicians . . . ." Though
accepted as conventional wisdom today—at least in rarefied circles—
then Robeson's remarks were, quite typically, controversial. He was
drawn into a "spirited discussion between an advocate of bebop and a
defender of the old New Orleans style," the predecessor. "I sat quietly,
drinking in this highly specialized talk, taking no sides," seeing merit
in both sides. "At a reasonably safe distance from the [New Orleans]
pro-Dixielanders, I am grateful to the arrival of Messrs. Gillespie,
Parker" and their New York based colleagues.[94]

Despite such diversions, he found plenty of time to devote to the
organization he had helped to found and subsidize: the Council on
African Affairs. It was during the war that Kwame Nkrumah—then
residing in the U.S.—and Amy Ashwood Garvey, former spouse of
the then deceased Jamaican leader, listened raptly as Robeson spoke
about the colonized continent and what was to be done to alter this
state of affairs, a decolonized prospect hardly endorsed by the prime
U.S. ally in London.[95]

This was accompanied by a massive 46th birthday party for him in
1944, featuring Duke Ellington, the musician; Joe Louis, the boxer;
and Richard Wright, the novelist,[96] designed to raise funds for the
Council on African Affairs (CAA). The coordinator of this tribute was
the prominent writer Lillian Hellman and joining her in providing an
avalanche of kudos were Cab Calloway, W.C. Handy, Walter Huston,
Lucky Roberts and Ed Sullivan.[97]

When the pre-eminent baseball slugger George "Babe" Ruth sent
him best wishes for this crowded gathering, it signaled Robeson's
exalted status in the U.S. stratosphere.[98] But signifying the breadth
of Robeson's appeal, Kwame Nkrumah—soon to be Ghana's founding
father—was also among the endorsers of this event.[99]

Thirteen thousand persons tried to squeeze into the crowded
locale and five thousand had to be turned away for lack of room.
Vice President Henry A. Wallace—soon to be defrocked in favor of

Harry S. Truman—delivered fulsome praise, as did the actor Edward G. Robinson and the labor leader Sidney Hillman. Mary McLeod Bethune, an acclaimed Negro educator, referred to him in awestruck terms as the "tallest tree in our forest," a label that was to stick to him for decades to come. A visibly touched Robeson, head bowed, occasionally dabbing at his moist eyes with his handkerchief, spoke movingly about his appreciation—and his sacred cause: the CAA and the liberation of colonized Africa.[100]

This was in Manhattan, but it was more than 3,000 kilometers westward, in Los Angeles, months later, when the CAA joined with celebrities in honoring Robeson—and raising funds for his favorite causes. Those lavishing pleasantries upon him were the famed actor and chanteuse, Lena Horne, who was explicit in her "love and gratitude" to him "for making the path so clear with the brilliant light of your artistry." Also joining in the amen chorus were Dalton Trumbo, perhaps Hollywood's most creative screenwriter and a talented novelist besides, who along with Robeson was to be persecuted after the war ended. Still, also on the list of those celebrating Robeson were distinguished actors, such as Gregory Peck, Boris Karloff, Gene Kelly, and Danny Kaye.[101]

The year of this celebration—1945—was to be yet another turning point for Robeson, his nation and the world. May witnessed the Allies' victory over Germany in Europe and August marked the horrific conclusion of the war in Asia with the atomic bombing of Japan. Finally, conditions were safe for Robeson to return to Europe. "We left New York Aug. 1st", said his accompanist, Lawrence Brown, with a "crossing of 29 hours" to Paris and were "on the go ever since. We have worked three performances, one ... for some GI's, and [a] radio recording," then "we will cover France, Germany and perhaps Austria . . . ."[102]

Robeson picked the concentration camp at Dachau as one of his initial stops. "I stood in Dachau in 1945," he said a few years later, "and saw the ashes and bones of departed victims," speaking of the most dastardly concentration camp established by the hated Nazis. "I might have seen the ashes of some of my brothers in Groveland, Florida just the other day—or in Martinsville [Virginia] a few months back," he wrote in 1952, referring to recently inflamed sites auguring the destruction of black life.[103]

However, Dachau was not the only shock that Robeson received in Europe. He was astounded by the "anti-Negro and pro-German attitude of our American troops" there. "I would never have believed it if I hadn't come abroad," he said. He spoke with U.S. officers and "found them to be anti-Russian and convinced that war with Russia was inevitable." He was similarly astonished to find that these men seemed equally determined to weaken the Labour Party in Britain and Social Democrats in Europe generally.[104] J. Edgar Hoover was informed that Robeson was disturbed to find that "Army officers and State Department officials" were in "open collaboration with Nazis and fascists in Czechoslovakia. Robeson said he knew this to be true because he was with these officers and officials in [Prague] while making a tour."[105] Robeson had a front-row seat in inspecting the U.S. military in Europe, an outcome that the brass themselves guaranteed when Major General Frank Keating invited him into their inner sanctum, requesting that he sing for the troops.[106]

Robeson chose not to retreat or yield since he had a sense of what he, and his comrades, were up against. It was also in 1945 that he addressed a large gathering in Los Angeles of the Joint Anti-Fascist Refugee Committee, where $17,000 was raised for those who had managed to escape the ravages of Europe. It was there that he enunciated the creed that was to animate his life for years to come. "We are standing at the crossroads of history," he said and "the American people do not entirely understand that we can have fascism here unless we learn to use our productive forces for the benefit of all people. We can't wait for fascism to die out and the oppressed peoples of the world will not wait."[107] Eagerly capturing his words were agents of the FBI, who thought they had reason to believe—as was to be said later—that actually Robeson had in mind becoming the "Black Stalin", a destiny the agency was bent on circumventing.[108]

6

"Black Stalin"?

Though there were indications that the U.S. would turn sharply to the right after the war concluded, thereby jeopardizing his livelihood—if not his life—Paul Robeson initially proceeded without evident signs that he sensed the wide and tumultuous dimensions of what was brewing.

In December 1945 Eslanda Robeson—still acting in a managerial capacity—was continuing to regard her chief client as "one of the greatest concert attractions in the western world," which was hardly inaccurate. She was negotiating with Sergei Eisenstein about producing a film about Felix Eboue, a hero of the Francophone world due to his stern anti-fascism. "When [Charles] De Gaulle was here in early autumn," she said, "I talked with him about the idea and he was enthusiastic . . . ." The couple spent a day with "Mme. Eboue in New York when she passed through on her way to Paris," and the great man's widow "was thrilled over the whole idea," feeling that "Paul will make a magnificent Eboue." Overly optimistic, she adjudged that "if the film is done correctly, this may be a fine chance for the Soviet Film Industry to enter the world film market . . . ."[1]

But even then it would not have been premature to assert that the U.S. was not only keen in preserving its domination of the global film market,[2] but that it was also determined to ensure that a man—Robeson—who could be a wedge in eroding this hegemony would not be allowed to flourish. As matters evolved, Hollywood became a major battlefield which increased the pressure on Robeson. He was to salute the Communist screenwriter John Howard Lawson, for his bravura upbraiding of inquiring Congressmen: it gave him a "thrill of pride," said Robeson, hailing the writer's "vehemence and eloquence."[3] He denounced the "low content and superficiality" and "conscious aversion to truth" of Hollywood, something he knew well, though it did little to enhance his popularity among moguls generally.[4]

Of course, Ms. Robeson's outreach to Moscow on her spouse's behalf should not be taken to mean their marriage had returned to the bliss of the early 1920s.[5] In May 1946 she told the press that her husband "had 10 days at home in the last year."[6] While performing *Othello*, Robeson leased an apartment in the fashionable section of Manhattan, 38th Street and Park Avenue, accentuating and facilitating his many absences from "home."[7] Still, this scenario does not account for Robeson's own ability—or inability—to sense that the warm relationship between Washington and Moscow was simply a function of the war and did not signal an ongoing entente.

For Robeson was thrown off balance by another contemporaneous development: the ruckus that enveloped the U.S. Communist Party. Robeson disclaimed membership but was certainly quite close to its leaders—particularly William Patterson and Ben Davis—and it was in 1945 that this group underwent a wrenching and painful split as their leader, Earl Browder, was ousted, along with the political approach he symbolized: seeing the friendly U.S.–USSR summit in Teheran in 1943 as emblematic of a long-term trend. The unrest generated by this instability disoriented Robeson's comrades on whom he relied for counsel at a time when clear and unsullied analysis was needed more than ever.[8]

Davis's summary of his conversation with Robeson about this controversy was captured by the FBI. "I saw Paul" and "had a conversation with him last night and then I had a more extended talk with him today"; he found that Robeson "didn't think much about our past policies" and "figured that at some later time it will be necessary for us to regard ourselves in the old party" way, meaning a return to the idea of confrontation—not conciliation—with the U.S. ruling class. A French Communist, Jacques Duclos, had denounced the recently installed policy of conciliation leading to the ousting of Browder after he spearheaded this now rejected policy and Robeson "didn't think much more about" the matter, until he "read Duclos' article" and that perusal made it "obvious that we went too far."[9]

Such a view expressing skepticism about the wisdom of the socialist lamb reclining comfortably with the capitalist lion was to brand Robeson as a hardliner, making him even more of a target for U.S. intelligence agencies. And this meant more probing questions from government interrogators determined to ascertain if he were a member of the U.S. Communist Party. This persistent query was posed in October 1946 by California State Senator, Jack Tenney, and—as ever—Robeson was just as dogged in rejecting the question and the questioner, telling the legislator that his committee was evidence that fascism lived. Robeson, as was his habit, characterized himself as a militant anti-fascist but made it clear that he preferred the CP over the Republicans, since as he travelled globally he found the former were "the first people to die, the first to sacrifice, and the first to understand fascism."[10] The FBI continued to insist that Robeson was in fact a card-carrying member of the U.S. party, registering under the pseudonym, "John Thomas."[11]

If a date can be ascertained for the formal launching of the Cold War and its handmaiden, the Red Scare, it would be 5 March 1946, when Winston Churchill journeyed to Missouri with President Harry S. Truman, who had replaced Roosevelt after his untimely death. There the pudgy, cigar-chomping, alcohol-guzzling British Tory announced that an "Iron Curtain" had descended across Europe, a reference to a divided Europe (and ultimately a divided world) with Communists surging to power in the east in the aftermath of Berlin's defeat: these radicals, he argued, intended a dire fate for those in their jurisdiction and those who struggled against them, who were presently beyond their purview. This was to lead to bloody wars in Korea and Vietnam, while continuing attempts to overthrow colonialism, were combated by the Washington–London led axis in the name of fighting communism. At a certain point, U.S. leaders began to question the sagacity of shedding blood and treasure to combat Communists abroad, while allowing these self-proclaimed revolutionaries to exist at home—particularly those like Robeson who had demonstrated a proven ability to attract millions.

Still, moving the U.S.—and the North Atlantic community generally—from the entente of the war to the confrontation of the Cold War was not a speedy process, taking a while for the new approach to trickle down to the frontlines. Surely, before Churchill's portentous words, the postwar glow seemed to be intact. Robeson was honored with the highest award of the NAACP at a star-studded reception at the Biltmore Hotel in Manhattan in October 1945. Unsurprisingly, Robeson praised socialism, which at that point was not considered beyond the pale.[12] The pro-socialist Robeson was asked by the publication of the rising Negro millionaire, John H. Johnson, to pose for their glossy pages. They wanted a "nice layout to be titled, perhaps 'All American Family', presenting the Robesons [in] their home," which "started me wondering," said the editor, "why someone does not do a book on the Robeson family the title 'All American Family.'"[13] Such was not to be and, if anything, soon the "Robeson family" was to be scorned—if anything—as an "All Soviet Family." Yet during that different era, Johnson himself asked Ms. Robeson to become a "contributing editor" of his infant periodical.[14]

In early 1946, Robeson's income was yet to come under assault, so his plush estate remained his hideaway on the few occasions he abandoned his demanding routine of concerts and political rallies. He had "promised" Ben Davis that he would "come up with me" to Enfield, "so that we could talk over many things, not to mention a few games of uninterrupted and concentrated chess,"[15] and perhaps some tennis too.

Davis, a frequent guest, had grown accustomed to the comfortably informal residence, which resembled the workshop of an absent-minded professor, appropriate for a man whose "secret ambition" was to be "a professor of languages."[16] As in London, bookcases were packed tight, lining many rooms, groaning from the weight of studied volumes. Even the top of the grand piano was used to hold tomes. Volumes of Proust and Chekhov abounded and various books in diverse languages, though Robeson conceded that, for many of these tongues, he read them better than he spoke them. He hoped some day, it was said then, to read Confucius in the original. Davis, along with Patterson, his closest friend and comrade, knew better than most that left to his own devices, Robeson—as he declared—had "only one ambition—to be a great scholar, a teacher." For "some day," he mused, "I'll give up the theater and join the faculty of a college," perhaps pursuing his true love: philology and linguistics. But that was not to be. Even then, during the height of his popularity in the U.S., before he became a recluse late in life, Robeson acknowledged,

"I always want the curtains closed and lights turned on in any room. I don't like to look out at the world."[17]

Robeson continued to build the Council on African Affairs, the vanguard organization in the U.S. campaigning against colonialism. In early 1946 Harlem witnessed what was described as "one of the greatest meetings ever held" there, when thousands gathered at a "famine relief rally", focused on suffering in Africa, that received expressions of support from the contralto Marian Anderson; Eleanor Roosevelt; Mary McLeod Bethune; and the Jamaica-born Communist Ferdinand Smith, then the highest ranking Negro in the trade union movement in his capacity as leader of the National Maritime Union.[18]

Even after the "Iron Curtain" speech, it seemed to be business as usual when boxer Joe Louis joined with Robeson in hailing a huge rally in Manhattan targeting South Africa and the colonized continent generally.[19] Days later there was Robeson linking a speedy end to both lynching and colonialism at a staggeringly large rally of 15,000 at Madison Square Garden in Manhattan; joining him was the dancer Katherine Dunham and messages of support were received from Nehru in India, A.B. Xuma of the African National Congress of South Africa, and Ken Hill, a leader of the union movement in Jamaica.[20]

The U.S. authorities had quite a chore in seeking to disrupt Robeson's anti-colonial ties. Just before independence, Nehru confided to "My Dear Essie" that "I often think of you and Paul."[21] Robeson was friendly with Norman Manley, the anti-colonial leader on the island of Jamaica, as he informed Robeson then, "we here follow your work with great interest".[22] Robeson made it clear there that when he spoke of "The Negro," he "mean[t] American Negroes as well as West Indians and Africans"; this also meant "in that very process of helping others," speaking of African-Americans, "we add to our own strength and bring nearer full freedom for ourselves." This also meant special attention to "uranium from the Belgian Congo for atomic bombs" and rubber for "Firestone," the U.S. giant corporation, taken from Liberia.[23] Disrupting this expansive view of "The Negro" became a priority for Washington whose strategy was to offer civil rights concessions to U.S. Negroes at home, while bolstering colonialism and neo-colonialism abroad.

Robeson's critique of U.S. policy toward Pretoria had become so strident that a future Secretary of State, John Foster Dulles, felt compelled to reply to him at the United Nations, excoriating the artist's alleged "misapprehension." Ironically and damningly, Dulles conceded in a way that undermined his own nation: "I did not feel that the United States, in view of its own record, was justified in adopting a holier-than-thou attitude toward the Union of South Africa"[24]—which was precisely the point and which was to doom ultimately both apartheid and Jim Crow to the dung-heap of history.

Robeson was then mulling a proposal to return to the silver screen, this time playing the lead role in a cinematic version of an acclaimed novel by his friend, Howard Fast:[25] *Freedom Road* was later to be made as a movie starring the boxer Muhammad Ali, in the role of a slave who rises after the U.S. Civil War to high political office.[26] One periodical allowed Robeson to assert—strikingly and truthfully— that if he "went to Hong Kong tomorrow the people there would know me because of the Chinese records I had made."[27] Even in 1947, the consul for the regime in Port-au-Prince told Robeson that "President [Dumarsais] Estime and his Cabinet would be delighted to be honored by you visiting them and spending a few days as the guest of the Republic of Haiti . . . ."[28]

Yet this buoyant global popularity was to be punctured and deflated and this process began in his homeland and, intriguingly, may have begun in the White House itself.[29] It was there in September 1946 that Robeson vehemently charged that it was hypocritical for the U.S. to take the lead in Nuremberg in indicting purveyors of race hatred, while lethargically engaging the same at home. "What is happening in Nuremberg is a travesty on democracy," said Robeson, "when the people of America are murdered by the same kind of men that are on trial."[30] Drawing a connection between the parlous domestic plight of Negroes and global trends, had touched the sensitive Achilles' heel of the republic for decades and this was bound to bring a forceful counter-reaction.[31]

The clear implication of Robeson's denunciation was that U.S. officials—President Truman included—were surely worthy of being dragged into the dock, an event that Robeson sought to ensure when a few years later he and Patterson filed a petition with the

United Nations charging their nation with genocide against African-Americans.[32] Soon Robeson made clear that "I heartily endorse the proposal of the Soviet Union to make race discrimination and hatred a crime."[33] At once, this linked tightly the most pressing global and domestic concerns, which simultaneously placed Truman himself in legal jeopardy. The president may have heard that Robeson was becoming the most unrelenting critic of what was called the "Truman Doctrine,"[34] the assumed right of the U.S. to intervene globally to combat socialism. Yet how could the U.S. move on this treacherous course, when African-Americans were being told by the most popular amongst them that this was decidedly inimical to their interests? The response was to erode Jim Crow—then toss Robeson and his comrades overboard.

Robeson's attorney, Leonard Boudin, felt that his client's real Waterloo was encountered when he led an angry delegation to Washington to confront President Truman about a spate of lynching, including the maiming of Negroes in military uniforms. There Robeson had an inflamed face-to-face confrontation with the Missourian, which led to the president banging the table, as if these blows were intended for the man across from him. With blood apparently rushing to his temples because of the anxiety induced, the purpling Truman was vociferous in his reprimand of Robeson—though not as pointed in his condemnation of lynching. It was just after that meeting that Truman moved to circumscribe Robeson's globetrotting, which was akin to cutting off his oxygen supply. It was during Truman's reign that Robeson's passport was snatched, which—according to his attorney—"destroyed ten or eleven or twelve creative years, the most important years in his life." Robeson, he argued, because he was a "black leader, created more anger," and even "fear" but "certainly anger in the white community."[35] Combined with the allegation that Robeson secretly wished to become the nation's "Black Stalin", the pressure on him to recant his revolutionary views became palpable.

But even before Robeson's fiery encounter with Truman, there were symptoms of the artist's deteriorating relationship to the state. Days after Churchill's pronouncement in Missouri, Robeson was to be found in Detroit, a bastion of labor and Negro militancy—whose future mayor, Coleman Young was as close to the Communist Party (if not closer) than Robeson himself.³⁶ Robeson was there at the founding of an organization—the Civil Rights Congress—with which he collaborated with the same level of intensity and commitment that he devoted to the Council on African Affairs. There Robeson was described as "rough, tough and angry" in his embattled remarks and received a "standing ovation" in return. "His broadcast speech read like an angry poem," said a reporter on the scene—"and he read it like a call to battle."³⁷

These pressures came to a head in Jefferson City—in the home state of the President—where Robeson had brought his anti-lynching crusade. There he was involved in a perilous automobile "accident" but investigation revealed that four bolts had been removed from the lugs of a tire and a fifth mishandled intentionally, preordaining that Robeson's car would be diverted—dangerously—from its intended course. That is, only one bolt was found on the hubcap, meaning that the others had been removed and the cap then placed in such a way as to conceal this defect. Without a doubt this was done while the car was parked, as the car had been driven only recently from St. Louis, scores of kilometers away, without incident. Yet Robeson was increasingly vilified at this point—soon he was to be labelled "Black Stalin"—thus it was mostly the Negro press that sounded the alarm about this attempted assassination.³⁸ Robeson "cheats death," said the *Pittsburgh Courier*, as "prejudice prompted [an] attempt on his life"; yes, it was concluded, the tire on his vehicle was "tampered with."³⁹ Months later Robeson was to tell the U.S. Congress bluntly, "I have been threatened with death . . . two or three times," and this incident may have been foremost in his mind.⁴⁰ Ms. Robeson was said to fear "killers", adding "each night before I go to bed . . . I put a broad-bladed hunting knife under my pillow, along with a portable burglar alarm. The police have turned down my request for a gun permit. But I'm terrified," she added tremulously, "that somebody might try to avenge themselves on me . . ."⁴¹

This murderous attempt was the response to Robeson's cry at a picket-line in St. Louis organized by Patterson's Civil Rights Congress where the artist announced that he was retiring from the concert stage and had chosen to "enter the day-to-day struggle of the people from whom I spring . . . ."[42] Thus, he said his intention was to "talk up and down the nation against race hatred and prejudice."[43] On the one hand, since his concerts were beginning to be boycotted by impresarios and booking agents in any case, this cry was simply making the best of a bad situation. Yet, later Robeson was to rue this decision, feeling that it removed him from the wellspring of what had been phenomenal support.

"I am devoting [time] mainly to assisting progressive causes and lending whatever aid I can to the fight," was his conclusion then. Thus, though in October 1947 he was singing before 7,000 in Norfolk, Virginia, "more than half of whom were white," as was to be the trend, the audience was also slated to hear a political message from him—except just before the program was to begin, the Chief of Police appeared and announced, "you've got to have these people separated", i.e. segregated. The organizer replied, "White people can get their money back if they don't want to sit with Negroes" but was told, "What kind of white people are these?" For, unusually, not a single one asked for a refund. Days later Robeson was in the Capital of the Confederacy, Richmond, at a program sponsored by his college fraternity, Alpha Phi Alpha. Again, the assembled were interrupted rudely by the authorities, as the police entered the hall and sought aggressively to enforce the state's segregation law by demanding that those defined as "white" not sit next to those not so defined—but not a single "white" person moved: though one Negro was arrested for failing to follow police orders to change his seat.[44] Earlier, Robeson had not been allowed to rent a hall in Albany, New York though a Nazi supporter had not been so mistreated.[45]

The worst was to come. Little concern was raised in the mainstream when it was reported that during a Robeson visit to Peoria, Illinois, the ultra-right threatened to "get" him,[46] i.e. inflict mayhem upon him. Forebodingly, this anti-Robeson alliance included executives of the region's major employer—Caterpillar, which specialized in earth-moving machinery—then being contested by a left-led union. Yet, these executives had recruited to their side the American Legion, war veterans, who included a goodly number of Euro-American workers, whose ultra-conservative influence was bound to move unions rightward.[47]

Robeson was appalled: the "whole city was subjected to terroristic control," he said. His unionized supporters were "immobilized," while the "Negro community was intimidated." The "struggle against fascism" was the nub,[48] he cried—but with his two bulwarks of support battered, Robeson was increasingly appearing to be a sacrificial lamb. No, said an anti-communist journalist writing for the liberal magazine, *The Nation*: In what was becoming a popular mantra, Robeson was stalked and rebuffed, it was said, not because of racism but because of communism.[49]

Vainly, Robeson sought to uphold the now tattered banner of working-class internationalism: "I have seen hunger at close quarters here at home and abroad," he reminded. "I have seen Sudanese workers in Egypt labor in the cotton fields from dawn to sundown on a meager diet . . . I have lived with Welsh miners, Glasgow dockworkers, French metal workers and Italian farm laborers"—but his dream, embodied in his determined study of languages, that the oppressed globally shared universal concern was being overridden by a contrasting tidal wave that uplifted "American Exceptionalism" and the companion notion that the U.S. stood hubristically apart from this global movement.[50]

By 1947 Robeson realized intently that a new stage in domestic and global politics had arrived, which called for a renewed stance on his part. He was never much of a writer: once, the lyricist Earl Robinson complained that "over a long period of experience with Paul and some of it quite close, I have never been able to get a written or even a wired reply from him. When I am with [him] in person," in contrast, "of course, the situation is entirely different."[51] A Communist journalist, who interviewed him more than once, echoed this consensus about Robeson, as did the imprisoned Ben Davis, hungering vainly to hear from his comrade.[52]

Surely, this reluctance of Robeson to write was not a useful political trait but now sensing the emergency at play, Robeson started penning weekly columns and eventually was to launch his own newspaper to highlight his and likeminded opinions. Robeson was "struck by the remarkable parallel between the valiant fight of the freed slaves during Reconstruction and the struggles which confront all darker peoples today"; similarly, the "concentration of power and wealth and white supremacy rule in South Africa, represent a threat not only to the whole of Africa but to India, Asia and the entire non-white world including"—he added pointedly—"Negro America."[53] Thus, Robeson heightened his solidarity with the union that best represented the kind of working-class internationalism he supported: the National Maritime Union, whose seafarers sailed into ports globally, and which was headed by a Jamaican, Ferdinand Smith—a man who the artist had the "highest respect" for and whose union he too held in "special" esteem.[54]

With Smith's aid, he also began to highlight the value of Jamaican independence, instructing readers that the "existence of a Negro-governed country so close to our shores is bound to have an important moral and political influence on the freedom struggle of 13,000,000 Negroes" on the mainland. "I have discussed West Indian problems with Arthur Creech-Jones, the present British Colonial Secretary; British Foreign Minister Ernest Bevin; Aneurin Bevan, the Minister of Fuel"; and "Sir Stafford Cripps," indicative of what Robeson acknowledged: "I am no stranger to West Indian problems,"[55] a major asset in New York City, which contained a large immigrant population from this region.

As such, Jamaica's premier periodical, the *Daily Gleaner* bellowed accurately that when Robeson arrived on the island shortly thereafter, he received a "hero's welcome."[56] Michael Manley, a future Jamaican Prime Minister, later called Robeson's concert "perhaps the greatest public performance in our history, a free concert—probably the first of its kind by a professional artist in the open air, attended by some 80,000 Jamaicans from every station of life."[57] Robeson was moved when he received this birds-eye view of the slum of Empire, which reinforced his anti-colonial determination: "I saw many families living in shells of old automobiles, hollowed out and turned upside down,"[58] he moaned, a dire state of affairs that was to impel shortly a mass migration to London. Monitoring him carefully, the U.S. authorities acknowledged that in Jamaica and Trinidad he was "feted by official and civic organizations"; this they knew since he was "under discreet surveillance" during his journey. This observer noted that during a "free open-air concert" featuring Robeson, "some fifty thousand persons" attended.[59]

Robeson also journeyed to Panama, a strategic territory whose labor force was heavily comprised of workers with roots in Jamaica and Trinidad. The U.S. legation in a "confidential" missive viewed suspiciously his recital sponsored by a "Communist led" union.[60] During his eight-day visit, Robeson reportedly "sang for children", a specialty of his, and to "silver communities," a reference to the apartheid designation of workers of African descent. He was honored by resident Spanish republicans, still thankful for his intervention in their homeland and—said the U.S. legation—"received a great deal of comment in the local press, stress being placed on his Communist sympathies."[61]

But retreating from the concert stage and advancing to the typewriter did not halt the decline in his popularity (though it fell least among Negroes). The man who for the longest was the sun around which all else revolved saw his income fall drastically from $104,000 in 1947 to $2,000 by 1950. Similarly, as the dark night of "McCarthyism" descended— the anti-communist witch-hunts often spearheaded by the pugnacious Senator from Wisconsin—artists who wanted to pursue a career found it safer to denounce him, rather than embrace him.[62] The doyenne of the Negro movement, Mary Church Terrell, who felt that Robeson was a "truly great man" who "made the supreme sacrifice," added that "it makes me dizzy when I think of the money he has practically tossed aside" by daring to confront the authorities.[63]

Soon some government investigators found workers to be suspect if they owned Robeson's recordings.[64] A celebrated physician, Samuel Rosen, admitted sadly that after his relationship with Robeson became known, "my practice dwindled to almost nothing."[65] Harry Keelan in Boston was denied a government security clearance since he happened to know Robeson.[66]

As the devilish implications of Churchill's demarche sunk in, Robeson correspondingly reeled. By 1948, his primary political vehicle, the Council on African Affairs (CAA), was spiraling downward as his erstwhile comrade there, Max Yergan, reversed field, denounced him as a stooge of the Reds and ultimately endorsed apartheid. Headlines blared that Robeson was part of a "Communist Plot" to seize the group he had founded,[67] while contrary words from anti-apartheid leaders generally went unreported in the mainstream press.[68]

Eslanda Robeson was astonished, reminding one and all that "more than 10 years ago in the drawing room of our flat in London," Yergan presented the kernel that became the CAA. "I was able to interest [Robeson] in the idea," and the organization launched. As for alleged infiltration of Communists—Yergan's charge—she reminded this man who once too had been quite close to the now despised Reds, "it was in his home on Hamilton Terrace [in Harlem] that I first met Earl Browder," the Communist Party's leader, who happened to be "the guest of honor there."[69] The U.S. Attorney General, Tom Clark, placed the CAA on a list of so-called subversive organizations,[70] which was a virtual death sentence. Taking the cue, British Kenya then chose to ban the publications of the CAA in Nairobi and elsewhere.[71] This attack on CAA was inopportune, arising—not accidentally—when it was enmeshed in generating a firestorm of protest about the precipitous deterioration of conditions in apartheid South Africa particularly.[72]

Robeson was summoned to Washington to testify before Congress on supposed Communist subversion of the nation, one of many appearances he was to make in coming years, to the point where it would have been understandable if he had leased a flat in this mostly black city for convenience. There he was in 1948 testifying on a bill co-authored by future U.S. President Richard M. Nixon, designed to illegalize—fundamentally—the Communist Party and sideline those like Robeson who objected, an effort the artist termed "fascist." Robeson was undaunted, telling the committee about his trip to the Balkans where he witnessed "peasants suffering," who were "perhaps nine-tenths of the population." In any case, he countered, "Communism began in England, not in Russia" —in other words, he saw this phenomenon as an inexorable outgrowth of the Industrial Revolution and the Dickensian conditions engendered. He warned that if Eastern European regimes were to be destabilized, then next would be Social Democratic governments with sizeable state sectors such as in Scandinavia, New Zealand—even Britain and its vaunted National Health Service. "I see Communism," he contended, "as nothing but an extension of great public ownership of the main means of resources", while his opponents preferred that plutocrats be allowed to extend their hegemony.

Robeson admitted what could not be denied. He had travelled to Moscow: "I was there for over a period say between '34 and '37, two weeks, three weeks, three months . . . ." And he refused to back down from his bedrock opinion: "I found in Russia," he maintained, "complete absence of racial prejudice." This was "the first time in my life, Senator," he argued, "that I was able to walk the earth with complete dignity as a human being," a contention that landed him in the contradiction of U.S. policy: simultaneously seeking to take halting steps away from Jim Crow while implicitly insisting upon the ridiculous: that this apartheid was normative globally, certainly was present in Moscow (an idea that was meant to shrink U.S. culpability) and any who disagreed were probably dupes of the Soviets. But Robeson whose experience in London and elsewhere on the continent had taught him otherwise, found it hard to swallow the new U.S. line.

The combative and burly Robeson told those assembled to be careful; "if somebody would suddenly call me a name here in the room, I don't think I would do anything about it but I would have a tendency to want to get up and knock the guy down." He defended his Communist comrades, asserting, "I don't think they do have as much allegiance to Russia, as certain Americans seem to have today, say, to fascist Greece or to Turkey or to Albania or Transjordan . . . ." What about human rights violations in Moscow, he was asked. " Well, he huffed, the Soviets had "not nearly . . . liquidated as many as the Negroes were liquidated in slavery" or that were "liquidated in many parts of the South."

Typically, Robeson sought to steer the conversation to broader ground encompassing Puerto Rico, Liberia and transgressions generally against Africans perpetuated by the U.S. and their allies, which did not endear him to the powerful. He had the temerity to raise the internment of Japanese-Americans during the war as part of his indictment. Then he was asked bluntly, "would you fight for America if [we] were at war with Russia?". The artist-cum-attorney then responded, "that would depend on the conditions of war with Russia, how the war came up and who is in power at the time,"[73] a reply that U.S. patriots found wholly unsatisfactory. Patriots were also furiously dissatisfied when Robeson refused to say if he was a member of the U.S. Communist Party and added that he would go to prison rather than answer this inquiry,[74] a response he saw as—minimally—providing a covering rationale for those Reds, not as well-positioned as himself, and unable to answer fully too.

Still, the Washington bird-dogs thought they knew the answer to the question they posed and that Robeson was being evasive for nefarious reasons, a perception seemingly buttressed when the artist was happily informed by a comrade, "Mr. Robeson, did you know that the largest Communist Party club in Winston-Salem [North Carolina] is named the Paul Robeson Club?" Robeson did not frown, nor did he object. Instead, he responded with a smile—"glowing like a sunrise," said his interlocutor—and answered, "No, I did *not* [know]! But I'm *mighty* proud to hear about it. *Thank* you! And he crushed my hand in both of his"[75] (emphasis original).

Effectively, U.S. patriots had determined that it was quite acceptable for their homeland to ally with Moscow a few years earlier to confront their antagonists—but unacceptable for Robeson to do the same after the world war ended.

Showing he was not cowed, Robeson remained in Washington to join 5,000 others who were picketing the White House because of inaction on anti-Jim Crow legislation. There he embraced Ben Davis, who had become the other prime target of patriots.[76]

"This fight Paul and I are in," said Eslanda Robeson, weeks after his angrily disputed testimony, was profoundly meaningful; this she admitted to Carl Van Vechten and his wife, a couple which like so many others had drifted away from them in the midst of this political storm. "It will probably give you a turn when I point [out] that you helped us get started with it, way back in the 1920s, you, along with a few other very good friends, encouraged us, gave us consistent moral, social and financial support," and though she was tactful enough to not mention it, this was no longer the case. "The fight then was intellectual, artistic and social. We Negroes were trying to be heard, to get started, to participate. You helped us all," she said elegiacally, "you were one of the first to help us," as "you entertained us in your home." But without noting it, she acknowledged that this fight was different, though it was "another phase of the same fight" since "now it is political", much tougher, intractable. "If you are not political," she told her soon to be ex-friends, "that's alright"—words she could have shared with other former allies who were fleeing in all directions from the Robesons.[77]

Meanwhile, Robeson himself was embroiled in what turned out to be a quixotic effort to elect former Vice-President Henry A. Wallace president—but on the ticket of the Progressive Party (PP), in which he played a prominent role. Robeson was present at the creation of this party, acknowledging he had conferred with Wallace "on the beautiful estate of Michael Straight," a man Washington considered to be a Soviet agent. "Straight told me that as a youngster he had watched my rehearsals and subsequently had attended several of my English recitals," said Robeson in words that won him few friends in Washington. Robeson had been present in 1943 in Chicago, along with Hollywood's Orson Welles and Walter Huston and labor's Sidney Hillman, when Wallace launched his unsuccessful bid to be retained as V.P.[78]

Robeson in turn denounced the Democratic Party, which had an influential pro-Jim Crow wing but which many Negroes backed because of the legacy of their former standard-bearer, Roosevelt.[79] Yet despite his most strenuous efforts, the PP suffered a stinging defeat in November 1948, though this was due in no small part to the reigning Democrats purloining the PP's anti-Jim Crow platform, eroding the PP's base among Negro voters. Robeson seemed to sense what was to occur, which did not improve his mood. The radical attorney, John Abt, was with him in Philadelphia that year for a party meeting; they had taken a train from Manhattan and shared a compartment. "Ordinarily the easiest person to be with," Abt recalled quizzically, "Paul was very unlike himself" as "he sat quiet[ly] and didn't want to talk." He was assured by Lawrence Brown, who was with the two, that "he goes through this before every performance," but Abt was seemingly unconvinced.[80]

Despite the uproars in Washington and Missouri, it was Paris that marked the sharpest assault against Robeson, for it was there that he again not only touched but battered the sensitive Achilles' heel of the republic. There in the spring of 1949 he was portrayed as telling a gathering of peace advocates that it would be unthinkable for U.S. Negroes to join in war mania against Moscow.[81]

It was on 20 April when a hall in Paris was jammed with delegates from 60 nations. When Robeson entered, the entire audience rose as one and cheered with 2,500 voices in unison. "I doubt if any other person on earth could have elicited such spontaneous tribute," was the accurate comment made by an astute observer—though present were Pablo Picasso and other notables.[82] If Robeson had not repeated his remarks at home, the controversy may have died a slow death in Paris but instead the Negro press continued to trumpet similar remarks made in New Jersey, e.g. "American Negroes must not be asked ever again to sacrifice on foreign shores. If we must sacrifice, let it be in Alabama and Mississippi . . . ."[83]

The eruption in the U.S. was volcanic, stoking more fury about Robeson. An alleged former Communist, now a friendly witness before Congress—Manning Johnson—charged that Robeson's ultimate aim was to become a "Black Stalin"[84] and to that end was involved in "certain intercontinental party work in connection with his concerts."[85] George Schuyler, the pre-eminent Negro conservative, renounced "Robeson's smearing of 14,000,000 Negroes as potential traitors," which "played right into the hands of our worst enemies . . . ."[86] Max Yergan, now one of his staunchest opponents, chimed in likewise.[87] Walter White of the NAACP, who had once sung his praises, now denounced him.[88] The Veterans of Foreign Wars picketed him.[89]

When the Robeson supporter and prominent Negro columnist J.A. Rogers wrote that "fear of Russia and communism, as well as outside criticism of the United States, have been the Negro's greatest benefactor in recent years,"[90] he was underscoring the ultimate importance of this furor: a wounded U.S. elite scrambled to erode Jim Crow so as to position the nation more effectively to confront Moscow, while pummeling Robeson to make sure that few would be prone to heed his sage advice.

Robeson's response demonstrated why the U.S. authorities found it necessary to clip his wings. In Belfast he held four concerts, all of them sellouts: "the English public [too] seems as fond if not fonder of Paul then ever," was Lawrence Brown's conclusion after alighting in London.[91] He addressed a cheering 16,000 in Copenhagen and a rousing 40,000 in Stockholm,[92] and tens of thousands more in Oslo, with his multi-lingual talent winning more adherents as the North Atlantic Treaty Organization (NATO) was being convened to confront what was thought to be his sponsor: Moscow. Surely his study of Norwegian paid dividends as this small nation was unaccustomed to seeing a cosmopolitan African address them in their own tongue. According to Ulf Christensen in Oslo, Robeson "sang and talked to the largest political rally held in Norway since 1945," as multitudes hung on his every word.[93] In Sweden, Robeson later noted, "some people in the American embassy tried to break up my concert" but were rebuffed forcefully. There he echoed what he had said in Paris: "why should the Negroes ever fight against the only nations of the world where racial discrimination is prohibited,"[94] he asked with ire, speaking of the emerging socialist camp.

Robeson delivered to U.S. audiences first-hand views of Europe that did not necessarily correspond with those of Washington. "If you want to see what fascism can do," he maintained, "walk through Poland," which he had done.[95] Inevitably, Washington concluded that wisdom dictated that his passport be revoked, his income reduced and his image tarnished.

The unapologetic Robeson insisted that "the emphasis on what I said in Paris was on this struggle for peace, not on anybody going to war against anybody"—but U.S. patriots saw this as a distinction without a difference.[96] "We of all groups have a right to some radicals," stressed Robeson speaking of himself[97]—but alleviating the quotidian oppression of Negroes would undercut this persuasive rationale, it was thought. The lauded left-wing playwright Clifford Odets hailed Robeson at the same time as "one of the most distinguished artists and gallant fighters our great country has ever produced", but soon even this otherwise courageous writer was seeking to salvage his own career and hardly had time to praise further the beset actor and singer.[98]

That same year—1949—Robeson testified at the federal court trial of the U.S. Communist leadership in a case designed to illegalize further this embattled group. He was the co-chair of the "National Non-Partisan Committee to Defend the Rights of the Twelve

Communist Leaders", derided as yet another "Communist front" by detractors. But Robeson's close friend and comrade Ben Davis was one of the defendants and the actor then recalled that a device he used to excite his nightly rage onstage in his performance as Othello was to imagine that Davis had betrayed him, an unthinkable prospect that drove Robeson to the witness chair.[99] Davis reciprocated, on one occasion telling Robeson, "a guy like you is born once every century," expressing feelings for his comrade so potent and "moving that I [can] hardly speak," leading the avowed Communist to consider "embracing you with a kiss . . . ."[100] Though he was only questioned for 19 minutes, the fact that Robeson had known the judge, Harold Medina, while a student at Columbia was thought to be important by some.[101]

The beleaguered Davis illustrated accidentally the dilemma comrades faced when he charged that Walter White was "afraid of Paul's influence in the NAACP"—but then was forced to add weakly, "I intend to develop this thesis as soon as I get time off from trial preparations."[102] That time did not come as Davis was then jailed, which illuminated why the trial occurred in the first place. Another incident in 1949 highlighted the same problem. While on tour in Britain in 1949, a burglar entered the room of Robeson's accompanist and systematically purloined items, leading to "3 sleepless nights and 3 frantic days"—"it was hell while it lasted," said Lawrence Brown,[103] an apt summary of Robeson's entire ordeal during the Red Scare.

Yet accusing him of another kind of betrayal was baseball celebrity Jackie Robinson, rapidly replacing Joe Louis as the pre-eminent star of sports in a culture obsessed with such competition. Robeson had campaigned tirelessly to desegregate the national pastime, making Robinson's career possible. Yet in 1949 it was precisely Robinson who excoriated Robeson before the House Un-American Activities Committee[104] and turned the knife further by ridiculing him as "silly."[105] Robinson pledged the "race's loyalty" and advised not to "think of radicalism in terms of any special minority group."[106] Robeson sent to Robinson "the true statements" he had made in Paris which occasioned the renunciation of him[107]—but to no avail. Simultaneously, the NAACP—which had honored Robeson a few years earlier—turned against him with a vengeance. At the group's 1949

Figure 6   Robeson testified on behalf of Communist Party-USA leaders during their pivotal 1949 trial in Manhattan. A chief attorney for the defendants was George Crockett, who was jailed because of his vigorous advocacy; however, this militant defense did not prevent Crockett from being elected to the U.S. Congress from Detroit subsequently, exemplifying the point that anti-communism was not as potent among African-Americans, the constituency that voted him into office and also buoyed Robeson. (Daily Worker and Daily World Photographs Collection, Tamiment Library/Robert F. Wagner Labor Archives, New York University, New York City)

Figure 7 Though he denied that he was a member of the U.S. Communist Party, Robeson was quite close to this organization, particularly the Harvard trained attorney Benjamin Davis (left), who was elected to the New York City Council from Harlem in 1943 and re-elected in 1945 before being ousted unceremoniously—perhaps illegally—as he was about to stand trial on political grounds. To Robeson's left is Henry Winston, longtime Chairman of the U.S. Communist Party. (Daily Worker and Daily World Photographs Collection, Tamiment Library/Robert F. Wagner Labor Archives, New York University, New York City)

convention in Los Angeles, Robeson's Progressive Party was vigilant, which, it was said, "toned down the NAACP crowd considerably," leading to a "lively battle," leading further to a "quite a victory . . . ."[108] But this was to be short-lived for the NAACP became the vehicle through which anti-Jim Crow concessions were channeled, providing a material basis for their defenestration of Robeson.

What had changed in 1949 was the Chinese Revolution, which increased the anxiety among U.S. patriots, bolstering the impression that the fight against Communists was waning, which augmented the assault on Robeson. This reaction heightened when a biography of Robeson by the Communist writer Shirley Graham, soon to be the spouse of W.E.B. Du Bois,[109] was translated into Chinese, bringing kudos from Nanking.[110] Days later, Ms. Robeson was asked by a prominent Chinese magazine to supply a story on her husband's "personal interest in China and his friendship with the Chinese people."[111] Was the war against Communists waning as evidenced by the tie between Robeson and China?

Also in 1949 a widely-circulated picture of Robeson was published: arriving from abroad, he was flanked by three uniformed police officers on his right and three more on his left.[112] He was headed to a clamorous rally in Harlem of 4,000 people at 155th Street and 8th Avenue, indicative of why he was under constant watch.[113] "When Robeson stepped off the train in Baltimore recently," said the leading Negro publisher, Carl Murphy, "he was followed by an agent of the FBI. He is constantly under surveillance."[114] Coincidentally, this Harlem snapshot exposed the kind of surveillance that was to blanket him until he breathed his last breath for from that point forward, he was constantly under surveillance to the point where he could hardly go outside without being accompanied by agents of the state.[115]

7

Robeson: Primary Victim of the "Blacklist"

By 1949, Robeson's income was plummeting, while his popularity was declining (in certain quarters). But even this unfolding annus horribilis hardly prepared him for what befell him in Peekskill, New York in August–September of that crucial year. For it was then that what he had encountered in Missouri a few years earlier came close to derailing him again: he almost lost his life.

He had come to Peekskill, north of Manhattan, for a concert on behalf of the Civil Rights Congress, headed by William Patterson who had helped to draw him closer to a commitment to socialism, more than 15 years earlier during a decisive conversation in snowy Moscow. Widely publicized, this concert was to take place in a lovely dale but what transpired was decidedly ugly. A howling mob of assailants brutally attacked those assembled with the idea of claiming the scalp of the star of the show: Robeson.[1] "They had tried to kill him at Peekskill," said his wife later. After Peekskill Robeson was compelled to travel with what she called "security" or the equivalent of bodyguards, whom if too meddlesome could keep him at arm's length from adoring crowds to his detriment.[2] Such a raucous unwelcome was nothing new for Robeson; later journalist Abner Berry recalled a similar disruption of a Robeson rally in Houston during the tumultuous presidential election campaign of 1948.[3] In other words, even before the turning point that was Peekskill and in the prelude to this disturbing event, there was a disturbing trend emerging of forceful—even violent—interruptions of Robeson's public appearances.

This, Robeson had not failed to recall. "I remember," he said, "our famous tour in the South in the 1948 election campaign,

Figure 8 Robeson was deeply influenced by William L. Patterson (right), who was also a Communist, political organizer and attorney. Beah Richards went on to become a leading Hollywood actor, receiving an Oscar nomination for her performance in *Guess Who's Coming to Dinner?* (Daily Worker and Daily World Photographs Collection, Tamiment Library/Robert F. Wagner Labor Archives, New York University, New York City)

standing before 4000 Negro and white citizens of Houston", amidst rowdy tumult.[4]

Yet that ugly moment in Texas hardly prepared Robeson for the tumult of Peekskill. "Behind the anti-Communist sentiments marshaled by [military] veterans," said the American Civil Liberties Union, speaking of Peekskill, was "prejudice against Negroes and Jews", egged on by "provocation of the local press", aided by "the mob spirit of youthful hoodlums." These "opponents of all sorts, numbering an estimated 10,000" eventuated in a vicious assault on the concertgoers "numbering an estimated 15,000." The local Republican Party, hegemonic in that region, was seen as the moving hand behind this outrage taking place in a region where a large prison was a major employer and where violence had deep historical roots.[5]

Ms. Robeson was understandably outraged, shocked by the presence of "about 1000" rioters, "armed with rocks and stones with knives, with hate and hysteria and whiskey with vile speech . . . ." There were police there too, "about twelve hundred of them—armed with guns and night sticks" but they seemed more determined to aid rather than detain the rioters seeking to massacre thousands of progressives. "The only serious interruption," she found, "was a police helicopter which circled noisily and low, directly over Robeson's head while he was singing, thus drowning him out . . . ."[6]

Undaunted, Robeson and his cohorts returned days later to demonstrate that they could not be intimidated. Instead, their opponents mobilized too and administered yet another stinging beating upon those assembled. Luckily, "only" 150 were injured during this second event—albeit six seriously—when hundreds of automobiles and scores of buses carrying Robeson supporters ran a gauntlet of stone-throwing demonstrators. There was a concerted attempt to drag drivers from cars. Effigies of a lynched Robeson abounded. Windshields and windows of these vehicles were shattered after the Robeson concert at the Hollow Brook Country Club, where Negro soldiers were taunted and one was struck in the face. A new epithet—"White Niggers"—was spat at those seen consorting with Negroes. The local hospital was jammed with the injured. One national newspaper was not alone in condemning this riot as "fascist."[7]

Validating this widespread perception was the chilling chant of the mob, "We're Hitler's Boys" and "God Bless Hitler"—and their favorite: "Lynch Robeson." Patterson was not singular in assessing that "the murder of Paul Robeson was a part of the official program of American reaction" at both events, which amounted to a "world event of paramount importance. Do you know," he asked heartrendingly, "what a mass organized attempt to lynch Paul Robeson means?" The car carrying Robeson was targeted for special attention, as even the police joined in smashing the windows of his vehicle before it escaped with desperation. Robeson headed promptly to his base in Harlem where 5,000 supporters greeted him elatedly.[8]

Another account estimated that 3,000 were present with standing room only—but 7,000 rallied outside. Yet left ringing in their ears was the throbbing cry: "Lynch the Fucking Niggers! . . . Hitler was a good man. He should have killed all the Communists and Jews!"[9] If it was any consolation to Robeson, he was not the sole target of abuse: even the foremost Negro pilot—Eugene Bullard—who had soared to fame in Europe, was beaten senseless with truncheons by state troopers,[10] as law enforcement joined the mob in the fray.

Even those not beaten continued to be harassed in the aftermath of Peekskill. When Norman Forer, a U.S. national, spoke at a peace rally in Manitoba, Canada, the Royal Canadian Mounted Police, reported his presence to the U.S. authorities since he was said "to have had a part in organizing guards to protect" Robeson during the uproar in Peekskill.[11]

Predictably, the victim was blamed as an official investigation invoked by Governor Thomas Dewey was tasked to ascertain "whether the meeting was initiated and sponsored [by the Civil Rights Congress] for the purpose of deliberately inciting disorder" as "part of the Communist strategy to foment racial and religious hatred," initiated by this alleged "quasi-military force." Dismissed was the targeting of Robeson since "resentment" was "directed against him not as a Negro"—the cause that was now losing popularity—but "as one whose reported acts and utterances identified him in the public mind as a leading proponent of Communism:"[12] the newer cause.

Unbowed, Robeson took off on a whirlwind tour, designed to rally support against the dangerous ultra-right pestilence detected. He addressed 17,000 in Los Angeles.[13] But more indicative was the denial of venues for him in Oakland and San Francisco (Berkeley emulated L.A. in welcoming him with open arms).[14] Further north, in Seattle, a battle royale ensued as to whether Robeson would be allowed a venue with those defending him losing their jobs.[15] Subsequently a department store sacked a Negro worker who sponsored Robeson's appearance in the Pacific Northwest.[16] Heading eastward to Minneapolis, Robeson was denied a venue to sing and lecture—even left-wing unions turned down an initiative backed by the National Negro Labor Council. The University of Minnesota campus acted similarly—after tickets had been printed for his appearance. Finally,

he found a private site in St. Paul—but then the American Legion
threatened to riot, a proposal that was joined by the Veterans of
Foreign Wars and local businessmen.[17] In short, as Cold War tensions
rose abroad, this was felt at home: the logic was that if real or
imagined Communists were not tolerated abroad, why should they
be countenanced at home?

Peekskill continued to haunt Robeson's appearances, with the
scent of violence hanging ominously, which was a deterrent to his
making public appearances. Two years later, Patterson lamented
after one U.S. appearance where thousands appeared and many were
turned away, that "it is true that the threat of violence and assassination hangs constantly over [Robeson's] head . . . ."[18] Despite this
miasma of fear pervading the atmosphere, Robeson refused to retreat
from his solidarity with Moscow—and vice versa—though this was
near the heart of the matter. Shortly after the Peekskill debacle,
Moscow affixed his statue atop a mountain peak in Kirghizia.[19] "In
Russia I felt for the first time like a full human being," he explained
later; "I did not feel the pressure of color as I feel in this committee
today," referring to the House Un-American Activities Committee.[20]

The Russian language and music, he mused in 1951, "seem to suit
my voice," perhaps because of the "kinship between the Russians and
the Negroes. They were both serfs and the music there [reflects the]
same note of melancholy touched with mysticism."[21] Thus, that same
year found him in Washington, D.C. singing, and lecturing, before
5,000 with Negroes comprising about 25 percent of the audience,
in a benefit for now Communist-led China and a local organization
considered a "Communist front" by the authorities. Confirming his
status as the reigning Russo-phile—and the embodiment of the then
Peking-Moscow alliance— he was proclaimed, once more, to be the
"Chaliapin of [the] race . . . ."[22]

Robeson, who had overcome his reticence about writing, also
penned a widely circulated pamphlet in 1950. "The Negro People and
the Soviet Union"—a mere 15 pages and selling for two cents—was
the text of an address he presented at Manhattan's Waldorf-Astoria
Hotel at a well-attended conference of the National Council of Arts,
Sciences and Professions, a left-led grouping. The occasion was the
anniversary of the Bolshevik Revolution, which led to his not only

praising Moscow but quoting Mao Zedong at length in a similar vein, which was ill-designed to win him favor in Washington. "Where indeed would the Negro people's struggle for freedom be today," he asked, "if world imperialism had not been critically wounded and its forces weakened throughout the world"; we should not forget, he insisted that "it was Roosevelt who in a letter to Stalin spoke of how civilization had been saved by the battle of Stalingrad," which—a fortiori—meant saving Negroes from further destruction. But even this gargantuan victory with its manifold significance did not spare U.S. Negroes from a dire fate: "last hired, first fired," lynching, unemployment, etc.—yet they were expected to enlist in yet another war, this time against the nation that had rescued civilization.[23]

He refused adamantly to retreat from his controversial remarks in Paris, seeming to suggest that African-Americans would not join in war against Moscow—remarks that had brought him so much grief. In December 1952 he proclaimed at a meeting of the National Council of American-Soviet Friendship, "it is unthinkable—as I said at Paris and I repeat it now—that the colored peoples of the world will serve their oppressors in such a war" against the socialist camp.[24]

But what he and his comrades did not seem to grasp was that the spooked U.S. authorities veered in a direction not predicted by most of them: oppression of U.S. Negroes was eased which made this base of support for Robeson less prone to lend him aid in his time of need.

An essential aspect of the clubbing of Robeson was seizing his passport, which occurred weeks after war had been declared on the Korean peninsula in June 1950.[25] Within months the foreseeable occurred: As Secretary of State Dean Acheson was informed curtly: "two agents" of the state "called on Mr. Robeson" and "advised him" that he was now "instructed" to "turn over to them the current passport which he now has for travel in foreign countries . . . ."[26] Later it emerged that this draconian move was made not least since Robeson's advocacy for decolonization was hostile to the best interests of Washington.[27] Carl Murphy, perhaps the chief Negro publisher, asked why Jim Crow advocates were not denied passports? "Haven't such persons done more harm than a score of Robesons?" he asked. "There are many whose expressed opinions are not in the best interests of our country. Some of them are in Congress"—so why weren't they penalized? Why was it only those of the left denied the right to travel, for example Robeson and W.E.B. Du Bois?[28] Another leading Negro journalist, J.A. Rogers, posed the query rarely asked during this tempestuous time: "Which is the greatest menace to America, communism or racism?"[29] He thought it was obvious that the correct answer was the latter—but his was not a view universally accepted in the U.S.

Still, as early as his passport being snatched in 1950, it was predictable that, ultimately, Washington would have to yield to unremitting pressure from abroad, India and Africa not least, and return Robeson's right to travel. For it was in that very same year that Robeson was part of a small group invited to attend an intimate reception in honor of India's Ambassador to the U.S.[30]

By 1958 his passport had been returned after a lengthy hiatus; he then told inquirers in Sydney that "his income fell from $100,000 to two [thousand] dollars in the next 12 months" after Peekskill.[31] "Here he was in 1947," said Carl Murphy, of Baltimore, speaking of Robeson "ranking among the first four as a singer or an actor, with 86 concerts scheduled which would average between $2500 and $3000 per concert"—then he spoke out controversially and all 86 were cancelled. "Money isn't everything," he opined but such philosophizing hardly diminished the significance of Robeson's loss.[32]

The loss included his Connecticut estate, which was put up for sale weeks after his passport was taken,[33] as the Robesons sought to retreat to Harlem. The Nutmeg State, once so welcoming, now too was hostile. In Hartford in 1952 a heated controversy erupted when he sought to hold a concert at a local high school.[34]

By 1952, said Ms. Robeson, they were then "undergoing terrific financial pressure because the Government will not allow Paul to work, nor to leave the country and go where work waits him" and it was difficult to unload a house with "12 rooms and 5 bathrooms". She was now "alone" in this drafty edifice, as her spouse scampered from coast to coast in a precarious attempt to rally similarly beleaguered left-wing forces, reeling from the gale force winds of anticommunism. Nowadays he could not "travel without a bodyguard," an added expense and a turnoff for audiences who desired close and intimate interaction with their hero.[35]

The harassment of Robeson, the denial of his passport and the like were designed to turn him into a non-entity. Making Robeson radioactive was the intention. Du Bois reported that he had been invited to make the commencement address at the predominantly Negro school in Baltimore, Morgan State University—but when the President realized that Du Bois had been present during Robeson's controversial remarks in Paris, he "begged" the elderly leader "frantically" not to come.[36]

To be fair, the U.S. authorities were reacting to another Robeson initiative explicitly designed to embarrass the U.S. authorities and as with his charged confrontation with President Truman in the White House in 1946, it was also designed to place in the dock the U.S. authorities. It was in December 1951 that Robeson, Patterson and the Civil Rights Congress presented a petition to the United Nations accusing the U.S. of perpetrating genocide against African-Americans. The petition was a sickening cataloguing of various atrocities involving state complicity if not action. The finger of accusation on the cover of the petition, sold by the tens of thousands in various languages worldwide, was that of Robeson. It was he who presented the petition to the authorities at U.N. headquarters in Manhattan. At a moment when the U.S. was charging the socialist camp with human rights violations, the Robeson petition was trumpeted globally as yet another example of Washington's hypocrisy and brutality. It also served to prod the U.S. authorities in response to ease the horrific maltreatment of African-Americans, setting the stage for what came to be called the "Civil Rights Movement."[37]

In this historic process, Robeson played the role of sacrificial lamb. His income and career and health were to erode, as the people he sacrificed for saw their fortunes improve, as the bonds of Jim Crow slowly loosened, most notably in the realm of colleges and universities. For it was certain that enterprises and entities on the west bank of the Atlantic were not inclined to ignore what was called, ironically, the "blacklist," which claimed Robeson as an early and hard-hit victim. A Negro journalist complained at the time that "as a whole, people in show business have less backbone than any other group of people in the world"[38]—and their mistreatment of Robeson did little to discourage this perception.

Still, this writer easily could have turned the microscope on his own industry for the flagship publication of the rising Negro millionaire—John H. Johnson's *Ebony*—opened its pages to brutal attacks on Robeson, including an abrasive rebuke by his erstwhile friend, Walter White. The National Association for the Advancement of Colored People (NAACP) leader admitted that Robeson "scared some American whites into a panic from which they have not yet fully recovered," bringing concessions for Negroes as a whole; but Robeson's words also led to an "anxious scrutiny by whites of their Negro neighbors," which could easily turn to violence. For Robeson's turn to revolutionary socialism, White blamed William Patterson.[39] Similarly, the NAACP journal scorned Robeson too[40]—repeatedly. He was the "lost shepherd," it was claimed.[41]

On the other hand, part of the approach to Robeson was to critique him in a "more sorrow than anger" tone, portraying him as upset with a Jim Crow now receding, manipulated by Svengali-type figures such as Patterson. Robert Ruark, one of colonial Kenya's staunchest defenders, went as far as to claim that Robeson "had a chance, maybe, to have been the first black President," of the U.S.[42] but allowed anger to get the best of him. Peter Blackman, a Robeson partisan in London, was unconvinced by Ruark's analysis. "If there are Negroes in America stupid enough to join in the witch-hunt against Paul Robeson," he chided, "they deserve all the Daughters of the Revolution can persuade the [Ku Klux] Klan to give them . . . ."[43]

Ms. Robeson, now a journalist of some note herself, took up the cudgels in defense of her hard-pressed husband. Yes, her spouse was "stubborn," reluctant to back down in the face of an offensive and, yes, "we lived in England for 12 years and lived very well indeed," as Robeson "achieved fabulous success." Yes, "we lived in many different sections of London—in Chelsea, Regents Park, St. John's Wood, Hampstead, Adelphia and Highgate" but, contrary to White, "never in Mayfair" (part of White's charge was that an affluent Robeson lost touch with the Negro masses, particularly during his years abroad). So, yes, they conferred with esteemed figures like Gandhi and Nehru—but why should that be held against them?[44]

This was one of many kerfuffles ensnaring Robeson during this conflicted era. He had become the personal pivot point on which progress for Negroes was said to turn. Dethrone his pre-eminence, Negroes were told, and an endless bounty loomed. Choose not to, and the height of lynching would seem nostalgically like the good old days. Peekskill seemed to mark an escalation of assaults on Negroes generally, as if they were being softened up to accept the marginalizing of Robeson while accepting in return anti-Jim Crow concessions, allowing for increased appointments to high-level government posts. "Some people remark," said journalist James Hicks in August 1950, "that never in their lifetime have they seen such unbridled hatred for Negroes,"[45] a reality inseparable from the developing phobia about Robeson. A quizzical Negro journalist chewed over this quandary and concluded that "in the United States today, many white people are asking this same question over and over again," i.e. "what are we going to do about colored people like Paul Robeson?"[46]

What not to do was to allow him the right to travel abroad to rally anti-Jim Crow forces. The U.S. authorities were quite concerned that with Indian independence, Robeson's pre-existing tie to Nehru could be leveraged on his—and his people's—behalf. Months before Peekskill, the U.S. legation in New Delhi desperately sought "corroboration" of a story of Robeson's "proposed visit" to India.[47] Disconsolately, the legation reported that "we should not count on GOI [Government of India]" to "refuse visa" for "such action when it became known here would cause a storm of protest from leftist elements and raise suspicion Nehru had aligned with U.S."[48]—a cardinal sin in the estimation of the potent socialist movement there.

Vijaya Lakshmi Pandit, India's Ambassador to the U.S., in contacting "Essie Darling," at a time when Robeson was under fire, termed her "the best kind of friend anyone could possibly have." She was now "drawing up my brother's programme" for his pending visit—referring to the Prime Minister, Nehru: "he has written to see you and Paul privately for a good talk . . . ."[49] But now such global contacts were being viewed by NAACP leaders as evidence of how Robeson had lost touch with the everyday Negro.

In short, Robeson could have made up for the shortfall in his income by touring abroad—independent India, for example— for the near lynching in Peekskill only served to heighten his popularity abroad, as many wondered what the mighty superpower was so concerned about. Invitations to visit poured in from Prague, Copenhagen, Paris—and Scottish miners: according to Robeson's newly organized periodical, *Freedom*, "the leading concert agency in Tel Aviv" requested a "series of ten concerts at an unprecedented fee" and were joined in enthusiasm by peers in "Bombay and Calcutta". Those described as "Japanese progressives" joined the clamor. "We would like to see Paul back in Norway again!" was the cry from Oslo.[50]

Circumventing the passport ban, two million young people from scores of nations—as was to become the pattern elsewhere when his passport was taken—lined up in Berlin to hear Robeson's voice over loudspeakers via telephone lines, as he sang in various languages.[51] This had become a trend. Earlier in the fall of 1950 at a well attended peace congress in Warsaw, Robeson's booming voice was heard in recording, singing two songs. Said one member of the audience, "the hall rang with the deep and vibrant voice of this dauntless soldier of peace," as "delegates were deeply stirred," expressed with a "burst of thunderous applause."[52] Among the partisans of peace who were Robeson supporters at this time were Pablo Neruda of Chile; Sekou Touré, the founding father of Guinea-Conakry; Pablo Picasso, Jorge Amado of Brazil; the widow of Sun Yat-sen, the Chinese nationalist leader; and the pre-eminent Britons, Ivor Montagu, J.D. Bernal and D.N. Pritt.[53]

Robeson's disembodied voice became a staple at revolutionary and socialist meetings globally, providing an implicit eerie condemnation of the misdeeds of U.S. imperialism. Robeson's aide, Louis Burnham, was involved in preparing a "series of messages and songs" from the artist, "which may be sent to peace meetings in the various countries of Europe, Asia and Africa."[54]

Robeson's embodied voice was heard in Canada, as when he arrived in the Pacific Northwest in 1953 to sing to 40,000 across the border in British Columbia.[55] Reputedly, this concert broke "all records for public gatherings" in the region.[56] Robeson had been stopped from entering this northern neighbor of the U.S., though U.S. nationals did not need a passport to do so. Yet, a special order barring him was implemented, which could have meant five years imprisonment and a hefty fine if he had chosen to violate this edict.[57] Later, Robeson's son argued that "American personnel at the Canadian border had been ordered to use force to prevent my father from <u>leaving</u> the United States. He was locked <u>in</u>, not <u>out</u>" [emphasis original].[58]

In London, where his popularity remained steady, the Workers' Music Association lamented in 1951 that although they "still get constant enquiries from all parts of the country", many from an "ever growing body of people anxious to secure recordings" of Robeson's handiwork, including "Joe Hill" and "Scandalize my Name", the group felt "very keenly the loss of the movement here;"[59] a loss which was aided immeasurably by the marginalizing in the U.S. of a titanic figure like Robeson. It is difficult for an absent artist to maintain popularity—even a Robeson in London. "There is a considerable demand for records of Paul Robeson" in London, said one recording company: the "demand and popularity of Paul Robeson" remained high, even in 1953. Yet, given the emerging reality of an indebted London, battered by war, becoming more dependent upon Washington, there remained "difficulties that our Authorities . . . put in our way should we wish to purchase the records themselves from you," foiling Robeson's own effort to distribute his work.[60]

London felt constrained to take such strict measures because of his continuing popularity in Britain, which complicated relations with the U.S. ally. "I get letters daily," said Robeson in October 1951, "especially from England" asking wondrously, "'is it true Paul that you can't sing, that there is danger when you sing? That you can't play in the theater, that you can't be on radio and television.'" Robeson affirmed this blackout, then contrasted it by asserting, "you would be interested to know that in every section of English opinion in the theater, in music, in every field they have begun as in the case of the Scottish miners to say to this government: 'We want him over here to play 'Othello' again.'" Robeson concluded in his twentieth-century version of "Workers of the World, Unite!": "we must see the necessity of unity between all sections of labor in this land and throughout the world."[61]

Internationalization aside, the fountainhead of Robeson's support remained Britain, a reality that became evident when in 1951 students at the University of Aberdeen nominated him for the post of "Scottish Lord Rectorship."[62] In September of that year William Pearson, General Secretary of the National Union of Mineworkers in

Scotland, told Robeson candidly, "my organization is very perturbed at the fact that you are not allowed to leave America and come to this country."[63]

Neighboring Canada—or at least thought U.S. officialdom—was quite concerned about Robeson's influence. Earlier, the embassy in Ottawa was told anxiously that "the situation" in Vancouver was "becoming more involved every day. The Communists are becoming more bold and the authorities are becoming somewhat concerned" since Robeson supposedly "made a speech at the University of British Columbia which was openly communistic," then the artist "made arrangements for Henry Wallace and Senator [Claude] Pepper [of Florida] to speak here"; the legation was in "daily contact with the RCMP [police] and the military authorities" but was worried nonetheless.[64]

Robeson did find the time to appeal for freedom of the celebrated Turkish poet, Nazim Hikmet,[65] persecuted for refusing to remain silent about earlier massacres of Armenians and Kurds. Writing him from a dank prison where he had been entombed by Washington's Turkish ally, Hikmet, after informing Robeson that "I have heard your name for a long time" and "have seen your picture in my prison," then told him, "at Peekskill the American fascists howled at you" but this did not shake his admiration: "I love you my brother," he said,[66] adding, calling him "eagle singer, Negro brother." He told Robeson, "they are scared . . . our songs scare them,"[67] which was a response to Robeson's impassioned appeal.

In any case, despite not holding a passport, Robeson was not cut off altogether from international contact. He was a regular presence at the embassies and legations of the Soviet Union and Czechoslovakia in Washington and United Nations' missions of these nations and those of Poland, Hungary, and likeminded nations.[68] It was in November 1951 that Robeson was to be found at the Soviet legation in Washington with 800 other guests—including Iranian Prime Minister Mohammad Mosaddegh, soon to be overthrown in a joint U.K.–U.S. enterprise, marking the anniversary of the Bolshevik Revolution.[69]

Blocked from traveling abroad, Robeson turned with renewed commitment to events at home, starting a newspaper based in Harlem. By 1949 there were 183 Negro-owned newspapers in the

U.S. and 98 magazines of various types; the *Pittsburgh Courier*, a newspaper with an impressive circulation of 282,000 was suggestive of the reach of these organs. Robeson's *Freedom* never reached this realm but it distinguished itself by offering more coverage of trade unions than its peers, though when newsstands refused to sell it, its abortive destiny was guaranteed.[70]

He continued to lead the now besieged Council on African Affairs, whose mandate to undermine colonialism was vitiated by the reigning U.S. idea that anti-colonialism was merely shorthand for communism. From Mombasa, Kenya, the U.S. legation reported in early 1950 of an "alleged liaison between East African and American Communists," i.e. "one N.V. Charles, an intelligent and well educated Negro presently" there "has been receiving from American Negroes . . . small quantities of Communist propaganda." Mr. Charles was "in contact with Paul Robeson, Jr." and his "father was an American Negro missionary in Uganda"; but what really seemed to irk the U.S. delegate was Charles being "extremely resentful of the inferior role assigned to members of the Negro race in Kenya."[71]

Yet the U.S. authorities had a real problem in seeking to maintain Jim Crow at home while isolating Robeson from his constituency in Africa. This difficult reality emerged awkwardly when a diplomat from one of the few independent African nations—Ethiopia—was ousted from his seat at Washington's Constitution Hall because of Jim Crow. The Ethiopian leader, Ras Imru, warned correctly that this "insult" was "prone to create serious implications, especially so because the offense occurred in a public place and in the presence of the President of the United States."[72]

Speaking in his capacity as Chair of the Council on African Affairs (CAA), Robeson swiftly expressed his "indignation and protest" at this outrage. This was "no accidental mistake" when this eminent dignitary was requested to "move to another section 'reserved for his race' . . . ." Nor, charged Robeson accusingly, was this emissary "the only foreign diplomat to fall victim to the insult of color prejudice while a guest" in the U.S.[73] An embarrassed U.S. Chief of Protocol clumsily lamented this "regrettable incident" that was "occasioned by a series of misunderstandings that had no connection with racial discrimination or segregation," contrary to Robeson's assertion.[74] The response from Ethiopia found this rationalization "unacceptable."[75] Sheepishly, the U.S. legation in Moscow reported that this incident created a stir there, doubtlessly confirming the pre-existing belief that Jim Crow was the U.S. Achilles' heel.[76]

A similar report was filed from Bombay (Mumbai), observing that periodicals there "carried" this news, given the "hyper-sensitivity" of the Indian people to the color question; attached to this report was a news story discussing how Robeson's Progressive Party was forcefully mounting a "challenge" to the "colour bar in parks" in Louisville. Also attached was yet another article questioning how a "Negro baiter" like Herman Talmadage could become a governor in Georgia.[77] By this point, Robeson had taken an active leadership role in the left-leaning PP, which was mounting a vigorous challenge to the two major political parties. In India, said the U.S. delegate dejectedly, this incident was "carried in every Calcutta newspaper."[78] The U.S. response was equally swift: further battering of Robeson and easing of Jim Crow to foil such incidents and the ability of the CAA to gain momentum in protesting same.

Unmoved, the CAA continued to press the question of anti-colonialism, particularly as to Britain's most important colony in Africa: Nigeria. It was in 1950 that Robeson and Du Bois were pictured pressing a check into the hand of founding father, Nnamdi Azikiwe—an old friend from London—for the ongoing struggle of mineworkers.[79] In return a leading church in Nigeria before a crowd of 5,000, bestowed upon Azikiwe, Kwame Nkrumah of Ghana—and Robeson—awards denoting the three as a prestigious "Champion of African Freedom."[80]

Robeson's Harlem-based newspaper *Freedom* was one of the few periodicals—even among Negro journals—that highlighted the anti-apartheid struggle, placing Nelson Mandela on the front page as early as October 1952 and including messages from his comrade, Walter Sisulu, thanking U.S. Negroes—meaning those like Robeson—for support.[81] In turn, Sisulu and Mandela's future cellmate, Ahmad Kathadra of the South African Indian Congress, sharply criticized the denial of Robeson's passport, observing that "in this country"—meaning South Africa—"you would be discriminated against under our apartheid laws and treated as 'inferior' but we, the people, would welcome you with all our hearts."[82] Ruth First of the South African Communist Party echoed these words, informing Robeson's supporters, "I support you every inch of the way. We will do what we can here."[83]

That Robeson's star was not altogether diminished—at least not in Harlem—was revealed when a few weeks later he spoke to a rally of 5,000 at 126th Street and Lenox Avenue.[84] The issue bringing so many together was South African apartheid. Picketers also descended upon that nation's consulate, while at the same moment 15,000 marched in Johannesburg—to the tune of Robeson singing. There Mandela, Sisulu, Moses Kotane and other stalwarts gathered.[85] "I'm very proud," beamed Robeson, "that those African brothers and sisters of ours play my records as they march in their parades."[86]

At a time when he was a persecuted man in colonial Kenya, Robeson proudly told Negro unionists meeting in Cleveland of his own special relationship with "Jomo Kenyatta . . . with whom I sat many times in London . . . ."[87] Robeson compared the Kenyan patriot to his comrades, Davis and Patterson, while observing that "we Americans of African descent" are "especially interested in what our Government is doing in Asia and Africa, because Asians and Africans are Colored Peoples like ourselves."[88] In urging backing for "jailed leaders and freedom struggles in Kenya and South Africa," Robeson asserted, "we Colored Americans will especially want to support our African brothers and sisters,"[89] thereby prefiguring a renewed Pan-Africanism in the 1960s.

This put official London in a bind, which generally opted to stand with its ally in Washington more so than the popular idol that was Robeson in Harlem; in other words Whitehall could hardly ignore the mass popular support for Robeson—but found it difficult to echo his anti-colonial message. "We never thought that Britain would become that much of a junior partner to the USA," was the opinion of a disappointed Ms. Robeson in late 1950.[90] She knew more than most that "Empire never did them any good," speaking of the working class of Britain. "I remember the black areas, the marches to London, the bread, tea and cheese diets of the notoriously underfed Englishmen when I lived there." It was appalling—"what good did it do for the miners?" she asked rhetorically, speaking of colonialism.[91] She did not quite grasp, however, that Britain—battered from pillar to post during the war—was in the process of an anguished retreat from colonialism, as Uncle Sam patted John Bull on the back with one hand and picked his pocket of colonies with the other.

Robeson's role as chairman of the Progressive Party was smeared similarly,[92] particularly since he was so unsparing in his critique of the two major parties,[93] Democrats and Republicans: virtually any effort beyond a comforting conservatism and centrism were deemed to be subversive. Robeson castigated the powerful television network NBC for cancelling a program on the Negro in politics on blatant political grounds—i.e. his scheduled presence: it was the artist who was deemed to be subversive by most in the U.S., as NBC was expected by a good deal of the populace to bar Robeson.[94] Ms. Robeson, in contrast, condemned the company's "tyranny."[95] Indicative of how the once vibrant "popular front" had deteriorated was that the culprit ousting him from the airwaves was Eleanor Roosevelt, widow of the late President, a woman with whom Robeson had collaborated in better days.[96]

Undeterred, Robeson was present at the creation of the National Negro Labor Council in Cincinnati (NNLC), a left-wing effort to marshal unionizing campaigns that was likewise maltreated by the U.S. authorities.[97] The NNLC quickly became a pillar of support for Robeson, with future Detroit mayor Coleman Young playing a pivotal role. Young was instrumental in establishing a "United Freedom Fund" designed to raise funds to attack Jim Crow and back the anti-colonial struggle, Robeson's twin causes.[98] Young was the chief executive officer of the NNLC.[99]

John Pittman, a Negro Communist columnist, encountered Robeson in 1951 and found the hair around his temples was graying, as he was now well past the half-century mark in age. A slight cough dogged him too, a signal of deteriorating health to come. He had survived not only Peekskill and an attempted murder plot in St. Louis but armed thugs too who had been dispatched in Memphis and Pittsburgh to dispense with him. Emoluments and enticements were dangled before those who would denounce him. "So remunerative did they make the fad of repudiating Robeson that a smart character in the South was able to procure a new automobile and a sum of money for merely talking against him . . . ." Yet, like the stain in Macbeth, the prominence of Robeson could not be easily obliterated, for as an editor put it, "there is something of a Robeson in the brooding heart of every Negro . . . ."[100]

Moreover, de facto bribes in return for denouncing Robeson could lead to untoward consequences. The actor Canada Lee assailed him and was rewarded with a lead role in the early anti-apartheid epic, *Cry the Beloved Country*, filmed on location. But Lee was so moved by the horror of South Africa that upon returning home he found it hard to keep quiet about this anti-communist ally of Washington. The intensified pressure created contributed to Lee expiring prematurely of a heart attack in May 1952.[101]

Robeson himself had little time to brood, involved as he was in shoring up various organizations—including the CAA, PP, NNLC and the Communist Party—at a time when these were widely seen as an unholy quartet. (The most controversial relationship he endured was his tie to the CPUSA—though he repeatedly denied formal membership.) This was in addition to running his newspaper in Harlem which had attracted a talented corps of writers and artists, including Lorraine Hansberry, Alice Childress, and Beah Richards. It was in 1952 when the latter two artists were joined by soon-to-be extolled actors Sidney Poitier, Harry Belafonte, and William Marshall, along with choreographer Donald McKayle, in a Harlem benefit for *Freedom*.[102] Poitier was among those who endorsed the proposition that "the richness of Negro culture has received no finer expression than in the career of Paul Robeson."[103]

What had brought these future Hollywood celebrities to Robeson's now tattered banner was his latest activist initiative, adding to his commitments with the CAA, CRC, PP, NNLC, etc. The Committee for the Negro in the Arts was a pet cause of Robeson, who knew more than most the formidable barriers that rested in the path of those not defined as "white" who sought to make a mark as an artist. As he put it in late 1951, "finding jobs for colored actors, colored musicians, to see that the pictures and statues and the heads of colored painters and sculptors are sold, to see that the creations of Negro writers are made available . . . ." Special note was made of the field of "dance" where Pearl Primus of Trinidad also had made a contribution to political radicalism. "Where could there have come an Astaire, an Eleanor Powell and James Barton without" Negro hoofers e.g. "a Bill Robinson, a Bert Williams and Eddie Rector, a Florence Mills . . . ." "Where stems even Gershwin? From the music of Negro America joined with the ancient Hebrew idiom," he replied. Yet, "billions" of dollars had "been earned and are being earned from their creation and the Negro people have received almost nothing," amounting to an extension of slavery. And why were there not more Negroes on radio and television? "The final answer is 'the South won't take it'. Now I had a program myself in the '40s all set up by one of the biggest advertising agencies", he said, but "one morning they said, 'we made some inquiries and the South just won't have it.'" Cancellation quickly followed.

And then there was the sorry reality of the absence of the poor and working class from theaters, which he too sought to address by insuring cut-rate fees for entrance to these groups. "When we say that we are people's artists," said Robeson, "we must mean that. I mean it very deeply . . . ." For artists are simply returning to the masses [the very] art the latter created. Bach and the "chorale" for which he was famed was an example: "the people made it in the first place. Haydn with his folks songs—the people made it up in the first place"; that is, the culture with which we deal with comes from the people. "We have an obligation to take it back to the people."[104]

Such heartfelt words caused even those struggling to establish themselves—such as Sidney Poitier and Harry Belafonte—to flock to Robeson, despite the cost. It was in 1978 that Poitier, then at the apex of his celebrity, recalled that "Robeson used to meet with Belafonte and me. And we used to walk the streets of Harlem, just walk" and "we would talk about things; about politics, about art, about race, about Africa. And I found him to be overwhelming in his knowledge, formidable in his commitment. He had phenomenal clarity" and "we . . . were kind of worshippers at his shrine"—and "he had an [impact] on every selection I've ever made as an actor . . . ."[105]

Still, it would be misleading to suggest that the spreading Red Scare hysteria left Robeson unaffected—even among African-Americans. Such an impression would do little to explain his continuing disputes with the emerging heroes of Black America. First, there was the denunciation of him by Jackie Robinson. Then, his fellow luminary from the baseball diamond—pitcher Don Newcombe, also with the Brooklyn Dodgers—confronted him in a Harlem tavern in the early 1950s and, it was thought, intended to attack him physically. On espying Robeson, the hulking hurler scowled as Robeson smiled, then spat out angrily, "I know all about you Paul Robeson . . . They told me all about you!" Robeson, who matched Newcombe pound for pound—though considerably older than the youthful athlete— sought to reason with him, to no avail. "The same 'success' of a few of us does not change the picture" for all of us, was the reminder Robeson uttered that fell on deaf ears.[106] Unconvinced, Newcombe vociferously informed Robeson, "I'm joining the army to fight people like you."[107]

Robeson returned to Robinson too, sending him an "open letter", reminding him that if this baseball player wished to make a contribution to the cause of freedom, he too could be attacked from the right. Robeson pointed out that "in the recent record books the All-American team of 1918 and the nationally picked team of 1917 have only ten players—my name is omitted," airbrushed from the annals. "I can't get a passport," he said; "I can't get auditoriums to sing or act in. And I'm sometimes picketed by the American Legion," conservative military veterans. "I have some records on the market but have difficulty getting shops to take them"[108]—could not Robinson himself face such a dire fate if he deigned to carp militantly about Jim Crow?

It is evident that the rebuke of him by those like Newcombe and Robinson wounded Robeson. This emerged when he was summoned by the House Un-American Activities Committee to be grilled. Robeson was quick to tell his inquisitors, "I know Jackie Robinson . . . I was one of the people [to] speak to Judge Landis," baseball commissioner, "to see that Jackie Robinson had a chance to play baseball"; this was in the early 1940s. "I addressed the combined owners" of the sport in a successful administration of pressure—but the payback he received from Robinson and Newcombe was rebuke.[109]

Robeson advertised what had befallen him as a cautionary note instructing others inclined to walk in his footsteps. "Hall-owners, sponsors and even audiences have been intimidated," he said in

December 1952; "although I have recorded for nearly every major recording company and sold millions of records both here and abroad, these companies refuse to produce any new records for me"—then his own efforts to produce his recordings were hampered.[110] Robeson did not add, perhaps because it would have undermined his case, that broad swathes of liberals turned away from him, unable to overcome antipathy to his defense of existing socialism. For example, the American Civil Liberties Union backed the denial of his passport.[111]

Still, what marked the early Red Scare was the resistance to it by those who could not easily forget Robeson's sacrifice on behalf of the anti-Jim Crow movement. At the annual confab of the African Methodist Episcopal Zion church in 1952, Robeson was the honored guest. Bishop William Walls asked the audience, "everyone who is in favor of having Mr. Robeson's passport returned to him—stand on your feet." Instantaneously, 3,000 delegates stood as one—and two remained seated, one of whom was Edith Sampson, a frequent emissary abroad for the State Department.[112]

This was reflective of the reality that Negro churches—which filled a vacuum of leadership left when Negro union leaders such as Ferdinand Smith were marginalized[113]—continued to be one of Robeson's most effective means of reaching his public. When he was able to find a venue to perform, frequently it was in churches (though his outdoor concert in Chicago in July 1953 drew 15,000).[114] In this Midwestern metropolis, said Robeson, "no hall could be hired because of the terror", mandating this change. "Ten thousand people," he said, "most of them Negro workers from the steel mills and packing plants" attended yet another concert.[115]

To put this in context, few figures during the Red Scare could attract as many adherents as Robeson did. Even today in the U.S., it is unusual for a public figure to routinely attract so many.

Robeson's father and brother were both clerics and he retained a special relationship with the church, leaving a deep imprint upon him. Robeson recalled, "how as a boy I saw my father reading Hebrew, together with my brother Ben" and this early exposure to the Bible shaped his continuing multi-lingualism.[116] He viewed his brother Ben, the pastor, fondly, terming him a "gentle, gray-haired man of quiet dignity. He still adheres to the Republican Party," he added.[117]

Reciprocally, when Robeson sought picketers for demonstrations at the South African consulate in Manhattan in 1952, he instructed, "get your church to join in observing two minutes of silence on Sunday, April 6, at noon."[118]

Still, even Robeson's victories during this era were clouded; thus, his appearance before thousands—outdoors—in Chicago was prompted by the fact that a hall-owner there had been threatened with repercussions, forcing the masses to brave the elements.[119]

Thus, by May 1954 the U.S. Supreme Court ruled that Jim Crow was no longer the law of the land—though implementing this ruling unfolded slowly at best. However, the apparent easing of domestic apartheid combined with the pulverizing of dissidents like Robeson served to erode support for the now aging artist. The September 1953 edition of his periodical *Freedom* shrank in size dramatically and by January 1955 it was suspended due to "both technical and financial reasons," then quietly folded later that year.[120]

8

Britain Beckons

17 May 1954 marked a departure in the torturous journey of Africans in North America, for it was then that the high court ruled that Jim Crow should no longer obtain. The process unleashed—which continues to unfold—also marked a departure for Robeson: it vindicated and validated his outspoken activism on this front. But it also eroded his base of support among— particularly—middle-class African-Americans who were slated to benefit from this turn of events. Yet the retreat of Jim Crow also undercut the rigid conservatism that had undergirded the snatching of his passport and buttressed his general marginalizing, which meant that he now would be free to travel abroad—notably to his beloved Britain—and replenish his severely diminished income.

Yet the murder attempts, the rioting mobs targeting him, and the like all exacted a toll, contributing to a steep decline in his health and well-being that was to hamper his ability to take advantage of his dramatically changed circumstances.

Robeson could have been a major beneficiary of these Copernican changes on the anti-racist front—if he had been willing to cut his views to fit the prevailing fashion. But he would not. Weeks before May 1954 he demonstrated that he would not repudiate his remarks in Paris in 1949 that caused so much consternation in Washington. "I ask again," he said defiantly, "shall Negro sharecroppers from Mississippi be sent to shoot down brown-skinned peasants in Vietnam—to serve the interests of those who oppose Negro liberation at home and colonial freedom abroad?"[1] An irate Robeson proclaimed that "no one could miss the popular alarm and protest that flared up all over the country when [Vice President] Nixon recently suggested that American soldiers be sent to fight the Vietnamese."[2]

Ultimately, the NAACP answered a rousing "yes" to this query about combat in Indo-China, deepening a cleavage among anti-Jim Crow advocates to the detriment of both sides. Robeson's voice, by way of contrast, was used to bombard U.S. prisoners-of-war in North Korea and China, as the high court was ruling. Like anti-apartheid marchers in Johannesburg, the military authorities in northern Asia provided those incarcerated a daily diet of his singing, which was meant to alienate them from their homeland, the U.S. Yet one visiting Negro journalist to these camps found that "many of them have [said] to me in secrecy that they 'have nothing against Paul Robeson' or that they [have] 'a certain admiration' for him:"[3] neither postulate was crafted to win Robeson friends in the halls of power at home. "How do you go along with Paul Robeson's ideas?" was the question put to Negro prisoners particularly; "do you think he's doing a good job for you and your people?"[4]

The State Department did not find the request worthy of reply when Robeson's lawyer demanded the return of his passport so he could travel to China to speak on the centennial of the publication of the work of poet, Walt Whitman.[5] Of course, Robeson was "honored and happy to accept your invitation,"[6] referring to his Chinese comrades.

But the calcification of U.S. politics was in the process of crumbling and not only because of the belated rendering of Jim Crow unconstitutional. For 1955 also delivered the exceptionally profound gathering of mostly African and Asian nations en route or already arrived at independence. Their rise placed a harsher spotlight on South African apartheid which also served to discredit Jim Crow, to the benefit of U.S. Negroes and Robeson alike. "How I should have loved to be at Bandung!" Robeson exhorted, a meeting which he termed—accurately—a "historic turning point in all world affairs . . . ."[7] Two years later Robeson joined Du Bois in Harlem in marking the "Second Anniversary of Bandung" and "the Rebirth of Ghana," speaking of the nation that surged to independence with Nkrumah, an old CAA colleague, at the helm—with both epochal events being inextricably linked.[8]

Nevertheless, the depth of the problem faced by the left was exposed when Robeson felt compelled to reprimand one of two U.S. Negroes allowed in Congress. Adam Clayton Powell of Harlem had a merited reputation as a fierce fighter for civil rights at home—but like so many others, he felt compelled to trim his sails when entering international waters, endorsing the predicates of U.S. foreign policy. "The aggressive war policy of the Republican" party "receives his support," Robeson charged. He wanted the Congressman to "debate with me in your pages,"[9] referring to the London *Daily Herald*, but Powell wisely declined.

In short, Robeson continued to be featured in the foreign press while he was ignored—or scorned—in the press at home. Nevertheless, Robeson's voice continued to resonate abroad. This was not only because of his utilizing telephone lines to sing overseas via loudspeakers but also because of his presence in film (his being embraced abroad and battered at home was also an aspect of the unavoidable fact that the Cold War had driven the U.S. even further to the right than its foreign allies, such as London). This included the remarkable documentary, *Song of the Rivers*, helmed by Dutch filmmaker Joris Ivens, which celebrates workers' movements along six major rivers: the Volga, Mississippi, Ganges, Nile, Amazon, and the Yangtze. The film poster was by Pablo Picasso, the score was by Dmitri Shostakovich, the lyrics by Berthold Brecht—with singing by Robeson. In a sense this was comedown for Robeson. He recalled his time in London and Hollywood: then, he said, "when I sang for films," there were "elaborate studios with perfect acoustics," administered by the "director, his assistant, the sound engineers, the conductor with his earphones, the orchestra in full sway, the small army of technicians . . . ." But now—in a metaphor for how the mighty had fallen—he was reduced to using the parsonage of his brother's Harlem church as a studio with his son, Pauli, an electrical engineer—"quite expert in making recordings"—at the controls. Millions in many lands saw this documentary, as it had commentary in Arabic, Japanese, Persian, Czech, Polish, English, Russian, Spanish, Chinese, French and many other languages—but, Robeson said in sorrow, "we here in America have been denied that opportunity"; as "American Exceptionalism" was exacted with brio, this riveting film was generally unavailable to U.S. audiences.[10]

Hence, Robeson was seen and heard abroad at a time when this was a major accomplishment at home. In 1957 a Londoner exulted that "it was a great joy to hear your voice coming over so clearly at St. Pancras Town Hall this evening", facilitated by a "new transatlantic cable [that] was laid quite recently—and it did not let us down. The audience", he added unnecessarily, "was very moved."[11]

Thus, Robeson remained a pariah at home but as the future Nobel Laureate, the Chilean poet, Pablo Neruda, informed him in 1955, "I am speaking about you and your case in a great meeting for public freedom here in Santiago" that "will be attended by delegates of all Latin American countries. 15,000 people at least will be present," he said happily.[12] "I have remembered many times the promise you did to me long ago: to sing for the Chilean people who admire and love you"; "we are prepared to pay your voyage and return," he concluded hopefully.[13] Neruda was reflecting a hemispheric consensus in that a dominant image of Robeson emerged from Mexico when the painter, Leopoldo Méndez —inspired by the wave of solidarity in favor of restitution of Robeson's passport—designed an engraving of the actor-singer, with chains breaking and doves of peace with wings flapping.[14]

Fortunately for Robeson, with Bandung and anti-Jim Crow measures in the U.S. cracking the solidity of reaction, an opening was created for his case to gain traction. What happened is that Robeson's consistent internationalism, his maniacal study of languages and cultures, was redeemed in a burst of poetic justice when a great wave of humanity demanded that his right to travel be restored. Ten days after the high court ruling, a "Paul Robeson Meeting and Concert" was held in Johannesburg.[15] Robeson's case became a cause célèbre in the land of apartheid. Walter Sisulu of the African National Congress spearheaded this effort, characterizing the artist as a "fighter for peace & freedom" at a forum that contended that he was "systematically victimized for championing" same.[16]

It was also in May 1954 that a select group of Israeli intellectuals—writers, poets, artists and musicians—demanded that his passport be returned.[17] It was during this time that a resident in a Kibbutz, tuned into a radio program of "Israeli and Arabic" music—and "American jazz," when "suddenly the voice of Paul" materialized.[18] This was a reflection of the special relationship that the Robesons enjoyed with the Jewish State—though like most of the left at that juncture, he was not on record displaying a similar solicitude for the Palestinians. There were personal reasons for this. "The more I learn about the history of the Jewish People," said Ms. Robeson in 1954, "the prouder I am that a substantial proportion of Jewish blood flows in my veins"— adding quickly, that this was a metaphor; that is, a "very unscientific statement" indicative of her Spanish Jewish heritage.[19] Robeson had a close personal friendship with the famous Soviet Yiddish actor Solomon Mikhoels and the Soviet poet Itzik Feffer, both of whom fell victim to Stalinist repression—and, according to Robeson, Jr., his father took sharp exception to what he saw as a recrudescence of anti-Semitism erupting in Russia.[20] Still, at a time when Israeli influence was growing in the U.S., this too played a factor in generating support for return of Robeson's passport.

Naturally, it was the British that were in the forefront of this movement, with the eminent Cambridge economist, Maurice Dobb,[21] joining the affluent filmmaker, Charles Chaplin,[22] in support of Robeson. "How deeply [am] I moved by your recent message supporting the struggle now being waged to restore my right to a passport," was the message Robeson delivered to the British born Hollywood star, as he complimented "your affirmation of life and beauty, so poignantly portrayed in your classic 'Limelight.'"[23]

In London Ivor Montagu resorted to history in detailing how "in [the] name of Magna Carta by which already in [the] thirteenth century Englishmen won [the] right of unimpeded travel"; this was now under assault in the republic.[24] Upon being deported to his native Scotland in the 1950s, the U.S. communist leader, John Williamson, immediately became a fount of support for Robeson. Yet he could not help but notice that other cases he worked on—for example, freedom for jailed Communist leaders and other victims of repression—"did not get the same broad support as the campaign for Paul."[25]

As with China, the idea was to invite Robeson overseas—for a concert in this instance—and then pressure the State Department to grant him a passport. This was the idea broached by Robeson to the Earl of Harewood.[26] Leaders of the Ira Aldridge Society in London—which included the great tragedian's relatives—requested that he come to perform *Othello*, a request that was joined by the anti-colonial leader Fenner Brockway; Joseph Dejean, Haiti's Ambassador; and

Chief Obafemi Awolowo, Premier of the western region of Nigeria. A "film script" on Aldridge was also developed that "opened with you unveiling the seat in the theatre dedicated to Ira Aldridge."[27]

As was his tendency, Robeson linked his admiration of Aldridge to the latter's admiration of the constituent elements of the U.S.S.R., recollecting that the leading writer of Ukraine, Taras Schevchenko, "was a dear friend of Ira Aldridge," who "visited the Ukraine and Russia in the middle of the 19th century." Robeson walked in the great actor's footsteps, having had the "privilege to visit Odessa, Kiev and Kharkov. I recall sitting at the quay at Odessa," he recalled later, "and looking over the beautiful waters. No wonder the immortal Pushkin loved this city," adding the father of the Russian language to this esteemed trio. "And in working on some ancient music of the Byzantine period, one finds the way inevitably to the culture of ancient Kiev . . . ."[28] To that end, a version of *Othello* filmed in the Soviet Union was also one of his ideas.[29]

In the spring of 1955 Robeson received a formal invitation to visit Britain, extended by "Sportsmen, Theatrical Workers and Cine Technicians." He was touched by this gesture, calling it "significant evidence of the united desire of the majority of the British people to have me continue my long personal association with them. This is very heartening. I look forward to the time when a similar united expression takes place in these United States to guarantee for all people the right to travel without arbitrary restrictions."[30] The U.S. Communist daily, observed admiringly in 1955 that "because of popular request," the BBC "has played a Robeson program daily for more than ten years", while Scandinavian countries—where the artist had drawn tens of thousands a few years earlier—"invited Robeson to become a citizen, as have a number of other countries."[31] Unfortunately, for Robeson, this wave of popularity did not necessarily translate into direct deposits in his bank account because of restrictions by the U.S. Treasury Department and the like.

According to Cedric Belfrage, one of his most active supporters, this "national affection" for Robeson in Britain was "best shown by the fact that although no new Robeson records have circulated here in a long time, the old ones are played over and over again on such top radio hours as the morning Housewives' Choice"; unsurprising since "his name is a household word", being the "perennial gift for which Britons are grateful to America"; worse for Washington was that "thousands of GIs [U.S. military men] stationed here . . . hear him sing on the British radio for the first time."[32]

In Jamaica, to which Ferdinand Smith had been dispatched unceremoniously after years of union leadership in the U.S., the Communist informed the artist that the national radio station had just launched a "'Paul Robeson Day' featuring about a dozen of your recordings."[33] It was in 1957, in the former British colony of Canada—Vancouver in this case—that Robeson supporters moved to organize yet another concert there by Robeson in support of his cause.[34] Canadians were in for a treat since it was in that year that he announced portentously, "I just recorded the other day what I think is some of the greatest singing I have done in the last 20 years . . . ."[35]

The *New Statesman* explained in 1955 that this British reaction was utterly predictable, particularly since "in England there was no racial discrimination to narrow the scope of Paul's sympathy with Left causes"—at least not to the same degree as obtained in the U.S.[36] Thus, at the Labour Party confab in Blackpool in 1956 there was considerable activity publicizing Robeson's cause; it was "beginning to snowball," said his friend, Cedric Belfrage with pinpoint accuracy. "We need another tape," Robeson was told, as recordings of his speeches and songs were stunningly effective in galvanizing support for his case. Whereas he was banned from "commercial TV" in his homeland, efforts were then being made to place him in the same medium in England. Actually, said Belfrage, he was informed "we could get [a Robeson program] shown on TV in most European countries," which "would be a very big thing,"[37] not least in revealing a rift with nations thought to be the closest allies of the U.S. There was a "National Paul Robeson Committee" which in 1956 held a major conference in Manchester.[38] Members of Parliament, union leaders and religious figures were among the 150 attending this December gathering.[39] Months later, 27 parliamentarians demanded that Robeson be allowed to visit London.[40]

London was befuddled by the persecution of Robeson. "Were I an American and frightened of Paul Robeson's political opinions," said Earl Baldwin of Bewdley, "I would not hinder his political opinions[,]

I would not hinder his departure and should be only too glad to get rid of him"; in fact, he demanded irritably, "send him to us. We should be honoured by the presence of such a fine artist."[41]

But it was not just London that was baffled by the vitriolic response to Robeson among the U.S. authorities, as his popularity abroad continued soaring. A visitor to a bookstore in Bucharest in 1955 watched as a man bought a reproduction of a Soviet painting, "Song of Peace," depicting Robeson at Peekskill, while in Budapest a student proudly displayed his excellent etching of Robeson singing. In Cracow, a lad started singing "My Curly Headed Baby"—in Polish—in an uncanny voice emulating Robeson's voice and manner.[42]

Robeson had been catapulted into legendary status in the first place because of his popularity abroad and, unsurprisingly, when the time came to rescue him from the clutches of his antagonists, the international community weighed in emphatically, creating domestic ripples hard to ignore, particularly among religious figures. By 1955, 300 clerics—befitting a man whose father and brother were pastors—from Baltimore and Washington demanded that his passport be returned.[43] They may have been influenced by the crusading of the Civil Rights Congress (CRC), then—like CAA—in its death throes but with its leader, Patterson, still capable of effectively placing the passport denial in the context of Robeson being a vector for global revulsion at the horror of Jim Crow and colonialism.[44] It was true that other institutions were emerging to fill the vacuum left by the impending demise of the CRC—those tied to Dr. Martin Luther King Jr. in the first place. However, these new groupings did not have the international ties of the CRC, nor the global reach of the CAA, which amounted to a net loss for African-Americans and their allies.

Feeling the heat, within months the House Un-American Activities Committee (HUAC) beckoned him to appear for a theatrical berating. Robeson was unrepentant, participating in what was reported as a "shouting, table thumping and gavel banging hearing."[45] It was a "dramatic thing," said Robeson's attorney, Leonard Boudin, "a very traumatic confrontation", which did not leave Robeson—a "very warm, intense, serious person" (though prone to anger when pushed)—unaffected.[46] A surprised reporter later asked Robeson about the contention by HUAC's counsel, Richard Arens, who claimed "you spat in his face each time before you answered his queries and he wanted to crash [a] chair over your head . . . your comment?"[47]

"I have sacrificed literally hundreds of thousands, if not millions of dollars, for what I believe in," was his direct message to the committee. "I have read a lot of Marx," he said, a regimen that began not in Russia—"[I] started to study that in England." Indeed, he stressed as he so often did, "all my political education, strange to say, came in England," that is, "my Marxist education" was also influenced by the "Labour Party . . . ." His hairline now receding but his voice booming and advancing as usual, he told the legislators, "I knew all the members of the Labour Party, so you cannot blame that on the Russians. You will have to blame (my Marxist education) on the English Labour Party." Then twisting the knife further, he added with mock whining, "They have just invited me to come to London next week to sing to 140,000 miners up in Yorkshire. Do you think that you could let me go?" He balked at disowning his friendship with Ben Davis, who he termed "one of my dearest friends, one of the finest Americans you can imagine . . . a great man." But he also balked when asked if he was a member of the U.S. Communist Party, registered under the name "John Thomas."[48]

Robeson's critics were disgusted with his words, particularly his contention that the republic was "built on slavery," which caused the U.S. to seem the hypocrite when assailing the socialist camp. The *Milwaukee Journal* epitomized the outlook of his belittlers when they reviled a "tragedy of intellect and talent, a tragedy of his race, a tragedy of America"—all encapsulated in the "tragedy of Paul Robeson."[49]

Robeson's bravura performance before HUAC did not win him many adherents in official Washington. Boudin, his lawyer, found it to be quite unusual when higher-ups in the State Department handled the passport dispute, indicative of how seriously it was taken. After the blowup at HUAC, Robeson conceded, "I have been doing a great deal of thinking," in other words, "about taking my case to the Supreme Court," but now was reluctant. "Supreme Court action is expensive," he said, "and therefore financially impossible for me to undertake," given his straitened circumstance. "Practically the whole burden falls on me," he groaned, "and I am not in a position to assume these burdens any longer . . . ."[50]

With Jim Crow easing, Washington strained to ensure that Robeson and the radical left could not take advantage by making sure their time was expended heavily in courtrooms and legislative chambers, converting them into firefighters focused on dousing flames at the firehouse. Months after the anti-Jim Crow ruling in the high court, the CAA was in federal court seeking to halt liquidation. Demanded by the authorities was all of their correspondence with Mandela's African National Congress.[51] Demanded was that the CAA register with the fearsome Subversive Activities Control Board, which meant providing a license for escalating harassment, for once information was provided to this agency, it was often used for enhanced persecution.[52] Washington well knew that despite the propaganda about the Soviet Union, one of the closest international relationships that involved Robeson was his tie to anti-apartheid forces.[53] Robeson well knew that a central reason for denying him a passport was his anti-colonial and anti-Jim Crow activism, via the CAA—and CRC.[54]

This bare-knuckled legal brawling was also costly, expenses that Robeson and his cohorts could hardly afford. A symbol of the financial sacrifice forced on Robeson because of his politics arose when Patterson "spoke with Paul about participating in the meeting against intervention in Guatemala. He agreed to do so," asking only if it was "possible to pay an honorarium of $25 to Paul's accompanist."[55] The U.S. overthrow of this Central America regime on spurious grounds of "Communist infiltration" was a mordant symbol of the Red Scare, as was Robeson's protest of this violation. Yet the point here is that an artist who once commanded a six-figure income was now reduced to performing—in his homeland—for nominal fees. For it was not only solidarity events with Guatemala where Robeson was compelled to perform for peanuts but in other venues too that in past days would have delivered adequate compensation. Contemporaneously, the *New Statesman* confirmed that in 1948 alone when he made an estimated 500 free appearances in support of the Progressive Party, "he was giving away the equivalent of $750,000 at the box office to help win votes for Henry Wallace."[56]

In sum, Robeson was not without weapons, as evidenced by the spectacular reception globally of the Genocide Petition filed at the United Nations. This prompted Senator John Bricker of Ohio—

Figure 9   When Robeson joined with Patterson in filing a petition at the United Nations charging the U.S. with genocide against African-Americans, he outraged Washington, which promptly seized his passport, preventing him from travelling to earn a living abroad, while simultaneously "blacklisting" him at home. (Daily Worker and Daily World Photographs Collection, Tamiment Library/Robert F. Wagner Labor Archives, New York University, New York City)

with substantial domestic backing—to propose constitutional amendments restricting the scope of international treaties (e.g. the Genocide Treaty) on the U.S., yet another attempt to forge "American Exceptionalism" but also a signal of grave apprehension about trends overseas.[57] The restrictions on his traveling north of the border were eased allowing Robeson to inform "dear friends in Britain" in May 1956 that "last February I sang in Massey Hall in Toronto and for the metal miners in Sudbury, Ontario" finding immense "warmth of these audiences," meaning a "trans-Canada tour was planned." A startled Ottawa then "decided to bar me from entering Canada", and joined their U.S. counterpart in "attempting to prevent me from making a living"[58]—but the impression left in Canada could not be erased, nor downplayed.

Because he remained one of the better known public figures in the republic—and definitely the most radical of this small circle—Robeson was even more in the crosshairs of Washington's political snipers as the overall political atmosphere thawed. This was recognized by Alice Childress, one of the coterie of artists—she was a noted writer—who worshipped him. "Your encouragement and faith in my ability to produce is in great measure responsible" for her recent explosion of productivity; "things will change for you," she insisted, since "times are changing"; yet "because your stand has been a stronger and bigger one . . . you will be fought the longest."[59]

He was fought the longest in part because he was among the most steadfast. After the death of Josef Stalin 1953, the Soviet intervention in Hungary in 1956, and the Stalin devaluation in Moscow that same year, as the Communist Party in the U.S.S.R. renounced and condemned their long-time leader, confusion erupted in the ranks of U.S. Communists with some calling for a break with the Soviet Union. This was occurring as another brushfire was lit in the wake of the rise of Dr. Martin Luther King, Jr. and halting steps toward desegregation, with some Communists arguing for a ditching of the party's view that Negroes constituted a nation meriting self-determination. In these "party wars," Robeson, as to be expected, stood stoutly alongside Davis and Patterson, who leaned toward overthrowing the "Negro Nation" thesis and refusing to break with Moscow. "This is a moment when steadiness is especially necessary in Left ranks," counseled CP patriarch, William Z. Foster, who too was part of the Davis-Patterson camp. "Undoubtedly," he continued "there has been much confusion and vacillations caused by the Stalin affair [and] especially the tragedy in Hungary"; signifying that Robeson's counsel too was desirable on such fraught matters, Foster announced that he "would be glad to have a chat with you" about all this.[60] The leader of U.S. Communists also sought to confer with Robeson on the "Negro Nation" thesis, telling him "the American Negro question is theoretically a very complicated one."[61]

The FBI thought that Robeson merited added scrutiny given his "background, intelligence and nationalistic sympathy", which suggested he "may well be one of the real leaders or possibly the real leader behind the Foster-Davis faction" of the CP. "Because of former trips to the Soviet Union and to Europe, [he] may be the one who is actually giving the line"; i.e. Robeson was deemed to be "much more dangerous to the security of this country than" even Communist leaders.[62]

Robeson placed the blame squarely for the unrest in Hungary on the shoulders of the ultra-right.[63] His interpretation of these events was placed prominently in the pages of the *Baltimore Afro-American*; "he got more space in our press," said George Murphy of the family that controlled this important organ, "than the Dean of Canterbury got in most of the daily papers of the U.S. That to me is important."[64] That it was. Robeson's voice continued to carry weight among U.S. Negroes and it was hard for it to be otherwise as long as Jim Crow reigned.

It was in late 1956 that a mostly Hungarian-American assemblage responded by picketing his speech at the annual gathering of the National Council of American Soviet Friendship. Early arrivals were showered with eggs, tomatoes and sticks, as—typically for the era— police watched idly. There were virulent taunts of "murderer" and "priest killer" and "Communist traitors", while Robeson particularly was targeted with a well-aimed bottle filled with ammonia.[65] In a sign of progress, unlike Peekskill, no racist imprecations were reported.

Foster may have heard what Robeson told an Australian journalist a few years later when—after describing himself as an "ardent advocate of socialism"—he called the Budapest revolt "fascist". A socialist planet would surely rise—"without too much violence, maybe"—he opined, while rehashing his controversial remarks in 1949, he said bluntly that if the U.S. fought the U.S.S.R., he would be found "on the side of Russia."[66]

This attack on the Hungarian revolt carried a cost for Robeson. His staunchest supporter in London—Cedric Belfrage—who was also close to the radical left in the U.S., warned him about "taking a position of all-out defense of the Soviet troops in Hungary," since this intervention "has demoralized, discouraged and confused British progressive forces much more gravely than any other of the USSR's controversial actions . . . ." In Britain, for example, "the CP is split down the middle," a convulsion that engendered mass resignations. "British support for the USSR over Hungary outside the

CP is virtually zero." He fretted about the impact on the "Natl. Paul Robeson Committee" which had been organized "on a non-political basis" but now "this particular issue is so all-pervading that, if you are known to take an uncompromising position on it, we would be unlikely to be able to head off the effects. There are now some 150 organizations participating in our campaign to get you to this country to sing," now jeopardized, he thought.[67] Robeson ignored this counsel though, contrary to Belfrage, it had no appreciable impact on his British support.

Indeed, months after Belfrage's dire warning, he was told a "world wide action" on Robeson's birthday was brewing. "Chaplin would be in it, of course, and so would Sean O'Casey, Sartre, Picasso, Herman Hesse, Ulanova, Shostakovich, Laxness and why not Graham Greene, Louis Armstrong, Arthur Miller, Jussi Bjorling," along with "Ingrid Bergman, Gina Lollabrigida," and the brightest stars in the film firmament.[68]

Thus, by the mid-1950s Robeson had managed to survive the sturdiest blows of his opponents and was dishing out a few of his own. The liberalizing climate had facilitated an anti-Jim Crow ruling and slightly improved relations with Moscow, all of which helped to propel a reinvigorated attempt to restore his passport, thereby allowing him to benefit from the continuing adoration of audiences abroad.

But as in a deadly chess match, the U.S. authorities responded forcefully. The denial of his passport was upheld by a federal court in 1955, with his reluctance to file an affidavit attesting that he was not a member of the U.S. Communist Party being at issue. As the cameras rolled outside the courtroom, Robeson—perhaps thinking of his yeoman duty during the anti-fascist war—resorted to Shakespeare in his deep and rolling cadences: "I have done the state some service and they know it . . . I pray you in your letters when you shall these unlucky deeds relate, speak of me as I am nothing extenuate, nor set down aught in malice." Topping off this impromptu performance was his singing verses from "Water Boy", along with several lines of a song in Russian—the latter was akin to poking a stick into a hornet's nest.[69]

He lost his court appeal on passport restoration in mid-1956.[70] This occurred despite a brief filed in his behalf signed by Du Bois

Figure 10   Robeson was one of the best-known U.S. citizens abroad because of his multiple roles as political activist and artist—and also because of his ability to converse in numerous languages, a rarity in his parochial homeland, then as now. (Daily Worker and Daily World Photographs Collection, Tamiment Library/Robert F. Wagner Labor Archives, New York University, New York City)

among other dignitaries. Recalled was the visit to India by J. Saunders Redding, a liberal Negro intellectual allowed a passport, who while there was asked repeatedly, "why has your government denied a passport to Mr. Paul Robeson?" After returning from Germany, Austria, Italy, and France, Congressman Adam Clayton Powell, Jr., said, "In every country I was asked the same questions [all] about Paul Robeson." A Negro journal in Los Angeles asked mischievously if Robeson would receive a passport if he vowed not to enlist global support for African-Americans.[71]

And then unleashed upon him was the feared Internal Revenue Service—the tax gatherers—who requested an audit of his finances,[72] a process that in the worst case could lead to a prison term. "They have been trying for years to send Paul to prison but haven't been able to find any grounds for doing so," said Ms. Robeson. "Income tax, which is the usual method they use, is impossible in our case, because for years our lawyer who is an expert on income tax, has handled all our money."[73]

The IRS seemed to take notable umbrage at the awarding of the Stalin Peace Prize to Robeson, which had brought him $25,000 in 1953.[74] Still, because of his charitable donations and his lax administration of his finances, Robeson's adjusted gross income in 1955 was a paltry $10,685.04—still an uptick from a few years earlier. By 1956, this figure was $15,299.19 but had dipped again to $9,685.52 the next year. However, by 1958—as his right to travel was restored—his income had leapt to $39,095.11, with the increase largely attributable to British sources.[75] Since in early 1957 his law firm presented him with a bill for services of $4,382.81, mostly for efforts to regain his passport, this increased income arrived not a moment too soon.[76]

Washington was not inclined to unfurl the white flag of surrender simply because Robeson was being applauded abroad. This Robeson well knew and in case he had suffered memory lapse, there to refresh his recollection was Davis, still languishing in a jail cell after his 1949 conviction in federal court—fundamentally on the specious charge of simply being a Communist. The heralding of Robeson in prisons was akin to an invitation by the authorities to place the artist among his ardent fans. Davis had "lost none of my old starry eyed admiration for you" after "more than a quarter century of personal friendship," poking his comrade with the point that "there are legendary stories of you in every prison in America. The Negro prisoners, in their own way, speak your name in hallowed tones . . . ." Bulging with respect, even as he remained trapped in an iron cage, Davis told his friend that these prisoners' "knowledge of you is their passport to pride in their people . . . ."[77]

But this burst of good news was accompanied by concern for Robeson's health, which had deteriorated sharply, a result of irrepressible travel and concomitant loss of sleep, an inadequate diet, tension delivered by murderous plots, etc. By late 1955, George Crockett—Davis' attorney and a future Congressman representing Black Detroit—was happy to hear that Robeson was "on the mend and should be your usual hardy self within a few more weeks." This was not to be: Robeson was on a downward slide physically that would restrain his travel—and his income—and lead to his death in early 1976.[78]

Robeson had sought to escape traveling to Washington to testify before HUAC earlier in 1956, a request roundly rejected. HUAC demanded that an "independent medical examination" occur.[79] They looked askance at the report from his urologist who had had Robeson as a patient since he endured major surgery in October 1955, which left him confined to his Harlem residence for months, the result of a recurrent infection in the urinary tract that was "quite disabling" and necessitated "further surgery." Dr. V. McKinley Wiles emphasized that "stress" had "left him in a weakened condition",[80] which was catnip for HUAC, who thought that enhancing his stress was a neat idea. The press reported that Robeson had a "major emergency stomach operation."[81] Further surgery did occur in November 1955—according to his physician at Harlem's Sydenham Hospital—"for a prostatic hypertrophy with acute urinary retention and massive hematuria," along with "cardiac enlargement"; there was "left ventricular hypertrophy and myocardial damage," all of which was extremely serious for a man not yet 60 years of age. Travel, advised Dr. Aaron Wells, "would affect unfavorably the status of his heart"—which was akin to an invitation for HUAC to subpoena him forthwith.[82]

Robeson was in bad shape. Worsening his health was his extreme susceptibility to heavy colds.[83] "Paul has been so very ill," said his spouse as his HUAC appearance was unfolding, "that I have decided that he should not attempt any concerts at all" for "the operation was more of a shock than we had thought . . . ."[84] Helping to sense his mortality was his attendance in March 1955 at the funeral of his once friend, now sparring partner, Walter White of the NAACP.[85] He had ridden the wave of anti-communism, becoming a confidante to presidents in the process but did not seem to realize how the continued viability of those on the left like Robeson bolstered his high level access.

Nonetheless, Robeson had access to medicine that money could hardly buy. As the impact of the second surgery loomed, Pablo Neruda told his fellow writer, Howard Fast, "if you see Paul Robeson, tell him please his song was given to the charcoal miners only two days ago, introduced by myself . . . ."[86]

As ever, some U.S. artists found it easier to speak up against Robeson's persecution when artists of the stature of Neruda did so.

Still, Lorraine Hansberry probably required no prompting, as she had received her first break as a young writer when she was hired by Robeson to work for *Freedom*. Citing the credo of Cyrano de Bergerac, whose stark words she put in Robeson's voice, she posed questioningly, "what would you have me do . . . eat a toad for breakfast every morning?. . . . wear out my belly groveling in the dust? No thank you!"[87] A writer in the Negro press imitated her vigor by asking why should a passport be revoked because of an anti-colonial position?[88]

Hansberry, who went on to become a prizewinning playwright on Broadway by dint of her work *A Raisin in the Sun*, was courageous to speak up on Robeson's behalf for contemporaneously her peers were being hounded for similar relationships. The FBI reported that the poet and playwright once known as Le Roi Jones—then Amiri Baraka—was sufficiently bold to attend Robeson lectures,[89] while this agency sought to have poet, Sarah Wright fired from her job because she was supposedly, an "admirer" of Robeson.[90]

Naturally, all writers did not agree and this list included Carl Rowan, the Negro who was to serve as U.S. Ambassador to Finland. Responding to his writing for the flagship publication of the now affluent John H. Johnson's growing media empire headquartered in Chicago, he observed provocatively—not inaccurately—that "most white persons in this country definitely regard Paul Robeson as an enemy of the United States"; his interlocutor conceded that if he were to interview Robeson in a mass media platform, "I think NBC"—the television network—"[would] probably be boycotted and picketed and maybe shot at," confirming at once both the venomous hostility to the artist and why he was being treated like a non-person.

But it was left to Rowan to confirm the verity that global pressure was to assuage a declining internal situation: "a member of the Diet in Japan looked at the situation in this country and said, 'well if these Americans feel superior to Negroes who've lived there and fought and died for their country, what must they think of us?'"[91] After the release of Robeson's well received memoir, Kenzo Nishikawa of Japan, who had read the translation, told the artist that he was "now winning a greater reputation than ever"; with enthusiasm he told Robeson "you have shown you are superior to the white in mind and body, both in ability and strength. That's our pride and the highest and glory of our coloured races . . . ."[92]

Rowan's suggestion that Robeson had "betrayed the Negro" was not a notion accepted universally. "On the contrary," said Frederick Seabrook, "the Negro and America have betrayed Paul Robeson . . . due to fear." Rest assured, he asserted, "the State Department, the press and even our very own professional race hustlers will never succeed in dethroning Paul Robeson in the hearts of the masses of Negroes."[93]

Nevertheless, confirming further the breadth of the effort to marginalize Robeson was not only a scholar's contention that press coverage of him in the so-called newspaper of record—the *New York Times*—declined sharply during the 1950–58 era: the period when he was under de facto house arrest. What was also striking was the contention of Paul Robeson, Jr. that "most newsreel and film footage" of his father "had vanished" and that "most of newsreel footage which is available has had the sound-track erased from it . . . ."

But this same scholar also exposed why this information blockade had begun to crumble. It was in 1957 that the launching of Sputnik by Moscow shook the confidence of Washington, leading to agonizing reappraisals including whether it made sense to maltreat so atrociously the vast human capital that reclined in the African-American community, thereby curbing market potential and ill preparing a sizeable sector of the labor force to propel a complex economy—and compete, for example, in rocket science. It was also in 1957 that an attempt to desegregate a high school in Little Rock, Arkansas led to riots by the working class and middle class defined as "white," bringing a black eye to the U.S. globally and hampering its ability to charge Moscow with human rights violations. A missionary in South Africa then reported that "hundreds of Africans" and "non-whites asked him about Little Rock and [Robeson]".[94] In fact, said Dr. A. Chester Clark, executive secretary of the Missionary Department of the African Methodist Episcopal denomination, the "most frequently discussed topics among South African non-whites" was the conjoined matters of Robeson and Little Rock.[95]

Ms. Robeson, who by now had established an enviable reputation as a journalist, had a direct pipeline to a leader of the desegregation fracas. Daisy Bates was head of the statewide NAACP and also, she said, had the "pleasure" of "hearing from" Robeson, who sent her a "lovely family photo. The next time I am in New York," she enthused, "it would indeed be an honor if I could visit you and meet the family."[96] Ms. Robeson wrote about Bates' desperate struggle in global periodicals, telling her that "my colleagues from all over the world were simply enthralled by the Little Rock affair and I was a reference point for their clarification. I was the one Negro available," she boasted with some accuracy, "who didn't bite her tongue and called a spade a spade."[97]

Despite their tireless efforts, the U.S. authorities—as the political climate shifted—were unable to block the Robesons altogether from the emergent anti-Jim Crow forces, notably in Dixie. Earlier, Robeson had offered his "wholehearted support" in the aftermath of yet another example of racist outrage when Emmett Till, an African-American teenager from Chicago was slain by ultra-right racists in Mississippi in 1955. The "outrageous acquittal of lynchers" stirred his conscience, moving him to "offer all that I have—my art, my strength, my devotion—to our common cause."[98] The reaction to this slaying detonated an explosion of protest from the Atlantic to the Pacific.

Even Ralph Bunche, now safely ensconced in the highest reaches of the United Nations and distancing himself furiously from his former left-wing background, found it possible to contact the Robesons after years of hiatus. "Ruth [his spouse] and I thank you and Essie most warmly for the inscribed copy of your book," adding, on U.N. stationery: "no doubt there will be a family 'row' as to which of us gets first crack at it."[99]

The premier boxer, Archie Moore—also an African-American—contacted Robeson from São Paulo, where he had "just won a bout with the champion light heavyweight boxer of Brazil who happens to be colored . . . ." But the details of this pummeling were not the purpose of his message. "For me," he proclaimed, "you have played a great part in my life," notably since "I have followed you many years . . . ." To be sure, he added quickly, "I am not a hero worshipper by a long shot but there are men I admire and you are one of the few . . . ." Inspired by the artist, he admitted, "I believe I was put on earth to do something greater than just be a champion athlete. My greatest desire is to meet you in person," so "please call collect."[100]

That Moore was able to travel while Robeson was not was hardly lost on Ms. Robeson, though she chose to focus on the musician Louis Armstrong and those like him. Their jazz "tours abroad sponsored by the government" were the "reverse side of the coin in the State Department fight against Paul Robeson—denying him his passport because when he goes abroad he criticizes the treatment of Negroes in the United States"; ergo, Robeson "must be kept at home, must be immobilized, must be silenced."[101] Her own activism attracted the attention of congressional bloodhounds, as she was summoned for questioning by Senator Joseph McCarthy himself.[102]

Noah Griffin, NAACP leader in normally liberal San Francisco, was effusive in thanking Robeson "for the inspiration which you gave my son" during a recent concert there. "He brought home an autographed program of your recent concert" at "Third Baptist Church."[103]

Actually, by August 1957 Robeson had appeared five times in the Golden State in recent months, performing before 10,000 in the city by the bay and Los Angeles.[104] Negro churches had become a kind of sanctuary for his performances, offering as they did, attractive terms to the artist. "Terms for church concerts," advised Ms. Robeson, "are usually 60–40% of the net, that is 60% to him and 40% to the church, after expenses have been deducted" with a "guarantee of a minimum of $500 to cover the time and work."[105] Robeson's peregrinations had revealed a trend that was to shape U.S. politics for decades to come. Writing from their now "permanent address" at Harlem's Jumel Terrace, Ms. Robeson observed that her spouse "spends much of his time on the West Coast where the political and artistic climate is far superior to that of the East Coast . . . ."[106]

The FBI too had noticed this trend. Robeson, it was said, was not just performing in California but was seeking to "consolidate the left forces in the CP" there, as evidenced by his being "very close" to Pettis Perry, pre-eminent Negro Communist. To that end, Robeson—it was said—"plans to move to Los Angeles to live . . . ."[107] Robeson, said the FBI, was "becoming increasingly effective out on the West Coast among the Negroes and especially among some of the Negro clergymen." He had "approached the pastor of one of the more important Negro churches in Los Angeles" and "convinced the pastor to let him sing to his congregation. Robeson explained that the pastor could take up a collection for his church and the entire collection he could keep" because "he, Robeson did not want any of it. All he wanted was to sing and sing and sing. The pastor agreed" and "collected over $1100. This news spread quickly from pastor to pastor,"leading to a cascade of invitations from other churches. "In all these engagement," it was said with bitterness, "[Robeson] gets across one or more points in behalf of Communism and Russian viewpoints . . . ." An emboldened Robeson was now "planning to take a trip into Mexico" with the same approach.[108]

Slowly it was dawning that, perhaps, allowing Robeson a passport so he could resume residence in London was the "least bad" option.

This was the backdrop to yet another Robeson visit to Washington, this time arriving on 29 May 1957 at the State Department at 9:35 A.M.—and staying until 3:05 P.M.—in another attempt to regain his passport. He declined—per usual—to answer if he was a member of the U.S. Communist Party but immediately responded when asked where he would go if his passport was to be restored: Moscow? No, said Robeson, "I would go straight to London to do concerts first under the sponsorship of most of the leading composers of Great Britain", such as "Dr. Vaughan Williams . . . the Dean of English composers," the "greatest living composer" there and "also Mr. Benjamin Britten." But, yes, he would also visit Prague, "where Mozart had all his operas performed and where Haydn lived." Telling his questioners what they already knew, he seemed to take delight in discussing how "on Sunday night I sang into London where many of the English artists appeared in a concert at St. Pancras . . . and over the telephone I was broadcast into the hall and sang about 20 minutes of a concert and was able to accompany a Welsh choir . . . ." He reminded those who may have forgotten that "I sort of lived in Wales at different times and was very close to the Welsh people, even singing in their own language . . . ." Robeson also seemed to take pleasure in exhibiting that he was not the only one under pressure. He pointed out that of late in his judicial opinions, Justice William O. Douglas of the high court observed that it was "of importance that the [anti-Jim Crow] decision be taken because of world opinion—because of world opinion," he repeated. He linked himself to this trend by underlining that just recently he was at one of the major demonstrations on civil rights in Washington—tens of thousands amassing—and "many Negroes came to me and said, 'Paul we might not be on these steps [of the Lincoln Memorial] today, but for certain of the things you have stood by and fought for [—] for your people . . . .'" In other words, Robeson was part of this global movement that was forcing a recalculation by Washington that was to lead to his regaining his passport and his seeking to exert even more global pressure. "I know many of the men of Ghana," he said, speaking of the nation in the vanguard of African independence; "many members of the government were in college in London when I was there; I know many of them."[109]

Robeson's questioners also probably knew that he paid close attention to Little Rock, participating in a forum that suggested it represented the "symptoms of the evils of racism." He took note of the vote at the United Nations as early as 1952 denouncing apartheid, then advised that "leaders of the fight against racism in America should carry the struggle again to the U.N.," as had been done by himself and the CRC a few years earlier.[110] Like Du Bois, he seemed to become more militant—not less—as he grew older, as when he informed an inquiring New Zealand reporter subsequently that as for Little Rock, "I would have asked thousands of Negroes from all over the United States to go there armed," adding triumphantly, "I'm sure that nothing would have happened."[111]

Robeson's passport seizure and the crucifixion of him had begun at a time when a good deal of the world was colonized—but by 1957, a new world was awakening, particularly with the independence of Ghana, an epochal event that Robeson not so subtly brought to the attention of his interrogators. Surveillance of him would have revealed a point he did not note, that is, his growing closeness to populous India which—given this nation's historic ties to London and ongoing political relationship with Moscow, which persists in the twenty-first century—ensured that New Delhi would weigh in on his behalf. After all, he had known Prime Minister Nehru since the 1930s and had grown close to his daughter, Indira, a future Prime Minister in her own right.

In early 1958 Robeson had heard from an Indian official at the U.N. that he had an "urgent letter from Indira, asking that you send a greeting to the people of India via tape recording,"[112] a request that was satisfied promptly.[113] Yes, Robeson told the State Department with pride, "I happen to know many of the people in India . . . ."[114]

"Thank you so much for the beautiful silver dish," Ms. Robeson gushed in early 1958; "we are delighted that you received the book and tape . . . ." More to the point, "Paul is deeply moved, as we all are, by the fact that you in India have formed a Birthday Committee and that your father wrote a marvelous letter in support of it . . . ."[115]

Officialdom in Washington knew that the Prime Minister in early 1958 hailed Robeson as "this great humanist" to mark his sixtieth birthday in April 1958. The State Department took note when Nehru called this celebration "more than a tribute to 'a great individual'" since such occasions are "tribute to that cause for which Mister Paul Robeson has stood and suffered." Plans were afoot to "organize concerts and theatre and drama in big cities" on this hallowed occasion.[116] Even the *New York Times* temporarily eased the embargo on news about Robeson to inform its many readers of the "important fact that Robeson is a hero to most Indian intellectuals."[117]

With such surging support abroad, it became easier for domestic forces to support Robeson. The leading Negro newspaper, the *Pittsburgh Courier*, highlighted the fact of British support for Robeson's cause.[118] His wife was aware of this inextricable tie between the domestic and the global. She was "deeply grateful" for Nehru's avid backing of Robeson's case; thus, "the major press here" in New York City "was forced to give it coverage and this gave just the needed impetus for our friends in Actors' Equity."[119] "Actors' Equity," the union, "had a general meeting," recounted Ms. Robeson "[to] offer a resolution . . . " in the Spring of 1958, and "Ossie Davis, a Negro actor friend of ours, presented a Resolution appealing for a limited passport for Paul . . . ." Ralph Bellamy, "president of Equity, spoke against it," to small effect since it passed "by a vote of 111 to 75"; Robeson, she said, "is greatly heartened by this . . . ."[120] Punctuating this victory, in 1958 there were birthday celebrations for Robeson in all of India's key cities, with Nehru's daughter serving as Chair of the events.[121]

Finally, the dam broke: "We are literally packing our bags and will be off the moment we get the passport," was the harried message of Ms. Robeson in 1958, as the high court ruled that their friend and comrade, Rockwell Kent, could not be denied the right to travel, a ruling which encompassed the now delighted couple.[122] In anticipation, invitations had been flooding into their home from Britain. It was "extraordinary", she said; "they have been telephoning almost every hour . . . ." There was "great excitement about a wonderfully well-sponsored engagement for Paul to appear in the Palladium"; then there would be an event "on Easter Sunday in their special nation-wide television show." The latter "is one of the most important events in their entertainment world," carrying a "whopping fee" and "an amazing list of sponsors." In eager expectancy, "they have already put up huge advertisements all over London . . . ."[123]

9

Triumph—and Tragedy

The Robeson case had become a symbol and focal point of widespread British resentment against their former North American colony, at a time when Washington was in the process of supplanting the Empire in London's former colonies. Few Britons would have disagreed with the opinion of Louis Burnham, who worked alongside Robeson at "Freedom." "It is one of the shameful consequences of the Cold War that the American most honored abroad is most cruelly persecuted at home," he said, referring to his co-worker.[1] Robeson's uplifting message that "after all there is but one race—humanity" sounded dangerously subversive in his homeland though when he shared this thought with the BBC in 1960, it elicited neither groans nor skeptically raised eyebrows.[2] The U.S. was simply too conservative for a cosmopolitan like Robeson. "During the 8 years when Paul was denied the right to travel," said Eslanda Robeson, "he received many letters of sympathy and concern from all parts of the world, particularly from Britain and the Soviet Union."[3]

Unsurprisingly, these were the two nations to which the Robesons travelled as soon as the opportunity arose. However, he arrived in London first since, he said, "as a city it's one of the dearest and closest to me. I find it warm and comforting, like a person. And I feel it knows me too . . . ."[4] According to the well-regarded Guyanese conductor and journalist Rudolph Dunbar, then residing in London, this latter perception was wholly and reciprocally accurate. "Your prestige" here, he said, "has surmounted considerably and the great multitude of your followers has increased ten fold"—this is "without exaggeration," he emphasized. "What is most gratifying is that you have some of the most powerful organizations as well as, some of the most prominent people who [are] carrying on a relentless battle on your behalf. The reception that awaits you in the United Kingdom is something that would be etched on the memory forever. . . ."[5]

Thus, it was on 11 July 1958 that a crowd of British and African friends, including numerous dignitaries and celebrities, welcomed the Robesons as they stepped off a plane in London. Their intent was to make their base there, unwilling to get trapped in the U.S. again with all of the unfavorable consequences. The next day he was mobbed by crowds who spotted him in Trafalgar Square and on the Thames embankment. Two days later, some of these dignitaries and celebrities—including Claire Bloom, Simone Signoret, Lady Bliss, Kenneth Tynan, and Cheddi Jagan—held a formal reception welcoming him. That day was capped off when he dined with the Indian High Commissioner in London, an emblem of that nation's support, which along with Britain and the Soviet Union distinguished itself in backing his now successful case. Two days after that he was a guest of Viscount Stansgate at the House of Lords. Then he began rehearsing for the first of three half-hour television concerts for which he was being paid a record fee.[6] Tony Benn of the Labour left, was one of Robeson's most enthusiastic greeters.[7]

He had visited Britain briefly in 1947, performing before hundreds of thousands, but this was to be his first extended stay since 1939. He also brought a bracing message for London, then adjusting awkwardly to an influx from its former colonies in Africa and the Caribbean: "Whoever treats my people as equal to all other peoples, is my comrade," he maintained, and "who does not—is my enemy."[8]

Weeks later he was in Wales, where he was the official guest of honor for their most beloved event, the Eisteddfod of the Festival of Song, where he received a terrific welcome. The audience, 9,000 strong, joined him in singing the chorus of "John Brown's Body".[9] The miners there were the moving force in this boisterous welcome of those who had yet to forget "Proud Valley." These miners had sponsored the first transatlantic concert by telephone sung by Robeson from a New York studio to St. Pancras Town Hall in London.[10] "How they welcomed me into their homes," enthused Robeson about the Welsh—it was a sight to see.[11]

"Back in the twenties," Robeson recalled, "I was . . . building a career. I went to South Wales to sing and the Welsh miners took me to their hearts. I went again and again and once I carried a banner in their unemployed march. That was the turning point in my life, around 1930. For the first time I had white people who made me a true friend."[12] Robeson's attraction to Wales was not new. The Welshman, R.R. Roberts was on a ship to Britain that also had Robeson as a passenger. It was July 1922 and Roberts was en route to Wales, along with about two dozen of his compatriots, all with a fondness for song. They sang for an hour or more which drew a sizeable crowd and the following morning he encountered Robeson and asked him to join that evening. "You came with a roll of music in your arms," he said of Robeson years later; the "crowd was larger than night, the emotion was high and it must have influenced you as you were in great form and you entertained us for an hour. The next night you came again" and performed again, earning Robeson his first—among many—Welsh fans.[13]

The celebration intensified when he landed in Moscow in mid-August 1958. There he was besieged by Russian admirers, including a crew of U.S. Negroes in exile.[14] The FBI was impressed with his frenzied reception in the Soviet Union. "Besides heavy police guard, the army had to be mobilized to protect [Ms. Robeson] and Paul. When he sang at the Sports Palace, there were 60,000 persons inside and 60,000 more standing outside. [Ms. Robeson] said that she met and spoke to Khrushchev and his wife . . . ." The plan was for Robeson to be involved in "making 2 movie pictures in the Soviet Union, one will be his own life story, the other one a travel picture."[15]

When Robeson performed in St. Paul's Cathedral in London for his "people," a benefit for the anti-apartheid cause in this instance, the crowd overflowed. Every seat was occupied, 4,000 all told, when ordinarily there would be about 400 at the late Sunday service. Sizeable sums were raised for the defense in the so-called treason trial. Here in previous centuries John Wycliff had been tried for heresy and Bishop Tyndal's New Testament was burned publicly—but now a righteous cause was celebrated by Robeson.[16] Then the Robesons adopted a manic travel schedule, using London as a base and traveling across the continent repeatedly, a punishing regimen that may have not have been the best prescription for his deteriorating health[17]— and probably hastened his demise. Yet there were simply too many important demands on his time, not only performing to replenish his depleted bank account after eight years of de facto house arrest, but conferring with notables. One of these was Nnamdi Azikiwe, founding father of soon-to-be independent Nigeria who referred to Robeson as "my dear hero" and wanted to spend time with him,[18] a request hard to refuse. That was in August 1958 when Robeson was just settling in London but by 1960, Azikiwe requested his presence at "my inauguration on November 16, 1960" as "Governor-General and Commander-in-Chief". He offered to subsidize his "costs of air transport and accommodations."[19]

Even the U.S. emissary in Lagos realized that "Nigerians have been more interested in Paul Robeson's visit to England because many Nigerians studying in the U.K. in the thirties [recall] Mr. Robeson during his sojourn" there. Upon encountering Nigerian hero Hogan Bassey, Robeson opined that his own origins could be traced to the "Efik tribe of Calabar which produced" this international boxing champion. This was followed by a series of letters to the local press in Lagos all advocating collection of funds there to finance a Robeson visit.[20]

Robeson had a natural advantage in London and not just because of his ties stretching back decades. By 1958, Claudia Jones, a former leader of the U.S. Communist Party, of African and Trinidadian origin, had been deported and was residing in London. She initiated the *West Indian Gazette* and during this period became a beacon welcoming thousands of migrants to London from Britain's former colonies in the Caribbean and Africa. It was her paper that feted the Robesons formally and publicly at a festive event: because of Jones' efforts, the couple was greeted by famed percussionists from Ghana.[21]

The rousing welcome accorded Robeson did not escape the attention of the FBI dragnet. After it became evident that Robeson planned to establish London as his residence, a debate erupted at the highest level of the agency as to whether his status as a "Key Figure," should be revised in light of his domicile beyond Washington's ostensible jurisdictional reach. Being a "Key Figure" also meant holding a status that would allow for detention in case of national emergency; but since he would not be in the U.S., it might seem rational to change this. However, FBI Director, J. Edgar Hoover,

objected, because of Robeson's "importance and potential danger-
ousness from an internal security standpoint"; this would "require
his immediate apprehension in the event of an emergency"—perhaps
defiling Britain's borders in the process.[22]

Also contributing handsomely to the Robesons' enhanced income
was the publication of his memoir, *Here I Stand*. Notorious for his
reluctance to put pen to paper—"Paul just doesn't write if he can avoid
it," was the somber conclusion of his wife[23]—this made the success of
this slender memoir all the more remarkable. As his spouse's comment
suggested, though he spoke in strong political terms in these pages
and alluded to how his upbringing shaped him, this book was not
sufficiently lengthy to provide profound revelation about his life.
Still, quite typically it was embraced heartily by African-Americans
and overseas audiences. Dizzy Gillespie, the famed jazz trumpeter,
was among those who exhorted, "now that is one book [that] all
of you really ought to read." The U.S. Negro press was rhapsodic,
notably the *Baltimore Afro-American*,[24] which serialized it, followed
closely by the *Pittsburgh Courier*.[25] The only discouraging word from
the Negro press came from the organ of the NAACP.[26] (Intriguingly,
it was in 1958 that the FBI was "determining if [Robeson] had enough
political following to attempt to take over the NAACP on a national
scale.")[27] Yet, stressed Robeson's good friend Lloyd Brown, "no white
commercial newspaper or magazine in the entire country, so much
as mentioned Robeson's book," an astonishing comedown for the
man only viewed recently as the world's most famous Negro. Yet,
the London *Times* proclaimed that the book "commands attention
because he is a great artist"[28] and the Japanese edition received
widespread attention; ditto in India.[29] The reception in Japan was so
overwhelming that—like Nigerians—this island state too demanded
a Robeson visit.[30] The first printing of this book, which is still in print
in subsequent editions, was a healthy 8,000 in paperback and 2,000
in cloth, with the second printing raised to 9,500 and 500. As of 31
May 1958, a respectable $6,071.08 in "cash on hand" was available as
a result of this book's publication.[31]

After being barred from the stage for eight years, there was concern
among some of his most avid supporters that his skill in this arena
had deteriorated too. He wondered if he had the experience, style

and accent to play Gower in *Pericles* adequately on stage surrounded by actors better steeped in Shakespeare. Even his signature role as Othello gave him pause—according to his wife. It was only after "great soul searching" that he returned to this role since the character was a "foreigner, dark, different from the rest of the cast and it was a foreign-ness which he thoroughly understood and actually *was*"³² [emphasis original]. Nevertheless, Robeson—now a graybeard—had to die his chin whiskers in order to better accommodate this role,³³ which did little to stem an avalanche of positive reviews.³⁴

Then there were the roadblocks to his successful return to the stage that eluded his attention. Laurence Olivier, considered as Britain's finest actor, told a Robeson confidante, "it is possible that I might wish to play 'Othello' myself within the next two or three years and so I cannot be entirely unprejudiced in the matter or say with exactitude whether it is this that makes the idea of inviting Mr. Robeson to do the same not very attractive to me . . . ." With haughtiness unbound, he concluded, "Mr. Robeson has played the part in London and he has also played the part in New York. In neither event, I believe, was he thought to be supremely successful . . . ."³⁵

This pinched view hardly represented the British consensus. July 1959 provided a typical cross-section of Robeson's schedule, which proved to be too busy for his own good: after performing in *Othello*, it was off to the BBC for a series of interviews, then travel to Paris, then back to the BBC, then back to *Othello*.³⁶

The predictable occurred: Ms. Robeson informed George Bernard Shaw of "bad news. The doctors are still tracing Paul's dizziness and so far, are not at all satisfied with his heart condition"; the prescription was for Robeson to "avoid all sudden movements"—not ideal advice for a stage actor—"and he must avoid all strain of any kind . . . ." Robeson conceded that if he made a "sudden turn on the stage," he "might fall down . . . ." As if this were not bad enough, cancer had been found in Ms. Robeson's increasingly frail body.³⁷

This was a time for more sober reflection on Robeson's part, which was suggested when he told a reporter that when he "quit the concert stage because of politics,"³⁸ a reaction to the persistent pestilence of Jim Crow seating that had to be navigated, this may have been unwise in that it possibly hampered his mass appeal. This was an understandable reaction on his part but also served to illustrate the fiendishly difficult dilemmas he faced.

Seemingly with intentionality, Robeson embarked upon a series of interviews with the British press, providing something of a swansong as he sensed the end was near. The U.S. Consul General in Edinburgh took note of the lengthy interview he provided to the *Sunday Post*. "A lot of my spare time is spent studying music and languages," he said, making suspect instantaneously the idea that he was a wild-eyed subversive deserving house arrest. "I like to go to theatres and picture houses. If there's a good football match within reach, I'll be there," which contrasted sharply with his assertion, "I don't like to take too much exercise . . . ." What made this lengthy interview with Robeson so startling was that it would have been difficult for it to appear in a U.S. journal and, if so, the colloquy would have been a wearisome litany focused on whether he was a card-carrying Communist and did he have the appropriate hatred for Moscow.

But in Edinburgh he was asked if he was a "trained singer" to which he responded, "I've had a lot of instruction and have thrown most of it away. I've developed my singing by quite unorthodox methods. I look at singing as an extension of poetic speech and concentrate on trying to get the spirit of a song . . . ." He was asked, "what singer do you admire most?" and he responded instantly, "Chaliapin". And "the most outstanding book you've ever read?" The "poems of Alexander Pushkin—the Shakespeare of Russia. The words of Robbie Burns come a close second." As for music, he appreciated "especially Duke Ellington and Count Basie," for collecting their—and others'— records was his principal hobby. "I've got thousands of many kinds from many nations." What about friends in Scotland? "Loads. Two particular ones are Sir Patrick Dollan and Mr. Abe Moffat." There he was asked about his church rather than party membership. "Yes. I'm a member of the African Methodist Episcopal [Zion] Church". Instead of being asked about baying mobs tormenting him, he was asked about the "several hundred fan letters" he got "every week." He affirmed by now what had become rote: "Britain and the Soviet Union are the two [nations] in which I've been happiest because the people [there] have been kindest to me," with not so much as a perfunctory nod to his homeland.[39] Instead, when visiting Australia in November 1960, he informed an inquisitive journalist, "I won't go back to America—in case they take my passport."⁴⁰

It seemed that Robeson had not shed his special relationship to Scotland for he turned to newspapers there to unburden himself and ingratiate himself with the British generally. "I'm very pro-Scottish," he confessed, "but don't let them draft me into your nationalist movement here!" The *Edinburgh Evening Dispatch* in November 1958 was told further by him, "I don't pay much attention to clothes" and for those who saw an anti-clerical bent in him, he reminded, "I read the 'Christian Science Monitor' all the time," which was a "fine paper." "Some of the finest and warmest people I know are Christian Scientists," not least since "they're very liberal with racial matters." Unlike his son, who was a chess aficionado, Robeson "tried it for a while but it's like golf. Unless you're very good at it, it can be so discouraging."⁴¹ However, he said, "if you left me to it, I should study languages, their formation and relation to the peoples for year after year. Singing is a pleasure, but more of a hobby."⁴² Unlike their U.S. peers, the British press seemed willing to accept Robeson's admonition that "in my politics, I am a bit left of the British Labour Party."⁴³

Though this interview confirmed indelibly the special place held by Britain and Russia in Robeson's heart, the State Department seemed to think that it was independent India that merited most of their worry, perhaps because of the artist's close ties to the Prime Minister, which stretched back decades. By December 1958, the U.S. authorities had heard that he was planning a trip there. "This matter is important," it was proclaimed: "serious consideration should be given to counter-acting this." The matter was so important that the man designated as U.S. Secretary of State, Christian Herter, got involved. Val Washington "who is himself a Negro," the State Department was told, "had a long talk" with "Mr. P. Clark Ravatty who is a U.N. Delegate from India and also Permanent Secretary of the Congress Party" and was reported to be "very disturbed because [Robeson] is going to India in January or February and there is great stress being laid by the Communists to acclaim him as the greatest and most important Negro leader in the United States." Further, "Mr. Ravarty thinks they will do great damage among the darker Indians if Robeson gets away with the kind of propaganda he wants . . . ." This was all part of a Communist plot "to attract the darker races of the world . . . ."⁴⁴

There was reason to fret since the celebrations marking his sixtieth birthday in India "received considerable favorable publicity," a process aided immeasurably by the "blessing of Prime Minister Nehru" and the high-level role played by other prominent figures. Anticipating a trip that did not occur, the U.S. authorities mobilized to vaccinate India by constructing a wholesome picture of the desperate plight of U.S. Negroes. Therein one espies how revolutionaries like Robeson were influential even at a time when it was thought their direct impact was negligible; for the U.S. felt compelled to paint a positive portrait then move to reduce the gap between image and reality.

"Our efforts to counteract the visit must be handled very discreetly and carefully, since public knowledge in India of attempts by the United States Government to discredit Robeson"—their riveting goal—"would merely give added publicity to the visit, would not be well received by the Indian public and might embarrass the Government of India . . . ."⁴⁵ Such was the conclusion of U.S. officialdom.

But they did not stop there, as they expended untold taxpayer dollars and labor on a visit that did not occur. Consideration of an official U.S. government denunciation of the proposed Robeson trip was shelved since it "would make the situation worse." Instead they flooded Indian journalists with propaganda attesting to the well-being of U.S. Negroes then withering under the cruel lash of Jim Crow. Also, to counter Robeson the idea was concocted of dispatching other "famous Negroes" to India on junkets, including "jazz artists." Though supposedly freedom of the press was a hallmark of the U.S., the ambassador in Delhi had persuaded "American correspondents" there "not to publicize" the high-level endorsements of Robeson's birthday celebrations.⁴⁶

In short, the widespread appeal Robeson exhibited in 1958 was indicative of why the U.S. authorities were so reluctant to grant him the right to travel. He was able to bolster his income, garnering about £20,000 in Britain during a four-month period.⁴⁷ Yet the complexity of Robeson's life was exposed when it turned out that even good news potentially held the seeds of disaster. It was a "complicated job,"

Ms. Robeson was informed, to prepare his tax return to pass muster with the ever vigilant Internal Revenue Service, reflexively willing to bring criminal charges of tax evasion against him.[48] It would be "calamitous," said Robert Rockmore, "if Paul were considered to be a resident of England for the fiscal year of 1958/1959," since his "American income would then be considered as income in England and all of this would be on top of the fact that his American income . . . would be taxed in full in America without credit."[49]

It seemed that Robeson in order to elude draconian tax consequences could not simply reside comfortably in London, shedding light on his maniacal traveling during the 1958–59 period with resultant unfavorable health consequences: coincidentally or not, even by travelling Robeson was not able to evade the long arm of Uncle Sam.[50] Ritualistically, Robeson was dragged into U.S. Tax Court in 1959 but was able to escape relatively unscathed, though showing an adjusted gross income that year of $26,912.09.[51]

Enhanced income accompanied declining health. Thus, by early 1959 both Robesons were hospitalized in Moscow. He had what was described as a "terrific deep chest cold" and she was already displaying signs of the cancer that was to claim her life a few years later.

Before this collapse there were intimations of trouble, even in the elegant flat at 45 Connaught Square, the Robeson residence in the fashionable London neighborhood near Hyde Park. There were five ample rooms, carpeted wall to wall, with bookshelves everywhere groaning under the weight of old and new volumes: the centerpiece was a beautiful baby grand piano. There was a bed, seven feet long. There was work space for Ms. Robeson too, for her career as a journalist had taken off with emerging Africa as her central beat.[52] Still, the signs of normalcy and flourishing were not false, though this hardly conveyed the entire story of their existence.

Robeson's attorney expressed concern about the "long grind of 'Othello'" and the concomitant need for "the couple of weeks of relaxation" that followed. "I completely agree with you," said Robert Rockmore, "that the end of 'Othello' is a kind of period in a segment of your life's work. The height that you achieved in this production of 'Othello' is one that somebody else can shoot at but not you," since there is "no sense in competing with yourself . . . ." "You proved that you would even go into the theatre and show the professionals who made it their life work, that you could surpass all of them . . . ." It was now well understood that Robeson "could always [do] 'Othello' in the West End and pick up a lot of money. I wanted to guard against" this move, said Rockmore, warning him that because of his complex tax standing "it is extremely difficult to accumulate any money . . . ." Do not forget, he said, "each appearance drains a certain amount of energy out of you," meaning "it is not worth it . . . ."[53]

But Robeson found it difficult after years of ugly entrapment in the U.S. to turn aside loving audiences that longed to see him abroad. Moreover, the Robesons had not displayed a deftness in managing money, leaving them susceptible to seemingly attractive overtures. To be fair, even his attorney did not seem to recognize that the Robesons felt compelled to subsidize the less fortunate on the left, such as the family of their comrade Louis Burnham, left bereft after his premature passing.[54] After his income dropped vertiginously during the Red Scare, Robeson realized that "I had to live simply. I still do"—the problem was his penchant for supporting worthy causes.[55] Rockmore had a differing approach: "I have a theory that if you have too much money to your credit, either you or those around you will tend to indifferently expend it," whereas "my personal idea is the old Emersonian one, which is that not only should one plan to arrive at the destination of his voyage but to enjoy oneself on the way over."[56]

Before Rockmore's concern was expressed, Robeson was headed to Moscow; "the trip takes less than 4 hours," said his spouse; "they will meet me at the other end with an ambulance." She too was in bad shape, displaying early signs of the cancer that would ultimately claim her life: "Paul thinks I can make it," though "I am making slow progress but am still struggling with pain . . . ." Even those close to the Robesons were forced into punishing exertion. The "Australian impresario," said Ms. Robeson, arranging his tour Down Under, was worried that Robeson's passport would not be renewed, compelling him to jet from the island continent to Washington to explain personally: "that this was the biggest event in Australian Concert history, that the people had waited more than 20 years to hear Paul sing" and "bitter disappointment and resentment" would ensue if this trip was blocked because of a bureaucratic hitch over a passport.[57] However, the State Department had their own concerns: Robeson had visited Hungary, contrary to U.S. regulations; did that mean he would also visit China, also in contravention of U.S. regulations?[58] And if so, did he really merit a passport?

Rockmore then heard that Robeson was inclined to visit Africa, much of which was still under colonial control, with his stepping foot on the continent seen as a provocation. It "will be interpreted by our State Department as a calculated, political move," he advised.[59] Then Rockmore worried that Robeson was headed to the equally explosive "West Indies."[60]

At the same time Robeson's current tour was "nowhere as good as his first tour," financially and, said his promoter, "there is not too much money in Paul's account. His expenses for him and Essie over the past year have been rather enormous, because at Stratford-on-Avon he only receives [£60] a week and they have had to keep two homes going—one in Stratford and one in London"; as such there was "only roughly about [£1,500] in the account."[61]

By the spring of 1960, despite his peripatetic travel in Europe, Robeson was not only battling a persistent cold but Rockmore "had to lend Paul's account" a considerable amount for tax payments; then in "true Robesonian style," he added churlishly, the promoter "[Harold] Davison has been without funds for the moment,"[62] hampering the artist's ability make up the shortfall. Rockmore continued to carp about "the indifferent spending by both Essie and Paul without regard to the consequences," leading to "the old pattern" moving to "re-assert itself," meaning "his earnings will be frittered away in all kinds of directions including social and perhaps political trips . . . ."[63]

By May 1960, Rockmore was sounding a raucous alarm: "we are in a lot of trouble at the moment. The [U.K.] Home Office won't extend his work permit until his passport is renewed," which was now in doubt. Attached were a list of expenses, including "valet" and "hearing aid" for Robeson but he could have added the fine suits he felt compelled to wear during concerts.[64] The promoter Davison also found the Robesons to be in a "very difficult position," which would be compounded soon since "both he and Essie will probably be going to Ghana shortly, which means he will obviously need more money."[65]

The Robeson passport row was becoming an irritant in bilateral Washington–Moscow relations. It was in late 1959 that Soviet leader Nikita Khrushchev told U.S. journalists that "our people and a great many other people in the world like the great singer, Paul Robeson. Yet for 5 or 7 years I believe the American government would not permit him to tour any other country to sing there," which meant his "voice" was "jammed. A world famous voice" at that. "Well," he concluded triumphantly, "we jam the voice with which some of you want to speak to our people," referring to Moscow's derailing of U.S. propaganda broadcasts to the Soviet Union.[66]

By the summer of 1960 Rockmore was becoming almost hysterical, claiming that the "net result" of the Robesons moving to Europe was they were earning "tremendous sums of money," while "working extremely hard"—yet with "no money saved." Again, he warned the couple to "have some awareness of the consequences of free and extravagant spending of money . . . ." Why, for example, did they continue to maintain a residence in Harlem which they now hardly visited[67]and was mostly used by the impecunious Communist Ben Davis as a part-time residence? "Why the light bill is so much I can't imagine," said Davis since "I'm over there once or twice a week, play the radio occasionally and the TV only once since I had the key."[68]

A few months later, Robeson's daughter-in-law, Marilyn Robeson, was sorting through mail at the Harlem residence and found checks yet to be cashed that had been gathering dust.[69] Foreign licensees were then in the process of releasing Robeson recordings in Brazil, Colombia, Argentina, Japan, Israel—and throughout Europe—which helps to explain the difficulty of keeping up with the inflow of checks.[70]

The prospects for stanching this flow were not good since Israel was clamoring for a Robeson visit,[71] a rapidly radicalizing Cuba was doing the same, while word was that Robeson was "making plans for an extended tour to Africa,"[72] which even by December 1960 would not be welcome by Washington's European allies. The FBI was informed that it would be like a "national holiday" when "[Robeson] appears in Cuba." Ben Davis was cited for the proposition that Robeson "would be the personal guest of Fidel Castro in Cuba."[73]

A similar rapturous welcome was promised for the former British Guiana where their leader, Cheddi Jagan, told him, "when I first met you at Stratford-on-Avon I suggested that it will be a good idea if you visited" the region.[74] Further south, in Brazil, the FBI found that plans for a Robeson visit were accelerating.[75] Not waiting for a visit, hundreds gathered in Port-au-Prince, Haiti to salute Robeson. A U.S. agent present, noted that the audience was "equally divided between Negroes and Mulattoes," all listening to "playing of recorded songs" by Robeson; there was "circulation of a petition" backing him, as "speakers attempted to outdo one another in attacks on the United States."[76]

In Mexico, the exiled African-American sculptress Elizabeth Catlett reported that Robeson's popularity continued unabated: "when we celebrated your sixtieth birthday here, the National University of Mexico taped all your recorded songs we could collect."[77]

Gavin Greenlee, an Australia journalist toiling in China, from 1959–61, told Robeson that the "people of China are always looking forward to the day when you will be able to visit them. Your records always sell out in the Chinese music stores as soon as they arrive. I have seen groups of boys and girls sitting in the Wai wen Shudian music store in Wan Fu-Ching, Peking, mostly students and lovers of Western music of whom there are many in the Chinese People's Republic today enraptured as they listened to your recorded voice." Naturally, Robeson's rendition of the Chinese classic, "The March of the Volunteers", the National Anthem of the post-1949 regime, which he sang in Chinese, was a favorite of this audience.[78]

Yet India continued to be a locus of pro-Robeson sentiment, as evidenced by the continuing warm greetings he continued to receive from Nehru in Delhi.[79] The FBI took note of an editorial from the *New York Mirror* that asserted that Nehru was "whooping it up for American singer [Robeson's]" birthday.[80] "The people of India are eagerly awaiting his arrival" said K.P.S. Menon of the Indian Embassy in Moscow, speaking of Robeson.[81] E. Tomlin Baley, Director of the State Department's Office of Security observed sourly that in India, Robeson was "looked upon as the symbol of human aspiration and of the dignity of man"; it was conceded however that the "original inspiration" for global celebrations of his birthday came from Britain where there are "numerous Paul Robeson Committees . . . ."[82]

Though Robeson had stood with Moscow in its late-1940s dispute with Yugoslavia,[83] by 1958 all had been forgotten as Belgrade—it was said with emphasis—"definitely wants a tape suitable to use on their radio."[84]

Prying Robeson out of London would not be easy as he was becoming a fixture within left-wing circles. Colin Sweet of the British Peace Committee recalled fondly how Robeson had sung at a massive Trafalgar Square "March for Life" in July 1959 and again in 1960 and again in 1961 at the St. Pancras Town Hall, all the while bolstering what was to become one of the primary expressions of radical and anti-imperialist sentiment in London.[85]

While his attorney and promoter fretted endlessly about the Robesons' spending, Ms. Robeson expended a similar amount of anxiety in concern about her spouse's health (and her own). She was expecting "massive transfusions of whole blood and that will clean up my anemia some of this weakness and dizziness." Her "pain" had "now reached a new level," i.e. "lower . . . ." "His overweight is a serious problem," she said, meaning "I keep nothing whatever fattening in the house . . . ."[86] By the summer of 1960 he was receiving "gonadotrophin injections every morning," this "on a 500 calorie a day diet." The idea was to release the "abnormally stored fat" and bypass "the essential subcutaneous fat. Hence, he doesn't look gaunt but looks really wonderful. His skin [has] cleared up from all the splotches, his eyes are clear, the bags under them are gone" and his "voice is better. The tires around the middle and lumps of fat around the shoulders are gone, and he likes the way he looks now. He also doesn't waddle when he walks"; the goal was "to lose 40 pounds in 40 days and [he] has already lost 34." Also newsworthy was his passport renewal, which occurred "after much prodding from the Home Office here" in London which in turn "[was] prodded" by the "Australian concert people."[87]

With his health apparently in order, Robeson found time to travel to Paris where he spent time with his brother, Ben, who happened to be visiting then. He also found time to sing for the Nigerian independence celebration over the BBC. His success in dieting meant obtaining new suits, delivering mixed feelings to Ms. Robeson. "Tall, dark and handsome and slim too, as a fan said the other day! Of course it was a woman!!"[88]

Robeson was much more convivial, conversational and gregarious in dealing with the British press in a manner that he found hard to duplicate in his homeland, where reporters were fixated—and obsessed—on the singular issue of whether he was a member of the U.S. Communist Party, which dictated an approach to him that Robeson found odious. The more relaxed attitude toward Robeson was also characteristic of the BBC, which made the artist a fixture on their airwaves, leading to a series of revelatory interviews, allowing British audiences to see a side of him generally obscured in the U.S. He even appeared on BBC radio's *Desert Island Discs* in December 1958,[89] selecting eight "castaway" discs and his chosen luxury: a "Carved Benin head."

In mid-1960 in a wide-ranging conversation Robeson revealed that "the only love songs I sing about 'he' and 'she' are usually French or Elizabethan. My tenderness in song is in a lullaby for a child." His performance of "Sometimes I Feel like a Motherless Child" was "popular in all parts of the world" but "to the people of Poland it seems to have a special meaning. Maybe [it] suggests Chopin to them," he mused, "and whenever I've sung it over there I've had to repeat it not just once or twice but three or four times."[90]

"One of the things I do in London," he remarked, "usually very early in the morning before people start work, I like to walk through the city. It has the intimacy of a person—more than [any] other city in the world. And the centre of it all is St. Paul's. I wandered in there the other morning and I remembered being there on a Christmas morning some years ago, when the whole city lay deep in snow," to the point that he recalled "when I was a boy I had the idea that London was white with snow at least half the year."[91] By May 1960 he reported to the BBC audience about "singing in towns and cities all over England, Scotland and Wales," and a question that had arisen was "'why haven't you sung in opera?' Sad to say," he admitted, "I do not enjoy opera because I cannot sing a song which has no meaning for me and I cannot sing a song I cannot talk. To me, song is speech," a trend he then illustrated by singing from Handel.[92]

By December 1960 the Robesons had returned from a tumultuous tour of Australia and New Zealand featuring 21 concerts, all of which were packed to the rafters. Audiences had been playing his records and watching his movies for decades and now had the opportunity to see their hero in the flesh. But since these British appendages were now adjusting to a status more dependent upon Washington, there were those who felt they should reflect the official U.S. view of Robeson. He was "much too tired to make the Australian tour," was Ms. Robeson's opinion afterwards; "that's one reason he was so truculent, and quick to anger with the press. He was just bushed."[93] As Ms. Robeson saw it, her husband "became angry, very, very angry and went right on the offensive . . . ." Despite these bumpy encounters focusing on his Communist and Moscow ties they were entertained by New Zealand's Prime Minister in Wellington and greeted officially in parliament. Mayors from Auckland to Sydney welcomed the Robesons officially. Naturally, the Soviet Ambassador travelled from Canberra to Sydney in order to embrace the couple.[94]

Union leaders in Australia embraced Robeson with one analogizing the plight of the U.S. Negro to that of their own indigenous population. Robeson was saluted for not "forsaking principle for pecuniary benefit."[95] While in Sydney Robeson vowed he would return to the continent within six months to campaign for the indigenous because, he said, "You have a serious problem here in Australia."[96] In Brisbane among the 5,000 cheering and applauding was a delegation of union leaders visiting from China, who had been subjected to a violent demonstration earlier in the day.[97] Yet despite the welcome addition to their coffers, Robeson may have been better served by skipping the Australian-New Zealand tour. It was not only because of the exceedingly lengthy travel, no minor matter for a man with his parlous health, but also because what he saw there hardly improved his mood. He was now "angrier than ever," said his spouse in the midst of this journey, "and it makes me shudder, because he is so often angry at the wrong people, and so often unnecessarily angry. But that's Paul," she said, figuratively shrugging her shoulders.[98] In his declining years, Robeson was not keen to engage anti-communists pleasantly, which meant that his encounters in leading capitalist nations at times became unpleasant.

Upon returning from the South Seas, the Robesons got caught up in the ongoing Congo crisis: the attempt by leading North Atlantic nations to destabilize the newly independent regime led by Patrice Lumumba on spurious anticommunist grounds. The forced liquidation of the Council on African Affairs (CAA) a few years earlier at the hands of the U.S. authorities had not quelled their passion for African independence. "We have been both glued to the TV for the news of the Security Council Congo debate," said Ms. Robeson in February 1961. "I think they have unleashed the whirlwind," she asserted, "because no African worth his salt is going to forgive or forget the [Patrice] Lumumba murder. It was brazen assassination . . . ."[99] "If I had been Lumumba," said Robeson, "I would have asked Russia to kick the Belgians out of the Congo."[100] "You should not worry about Congo," Nkrumah assured the couple, since the "steps we have taken show that Ghana is giving every assistance."[101] Ms. Robeson, now an accredited journalist, was embraced by visiting heads of state during the Commonwealth conference in London during that time. "Paul and I spent a marvelous hour with Nkrumah," she asserted, which only served to enhance their fury about the Congo.[102]

But this rollercoaster ride of fury and anger was not the ideal recipe to be followed by a man now in his sixties and in declining health. As so often happened during Robeson's serpentine life and career, just as it seemed that he was at the mountaintop, about to soar from triumph to triumph, fate had another destiny in store for him. Looking back from 1963, Harry Francis of London who, he said, "has been close to Mr. Robeson ever since his return to Britain in 1958," was forced to elaborate on a debilitating series of maladies of his friend that had brought him to his knees. He blamed "the strain imposed upon him first by years of persecution he suffered in the [U.S.] and then by sheer hard work"; for example, "even in 1959 when playing 'Othello' at Stratford, he was already over-taxing himself," in a demanding role that won wide plaudits. "I personally feared that he was due for a crack-up in health before the end of that year." Then in 1960 "he undertook one of the hardest tours of his career in Australia where he found himself in argument, often quite violent, with sections of the Australian press," eager to demonstrate their fealty to the U.S., in the process of replacing the U.K., as a supposed guarantor of the continent's security. "His last public performance in Britain was on 5th March [1961]," but then en route to the Soviet Union he "became ill on the plane" and "entered hospital in Moscow." This led to a zig-zag between London and Moscow, which did little to improve his bearing.[103]

It was also in March 1961 that Robeson's son found his father in the bathroom of his Moscow hotel suite after having—it was said—slashed his wrists with a razor blade. His son asked ominously, "*was this a drug induced suicide attempt?*" [emphasis original], a reasonable suspicion he thought given Washington's "suspicious concern over my father's health beginning in 1955," at the time of his major operations and a moment when Jim Crow was thawing.[104] It is true that those who knew Robeson were taken aback by this turn of events. His passport attorney, Leonard Boudin, after being asked about a "nervous breakdown" of his famous client, replied with a scoff that Robeson was a "perfectly stable human being."[105]

It is also unavoidable that the U.S. authorities after being forced to return his passport did not simply forget about him. It was also in 1961 that Ms. Robeson complained, "I just don't understand why my letters don't reach you, or why they take so long to reach you. I remember at home in New York the Post Office used to send all our mail down to HQ, to be read and censored before they were delivered to us . . . ."[106] By 1961 Robeson had taken the unusual move of becoming a more faithful correspondent, generally not a sign of ennui. "Paul is writing these days," said his spouse; "I supply him with stamps, envelopes, and paper."[107] Still, Robeson's declining health worsened in 1961, a year of intense travel with the advent of a severe and chronic circulatory ailment with unpredictable consequences.[108]

Of course, Ms. Robeson was quite protective—in all senses of the term—of her spouse and what she reported was that he had arrived in Moscow for a two–three weeks' visit and fell "flat on his face with exhaustion and a slight heart attack. Obviously," a major cause was "from trying to do everything, everywhere for years . . . ." Now he was sited in a "gorgeous, luxurious sanatorium just outside Moscow. We have a cottage all to ourselves, with a bedroom for each of us, dining-room with TV, library with radio, sun terraced . . . big foyer

Figure 11   Eslanda Robeson was not only his wife; she was also the person who helped to propel Robeson's career as an artist. She also espoused socialism and, like her husband, was quite close to Communist parties, particularly those in the U.S. and Great Britain. (Daily Worker and Daily World Photographs Collection, Tamiment Library/Robert F. Wagner Labor Archives, New York University, New York City)

and bath . . . everything done for us, food, etc., nursing service and doctors on all 24 hours."[109]

Later, her analysis was supplemented: "it has been a long siege but he beat his brains out what with doing EVERYTHING, EVERYBODY, asked him to EVERYWHERE but he wakes up every morning, with no one to see, no statement to make, no concert to sing, no meeting to attend, etc., and he can't quite believe it"; the collapse, in sum, "was 40 years accumulating . . . "[110] [emphasis original]. Now the chastened couple, like lions in winter, "just sit and relax, walk, breathe, read, play chess, look at TV": she expected this reverie to last just a "month or two . . . ."[111]

This explanation apparently proved to be convincing to W. Alphaeus Hunton, yet another revolutionary African-American driven into exile: to Guinea-Conakary in his case. This former CAA leader, had kept the Robesons abreast of African trends with plenty of condemnations tossed at "French imperialists."[112] As a radio broadcaster, he had considerable access to news reports.[113] Just after the Robeson collapse, Hunton wanted the couple to visit Ghana, where he then resided. There were "quite a few other Afro-Americans here", he said enticingly, and "many of the Ghanaians with whom I talked expressed eagerness to have still more come" since "they continue to believe that all black Americans are ipso facto their brothers"[114] [emphasis original]. Robeson's long-time comrade, W.E.B. Du Bois, was already residing in Ghana then, leading U.S. Communist attorney John Abt to comment with exasperation, "what a commentary on the state of our country that the two finest and most talented of its Negro sons have been forced into voluntary exile!"[115] Writing from Romania where he was receiving medical attention, Du Bois added with acerbity, "America is impossible and I'm fed up . . . ."[116]

The Robesons' residence in London and frequent jaunts to Moscow suggested that they too were "fed up" with the former slaveholding republic. A few months later Du Bois and his spouse were too in London where they resided at the Robesons' flat.[117] A few days after that, Ms. Robeson was conferring with Dr. Martin Luther King, Jr., who was passing through town. "He asked very warmly after Paul and when I said Paul had asked me to give him his warmest welcome to London and best wishes," the human rights leader "seemed very pleased and said he hoped next time he comes to London to sit down and talk with Paul. He is only sorry that Paul is not well."[118]

At that point Robeson was contemplating joining Du Bois in Accra, invited by Nkrumah to be a professor of music and drama at a local university. "The pleasure of hearing the great Paul Robeson here in Ghana" was anticipated gleefully by Nkrumah.[119] The Prime Minister was planning to visit Moscow in May 1961 and informed Ms. Robeson, "I hope that you and Paul will still be there then."[120]

There was a problem, however. "Paul is still very ill," said his spouse in the spring of 1962; "the great trouble with Paul," she added, "is that when he begins to feel better, he goes all out for going here, going there, doing this, doing that"—while "doctors say that only a prolonged rest" will do.[121]

But Robeson was not to be in a position to experience this promised hospitality, since by the summer of 1962 he was in a nursing home in London.[122] The U.S. authorities had not taken note of his deteriorating condition and, instead, continued to besiege him, as if he were still a fire-breathing revolutionary on the frontlines of struggle. To renew his passport, he would have to sign a pledge that he was not a member of the U.S. Communist Party. "Paul himself refuses to sign anything, declares he won't sign anything, no matter what," said his spouse: "as usual very stubborn."[123] Stubborn was the term that could well be used to describe Robeson's unremitting denunciation of U.S. imperialism, even as his passport was up for grabs, as when he told a Budapest journal that Washington was the worst enemy of humankind.[124] Stubborn was also a word that could usefully be employed to describe Ms. Robeson's own counsel that "the Enemy is not Communism, not the Red Danger; it is colonialism, the White Danger."[125]

Fortunately, Robeson had options. His comrade Anna Louise Strong told him that "Ghana or Guinea or China"—the latter nation where she then resided—would provide travel documents if the U.S. remained obstinate.[126] Prime Minister Nkrumah was "sorry to hear about all the trouble that Paul has had with his passport renewal. I have a solution to his problems. Why doesn't he become a citizen of Ghana? I am serious about this."[127]

But by 1963 Robeson was reclusive; "except for one or two" persons, he had retreated into a cocoon. Yet, said his spouse, "we both want very much to come to Africa and to Ghana first" for "this [has] always been our idea and our wish."[128] The Prime Minister's practical solution was overtaken by events for soon Ms. Robeson had expired and her spouse's health deteriorated to the point that he was forced to seek refuge not in Ghana but in his sister's Philadelphia home.

10

Death of a Revolutionary

On 23 December 1965, Eslanda Robeson died at Beth Israel Hospital in Manhattan. She was 69 years old.[1] Weeks earlier she was slowly recovering from what she termed "my own big operation, cancer of the uterus"[2]—but she did not survive. This was a cruel blow inflicted simultaneously on the already tottering fortunes of her surviving spouse. They had relocated to New York earlier because of his nagging health problems which—it was thought—could be better handled while in the loving embrace of his son's family, which included two children. But it seemed that demands on his time were unrelenting to the point that before she expired, Ms. Robeson continued to complain that "Paul was very ill" and "exhausted" after returning from a long journey westward where he "got no rest at all . . . ."[3]

The passing of friends and loved ones had become a metronomic tone of Robeson's life, signaling his own destiny. It was in January of 1965 that Lorraine Hansberry breathed her last breath. Her career as a writer was launched years earlier at Robeson's periodical *Freedom*, which proved to be a springboard for her immensely procreative career as a writer, culminating with her prize-winning play, *A Raisin in the Sun*. Robeson eulogized her at her funeral and the singer Nina Simone performed. Her presence, along with James Forman, a leader of the shock troops then storming the barricades of Jim Crow in Dixie, was indicative of the reality that an emerging younger generation was well aware of Robeson's yeoman service and gargantuan sacrifice that had paved the path for the present.[4]

In September 1964 not long after crossing the Atlantic, he provided the major oration at the funeral of Ben Davis. This was his first public appearance since returning and hundreds of Harlemites turned out to pay their last respects—not just to Davis but, as well, to a kind of radicalism now in retreat. The overflow from the chapel spilled out into the street, blocking traffic. After a brief eulogy, which was piped outside through loudspeakers, Robeson had to make his way slowly through a huge crowd of friendly and sorrowful admirers; "the more he is attacked, the more devotion he seems to arouse in his [Negro] followers," was the opinion of an observer.

It was a thinner and more subdued Robeson that greeted an interviewer shortly after returning to Harlem. It was evident that family had propelled him back to a land that brought him mostly torment. He was proud of the engineering talent of his grandson, David: "I could never do anything mechanical with my hands," he said admiringly. The Robesons had become fans of the city's baseball team. "I watch a lot of [American] football. It's quite different from when I played pro football with Akron." Reminiscing he recalled, "I played against Jim Thorpe as a pro," referring to the heroic Native American athlete, "and man, he was one tough guy." In a nod to his age and health, Robeson had given up smoking.

The political trend that Robeson represented—revolutionary socialism—had been effectively undermined among black America, through a deft administering of bludgeoning of those like himself and anti-Jim Crow concessions. But filling the resultant ideological vacuum was the Nation of Islam, which had arisen in the 1930s when Robeson was then ascendant and did not begin to take off until Robeson appeared to be in eclipse. Now the NOI was proselytizing him in Harlem and he expressed appreciation for their "emphasis on the development of economic power among Negroes, discipline, responsibility and pride." He was also following closely the rush of events in the heart of darkness that was Mississippi.[5]

In this changing era, a Robeson revival was occurring, along with a downgrading—or remonstrating—of those who had rebuked him earlier. Thus, Malcolm X—who symbolized a Negro militancy that was a direct outgrowth from the mature Robeson—reprimanded Jackie Robinson, the baseball star, who had denounced the artist before HUAC. "It was you who let yourself be used by the whites," he charged, "you let them sic you on Paul Robeson . . . you let your white boss send you before a congressional hearing [to] dispute and condemn [Robeson] because he [had] these guilty American whites frightened silly . . . ." Retreating apologetically, Robinson awkwardly asserted, "I would reject such an invitation if offered now . . . I do have increased respect for Paul Robeson, who over a span of twenty years sacrificed himself, his career and the wealth and comfort he once enjoyed because, I believe, he was sincerely trying to help his people."[6] Prominent Negroes now saw little premium in assailing Robeson. When offered the opportunity "to talk you down," Robeson was told in reference to the rising star Harry Belafonte, the offer was refused unequivocally. "He thinks of you as 'Big Daddy'," it was reported.[7]

The responses of Belafonte and Robinson were further evidence—if any were needed—that Robeson was being embraced as the anti-Jim Crow movement deepened and the youth began to realize who had been the precursor of this epochal trend. Foremost among these was James Forman of the Student Non-Violent Coordinating Committee (SNCC) who thought it was an "honor" to be in Robeson's presence adding, "it was a great privilege to be able to tell you how much you mean to all of us."[8] Joan Baez, the songbird and voice of anti-war activism, "loves that man," speaking of Robeson, and "would love to sing for him . . . ."[9] She treasured the "many . . . hours" that "I listened to [your] thunderous and touching voice"; yes, "once every century or so there is a Paul Robeson."[10]

Even the otherwise staid National Urban League, whose budget was heavily dependent upon the largesse of the corporate sector, dubbed Robeson the "Father of the Civil Rights Movement" in providing him with an award.[11] The recently organized Congressional Black Caucus, comprised of African-American members of the U.S. Congress, saw fit to honor Robeson as a trailblazer.[12] Even U.S. Chief Justice Warren Burger, de facto leader of the judicial right-wing, hailed his artistry; he chose to "honor" Robeson and hoped "may all go well with you . . . ."[13] Arthur Ashe, the champion tennis player, termed "Brother Robeson" "an inspiration to 'all of us'" and lamented "'our' lack of courage" which had hampered the flowing of this sentiment.[14] Cesar Chavez, the Mexican-American labor leader too praised Robeson for his "courage."[15]

Of the torrent of messages that gushed into Robeson's mailbox, as it became clear that his life was rapidly expiring, perhaps the most heartfelt came from Congressman Andrew Young, former top aide to Dr. King. "Thank you for your beautiful life," he enthused.

> I heard you as a child and thrilled to the powerful image of Black Manhood you portrayed. You kept alive a legacy of hope through some of the darkest days of our history. But had you not done so in the 30s, 40s and 50s our accomplishments in the 60s would not have been possible and I would not be here in Congress, as the first black man from Georgia in 102 years.[16]

Still, he may have been exceeded in his appreciation by then State Senator—and future Detroit Mayor—Coleman Young who was "honored to call Paul Robeson my friend"; the "freedom struggle initiated by Paul Robeson many years ago might be looked upon as the opening gun in what is now commonly conceded to be the second American Revolution."[17]

However, there was no unanimity greeting Robeson's return to Harlem, with one columnist claiming she had received "hundreds of letters protesting" the return of this prodigal son.[18] David Susskind, who profited handsomely from the filmed version of *A Raisin in the Sun*, which he produced—it was penned by Robeson's pupil, Lorraine Hanberry—was insulted when asked "to participate in a Salute to Paul Robeson," commenting with contempt, "you must be joking—and what a bad joke it is."[19]

Still, many of this diverse array of supporters came together in April 1965 for a tribute to Robeson, which was a rebuff to those who thought his pro-socialist views should remove him beyond the pale. Instead, gathering to honor him were future Congressman—and present civil rights leader—John Lewis; the heralded writers, James Baldwin and John Oliver Killens; the top-flight musicians, Dizzy Gillespie and Pete Seeger.[20]

Times had changed. As the anti-Jim Crow movement gained strength, it compelled a retreat by reactionary forces, creating an opening for a hearty embrace of Robeson. Malcolm X grew to admire Robeson and sought to confer with him just before his brutal murder in February 1965.[21] Coretta Scott King—Dr. King's widow—continued her late spouse's pattern of saluting Robeson when in 1973 she joined former U.S. Attorney General Ramsey Clark and actor-activist Harry Belafonte in a celebration of Robeson's life.[22] According to her biographer, Ella Baker, who worked shoulder-to-shoulder with Dr. King and inspired the creation of the shock troops of the anti-Jim Crow movement—the Student Non-Violent Coordinating Committee—was a "close ally" of Robeson during his heyday.[23] James Baldwin, the pre-eminent writer and voice of the anti-Jim Crow movement, was a staunch defender of Robeson at a time when this was not universally popular.[24]

Refusing to forget him, 50 parliamentarians from London sent greetings,[25] including Michael Foot and Hugh Jenkins.[26] This was part of what was becoming an annual event, celebrating Robeson's birthday, which also took place in Ghana; "I venture to say," said W.A. Hunton then residing there, "that there were similar radio programs in other African countries . . . ."[27] Given the effusion about Robeson from Presidents Kenneth Kaunda of Zambia[28] and Julius Nyerere of Tanzania,[29] this was fair speculation. Moscow's ambassador in Washington, Anatoly Dobrynin, confirmed that Robeson was "known and loved in our country."[30] Further ratifying the perception that along with Africa, London and Moscow, Delhi was the epicenter of pro-Robeson fervor, Prime Minister Indira Gandhi, acknowledged that "we loved him because, although he was famous and so much in demand, he never said no to any request . . . . I deem it a privilege to be counted among Paul Robeson's friends."[31]

But with the passing of his spouse and the continuing decline of his health, Robeson could envision no option beyond retiring from public life and becoming more reclusive. His birthday continued to be an occasion for global celebration, with the one in London in 1968 being particularly festive, featuring as it did, Dame Peggy Ashcroft, Sir John Gielgud, and the law partner of Mandela and then leader of the African National Congress, Oliver Tambo.[32] Prime Minister Errol Barrow of Barbados proclaimed that it was his "privilege and honour to have known" Robeson for "thirty years."[33] It was Barrow who introduced Robeson to future Jamaican Prime Minister, Michael Manley.[34]

But these worldwide celebrations did not feature the guest of honor. Robeson moved to Philadelphia where he resided with his sister, Marian. Seclusion meant a concomitant fall in income: $5,277.37 in 1965, $8,812 the next year, $8,524.28 by 1967, $6,596.22 by 1968.[35] His mind was alert, as he continued to pay for music lessons at the rate of $8 per hour.[36]

By 1969 even Columbia Law School, pressed by student uprisings, saw fit to honor him. His old friend, Lloyd Brown, visited him during this time and "found him to be more like his old self . . . alert, responsive and affable . . . ." He discussed the "Nigeria-Biafra conflict, the religious conflicts in Belfast" with his usual insight, a reflection of an invigorated reality: "you can say I'm doing pretty good," said Robeson.[37]

That was true then. In 1974 Robeson's son, announced that his father "is now retired completely from public life and his health does not permit him to make public appearances"—but this unfortunate reality had descended years earlier.[38] Weeks earlier, Robeson was featured in the glossy pages of *JET* magazine, now the weekly of record for African-Americans. Recalled poignantly were the words of Benjamin Mays—Dr. King's mentor—when Robeson was awarded an honorary degree by Morehouse College, the Nobel Laureate's alma mater: Robeson, it was said, is "a man who embodies all the hopes and aspirations of the Negro race . . . ." But by this late date Robeson was portrayed as a virtual recluse, huddling in the twelve-room Philadelphia home of his devoted sister, a retired schoolteacher. He was depicted as virtually re-enacting his role as Othello, a man who had done the state some service—particularly during World War II—but was now cast aside cruelly. Yes, said this reporter, "he loved America too well but not wisely."[39]

How true. Though Robeson's relationship with the Soviet Union is often viewed in the U.S. mainstream as the source of his downfall, actually—like many of the U.S. left—he tended to misestimate the mass strength of ultra-conservatism in his homeland which contributed to naïve projections about the pace and prospect of progressive change.

Figure 12 Paul Robeson, Jr. shakes hand with eminent actor, Sidney Poitier, as Mayor Tom Bradley of Los Angeles (center) looks on as Robeson, Sr. receives the honor of being enshrined posthumously on the "Hollywood Walk of Fame." Though hounded during the darkest days of the Red Scare, increasingly Robeson is being viewed—particularly among African-Americans—as a visionary leader who sacrificed tremendously because of his unyielding devotion to the causes of anti-racism, peace and socialism. (Daily Worker and Daily World Photographs Collection, Tamiment Library/Robert F. Wagner Labor Archives, New York University, New York City)

* * *

In early January 1976 Robeson seemed to be in fine fettle despite the weight of an accumulation of various maladies and ailments. It was during this month at his sister's home in Philadelphia that he descended the stairs for dinner, dressed quite typically for that time in a suit and tie. But shortly thereafter he suffered a series of strokes and was taken to the hospital. On the morning of 23 January 1976 his son was in the train station in Manhattan on his way to see his father in Philadelphia when he heard a radio bulletin announcing that Paul Robeson had expired early that morning.[40]

Despite years of inactivity—forced and otherwise—he left an ample estate of $150,000 to his son.[41] Unsurprisingly, his funeral in Harlem was attended by a crowd that was overwhelmingly African-American. They—more than most—were aware of the sacrifice he had made on their behalf. The leader of the local branch of the NAACP said there was "deep anguish" afflicting "members" as a result of his death.[42] Wallace D. Muhammad, son of Elijah Muhammad, patron saint of the now ascending group known as the Nation of Islam, offered "our sincere condolences" to the Robeson family.[43]

Such sincere expressions from diverse sources were evidentiary of the unavoidable fact that Robeson had managed a difficult feat: at once, he was considered both a partisan of the most degraded sector of humanity—Africans—while being an advocate of a working-class internationalism that embodied universality.

Nevertheless, in certain circles the perception persists that Robeson's extolling of a largely disappeared socialist camp has been discrediting to his legacy. Yet, those who hold dear the victory over fascism do not as a rule argue that because this would not have occurred but for the collaboration with the Soviet Union, the triumph over Nazism is somehow discredited. In other words, the leaders of the capitalist bloc who presided over Jim Crow lynching and colonial terror have more leeway in saving their skins than do their victims. Moreover, if Stalin discredited socialism for all time, why didn't the African Slave Trade discredit capitalism for all time? This kind of apartheid thinking cannot—and should not—stand. Paul Robeson was sufficiently perspicacious and courageous to recognize that it required an international movement to save the world from fascism, colonialism—and Jim Crow. This multi-lingual descendant of enslaved Africans, whose dedicated study of languages was designed in part to illustrate the essential unity of humankind, continues to symbolize the still reigning slogan of the current century: "workers of the world, unite!"

Notes

Unless indicated otherwise, all citations to the *Paul Robeson Papers* and *Eslanda Robeson Papers* are from the collection held at Howard University, Washington, D.C. All citations referring to boxes are likewise from the *Paul Robeson Papers*, unless otherwise indicated.

Chapter 1

1. *Daily Worker* [New York], 13 April 1952. See also *The Worker* [U.S.], 5 January 1964: "Who can forget the cable dispatches which told how Africans on the march to freedom marched to the sounds of his golden voice," appropriate for a figure who "is of the stature of Frederick Douglass," the noted abolitionist.
2. *Jet* [Chicago], 16 April 1949.
3. *Freedom* [New York], July 1952.
4. Howard Fast, *Peekskill, USA*, New York: CRC, 1951, University of Texas-Austin.
5. *New Frontiers*, 4 (Winter 1955): 16, Box 31, *Paul Robeson Papers*.
6. Eslanda Robeson to Editor, 16 September 1957, Box 3, *Eslanda Robeson Papers*.
7. Pablo Neruda to Robeson, 15 September 1959, Box MB-PE Correspondence.
8. *The Worker*, 5 June 1968.
9. *TIME*, 1 November 1943.
10. *The Worker*, 5 January 1964.
11. Letter from Linus Pauling, 25 March 1973, Box 8.
12. *New Statesman*, 21 March 1936.
13. Coretta Scott King to Paul Robeson, Jr., 27 January 1976, Box 11.
14. Comment, *Race Today*, 16 (Number 4, 1983): 221–2.
15. *Daily Worker*, 17 April 1944.
16. Article, "The American," 137 (Number 5, May 1944): 28–9, 142–4, Box 22.
17. William Speer to Robeson, 24 September 1972, Box SF-WAL Correspondence.
18. *Edinburgh Evening Post*, 14 November 1958.

19. Quoted in Paul Robeson, *Here I Stand*, Boston: Beacon Press, 1988, xxvi.

20. Gerald Horne, *Negro Comrades of the Crown: African Americans and the British Empire Fight the U.S. Before Emancipation*, New York: New York University Press, 2013, 231.

21. Sergei N. Durylin, *Ira Aldridge*, Trenton: Africa World Press, 2014, 50, 25.

22. Robeson Remarks, December 1963, Box 21.

23. *New Zealand Herald*, 18 November 1960.

24. *Melbourne Age*, 16 November 1960.

25. Quoted in Jordan Goodman, *Paul Robeson: A Watched Man*, New York: Verso, 2013, 114.

26. Gerald Horne, *Black Revolutionary: William Patterson and the Globalization of the African-American Freedom Struggle*, Urbana: University of Illinois Press, 2013.

27. William Patterson to Paul Robeson, Jr., 10 February 1976, Box 11.

28. Doris Lessing, *Walking in the Shade: Volume Two of My Autobiography, 1949–1962*, New York: HarperCollins, 1997, 144, 167.

29. Pete Seeger to Paul Robeson, no date, circa 1965, Box PF-SE Correspondence.

30. Claude McKay to Eslanda Robeson, no date, Box KB-MA Correspondence.

31. *Christchurch Star*, 24 October 1960.

32. Ron Ramdin, *Paul Robeson: The Man and His Mission*, London: Owen, 1987, 38, 57.

33. Ibid.; Marie Seton, *Paul Robeson*, London: Dobson, 1958, 47.

34. *Guardian* [Melbourne], 1960, Box 34.

35. Diary, 22 October 1931, Box 16, *Eslanda Robeson Papers*.

36. See Gerald Horne, *The End of Empires: African Americans and India*, Philadelphia: Temple University Press, 2008.

37. Ben Davis on Robeson, *Daily Worker*, 10 May 1936 in Philip S. Foner, ed., *Paul Robeson Speaks: Writings, Speeches, Interviews, 1918–1974*, New York: Brunner, Mazel, 1974, 105–109, 105. See also Emile Burns, *Handbook of Marxism*, New York: International, 1935.

38. Lindsay Swindall, *Paul Robeson: A Life of Activism and Art*, Lanham, Maryland: Rowman & Littlefield, 2013, 81.

39. Panchanan Saham, *Rajani Palme Dutt: A Biography*, Kolkata: Biswabiksha, 2004; R. Palme Dutt, *Fascism and Social Revolution: A Study of the Economics and Politics of the Extreme Stages of Capitalism in Decay*, New York: International, 1935.

40. *People's Voice*, 30 August 1947.

41. Timothy Shenk, *Maurice Dobb: Political Economist*, New York: Palgrave, 2013; Maurice Dobb, *Studies in the Development of Capitalism*, New York: International, 1984.

42. Maurice Cornforth, *Dialectical Materialism, An Introductory Course*, London: Lawrence Wishart, 1952; Maurice Cornforth, *Historical Materialism*, New York: International, 1954.

43. Andrew Brown, *J.D. Bernal: The Sage of Science*, New York: Oxford University Press, 2005; J.D. Bernal, *Science in History*, London: Watts, 1969.

44. Ronald Clark, *J.B.S.: The Life and Work of J.B.S. Haldane*, London: Hodder & Stoughton, 1968.

45. Christopher Caudwell, *Studies in a Dying Culture*, London: Bodley Head, 1938.

46. Christopher Hill, *The World Turned Upside Down: Radical Ideas During the English Revolution*, London: Penguin, 1991.

47. Nikolai Vasil'evich, *A True Son of the British Working Class*, Moscow: Progress, 1972.

48. Colin Palmer, *Eric Williams & the Making of the Modern Caribbean*, Chapel Hill: University of North Carolina Press, 2006; Eric Williams, *Capitalism & Slavery*, Chapel Hill: University of North Carolina Press, 1944.

49. John Williamson, *Dangerous Scot: The Life and Work of an American 'Undesirable'*, New York: International, 1969.

50. Comment by Robeson, June 1953, Box 20. See also Robeson, "Robeson 'Discovers' Africa," *Fighting Talk*, 11 (Number 2, April 1955), Box 21: this is probably a South African publication.

51. Robeson Remarks, June 1953, Box 20.

52. Ramdin, *Paul Robeson*, 84, 98.

53. Peter Blackman, "Paul Robeson-Ambassador" [the box in which I found this article was denoted as #19 but it was probably #26, hence I will list it here as Box 19–26].

54. *Derby Evening Telegraph* [U.K.], 8 March 1960.

55. Seton, *Paul Robeson*, 122.

56. Goodman, *Paul Robeson*, 223.

57. Tributes, 1973, Box 8.

58. *The Scotsman*, 3 September 1938.

59. BBC Transcript, 20 May 1960, Box 35.

60. *Glasgow Herald*, 18 March 1960. In 1949, it was reported that Robeson spoke 19 languages: *Pittsburgh Courier*, 13 August 1949. Cf. Seton, *Paul Robeson*, 77: Robeson "embraced more than twenty-five languages

including Arabic, Basque, Chinese, Czech, Danish, Efik, Egyptian [sic], Finnish, French, German, Greek, Hebrew, Hindustani, Hungarian, Italian, Japanese, Kisswahili, Norwegian, Persian, Polish, Russian, Spanish and Yiddish." Robeson was capable of singing in 24 languages: *Orange Transcript*, 2 August 1956, Box 32.

61. Robeson Remarks, circa 1950s, Box 20.
62. Report from U.S. Embassy-Paris to State Department, 16 July 1958, RG 59, Box 121, 032robeson, paul, *NARA-CP*. [National Archives & Records Administration, College Park, Maryland.]
63. BBC Transcript, 8 June 1960, Box 35.
64. BBC Transcript, 3 June 1960, Box 35.
65. Gerald Horne, *The Counter-Revolution of 1776: Slave Resistance and the Origins of the U.S.A.*, New York: New York University Press, 2014.
66. Ibid., Gerald Horne, *Negro Comrades of the Crown*.
67. Ibid., Robeson, *Here I Stand*, 80.
68. Gerald Horne, *Mau Mau in Harlem? The United States and the Liberation of Kenya*, New York: Palgrave, 2009.
69. Lloyd Brown to "Rebecca," 25 March 1971, Box 39.
70. Gerald Horne, *Communist Front? The Civil Rights Congress, 1946–1956*, London: Associated University Presses, 1988, passim.
71. Interview with Carl Rowan, 1957, Box 19–26.
72. Robeson, *Here I Stand*, 10.
73. Daisy R. Onquir to Paul Robeson, 12 December 1946, Box MB-PE Correspondence.
74. Eslanda Goode Robeson, *Paul Robeson, Negro*, New York: Harper & Brothers, 1930, 10, 14.
75. Robeson, *Here I Stand*, 7, 10.
76. Ibid.; Seton, *Paul Robeson*, 18.
77. BBC Transcript, 13 August 1960, Box 35.
78. Robeson autobiographical typescript, no date, circa 1950s, Box 13.
79. Paul Robeson, Autobiographical Writings, no date, Box 20.
80. Remarks by Sam Woldin, 1969, Box 19–26.
81. Ibid.; Robeson, *Here I Stand*, 17, 25, 27.
82. Lamont Yeakey, "A Student Without Peer: The Undergraduate College Years of Paul Robeson," *Journal of Negro Education*, 42 (Number 4, Fall 1973): 489–503, 490, 491.
83. BBC Transcript, 8 June 1960, Box 35.
84. Robeson, Autobiographical Writings, Box 20.
85. Robeson on "Language Study," circa 1950s, Box 20.

86. Robeson Remarks, December 1963, Box 21.
87. Dorothy Ray Healey, *California Red: A Life in the Communist Party*, Urbana: University of Illinois Press, 1993, 209.
88. PP Press Release, circa 1952, Box 39.
89. "Press Book," Circa 1949, Box 22.
90. Samuel Rosen, *The Autobiography*, New York: Knopf, 1973, 68.
91. Ibid.; Yeakey, "A Student Without Peer," 491.
92. Cutting, no date, Box 41.
93. Gregory J. Kaliss, *Men's College Athletics and the Politics of Racial Equality: Five Pioneer Stories of Black Manliness, White Citizenship and American Democracy*, Philadelphia: Temple University Press, 2012, 13–14.
94. Eslanda Goode Robeson, *Paul Robeson, Negro*, 35.
95. Robeson, Autobiographical Writings, Box 20.
96. Robeson College Transcript, 1915–16 and 1918–19, Box 1.
97. "A Public Presentation of Four Negro Commencement Speakers...", circa 1919, Box 37.
98. Ron Ramdin, *Paul Robeson*, 23.
99. *People's Voice*, 26 July 1947.
100. *People's Voice*, 2 August 1947.

Chapter 2

1. Cameron McWhirter, *Red Summer: The Summer of 1919 and the Awakening of Black America*, New York: Holt, 2011.
2. Judge Raymond Pace Alexander to Paul Robeson, 14 March 1973, Box 8.
3. State of New York Affidavit for License to Marry, 17 April 1922, "Subscribed and Sworn . . . before this 17 day of August 1921," Box 1.
4. Ms. Robeson to Boris Morros, 1 February 1942, Box HT-MH, *Eslanda Robeson Papers*.
5. Cutting, no date, circa 1922, Scrapbook, Box 42.
6. Elizabeth Shepley Sergeant, "A Portrait of Paul Robeson," *The New Republic*, 3 March 1926, Box 22. Robeson, Jr. quote to be found on page 67 of biography cited in footnote 7.
7. Paul Robeson, Jr., *The Undiscovered Paul Robeson: An Artist's Journey, 1898–1939*, New York: Wiley, 2001, 69, 53–55.
8. *Birmingham Post*, 7 May 1959, Box 33.
9. BBC Transcript, 3 June 1960, Box 35.
10. BBC Transcript, 22 June 1960, Box 35.
11. *New York Call*, 7 April 1922.

12. Robeson to National Cyclopedia of American Biography, 7 September 1926, Box 1.
13. Ibid.; Seton, *Paul Robeson*, 9.
14. Interview with Robeson in *Sunday Post*, 16 November 1958, RG59, Box 121, 791.001/3–1958, *National Archives and Records Administration-College Park, Maryland* (hereinafter denoted as "NARA-CP").
15. Ibid.; Ramdin, *Paul Robeson*, 49.
16. BBC Transcript, 8 July 1959, Box 35.
17. BBC Transcript, 17 June 1960, Box 35.
18. Stephen R. Fox to Paul Robeson, 9 June 1964, Box 19.
19. Augustin Duncan to Eugene O'Neill, 23 February 1923, Box 6.
20. Ibid., Eslanda Goode Robeson, *Paul Robeson*, 76, 80.
21. Robeson to National Cyclopedia, 7 September 1926, Box 1.
22. *Negro World*, 26 March 1921.
23. *New York Amsterdam News*, 25 September 1933.
24. *Negro World*, 3 March 1923.
25. Eugene O'Neill to Agnes Boulton, 11 September 1927 in Travis Bogard and Jackson R. Bryer, eds., *Selected Letters of Eugene O'Neill*, New Haven: Yale University Press, 1988, 256–8.
26. *New Statesman*, 19 September 1925, Box 22.
27. *Opportunity*, 3 (Number 35, May 1925): 346–8.
28. Review, *Saturday Review*, 19 September 1925, Box 22.
29. Thomas Cripps, "Paul Robeson and Black Identity in American Movies," *Massachusetts Review*, Summer 1970, 408–85, 477, Box 24.
30. Interview with Robeson by Sidney Cole in "The Cine-Technician," 1938, Box 22.
31. Diary, 6 May 1924, Box 16, *Eslanda Robeson Papers*.
32. Robeson Remarks, 1960s, Box 21.
33. Ibid.; Seton, *Paul Robeson*, 32.
34. BBC Transcript, 13 February 1961, Box 35.
35. Diary, 27 August 1924, Box 16.
36. Diary, 17 October 1927, Box 16.
37. Frank Dazen, First National Productions Corporation, First National Studios, Burbank, California, to Robeson, 9 July 1928, Box 2.
38. Diary, 4 May 1925, Box 16.
39. Diary, 3 January 1925, Box 16.
40. Diary, 10 May 1925, Box 16.
41. Diary, 4 January 1925, Box 16.
42. Diary, 2 May 1925, Box 16.

43. Edward White, *The Tastemaker: Carl Van Vechten and the Birth of Modern America*, New York: Farrar, Straus and Giroux, 2014, 181.

44. Diary, 19 April 1925, Box 16.

45. Robeson to National Cyclopedia, 7 September 1926, Box 1.

46. Review, *Opportunity*, 3 (Number 29, May 1925): 160.

47. Robeson, *Paul Robeson*, 101.

48. Walter White to Paul Robeson, 6 January 1927, Box WAM-Z Correspondence.

49. Walter White to Eslanda and Paul Robeson, 25 April 1925, Box WAM-Z Correspondence.

50. Diary, 29 August 1924, Box 16.

51. Robeson, *Paul Robeson*, 100, 101.

52. Diary, 27 January 1925, Box 16.

53. Diary, 9 August 1925, Box 16.

54. Robeson, *Paul Robeson*, 105, 111.

55. Diary, 12 August 1925, Box 16.

56. Diary, 13 August 1925, Box 16.

57. Emma Goldman to "Dear Paul and Essie," 9 September 1925, Box DJ-HS, *Eslanda Robeson Papers*.

58. Emma Goldman to Eslanda and Paul Robeson, 18 November 1925, *Eslanda Robeson Papers*.

59. Diary, 22 August 1925, Box 16.

60. Eslanda Robeson, *Paul Robeson*, 105, 111, 112.

61. Review, *Theatre Magazine*, August 1925, Box 23.

62. Diary, 28 May 1925, Box 16.

63. Brigadier General G.F. Trotter to Robeson, no date, Box PF-SE Correspondence.

64. Kurt Honolka, *Dvorak*, London: Haus, 2004, 83.

65. Robeson on Dvorak, November 1954, Box 21.

66. Robeson Biographical Data, no date, Box 1.

67. BBC Transcript, 8 June 1960, Box 35.

68. *People's Voice*, 2 August 1947.

69. For an exploration of this phenomenon, see *Financial Times*, 3 April 2014.

70. *New York Amsterdam News*, 3 October 1928.

71. BBC Transcript, 10 June 1960, Box 35.

72. Robeson, *Paul Robeson*, 142. See also Robeson Remarks, circa 1960s, Box 21: "When I had a cold or had not slept well or felt badly physically, I could not sing."

73. Paul Robeson to Eslanda Robeson, 12 December 1927, Box 6, *Eslanda Robeson Papers*.

74. "International Who's Who Publications," circa 1946, Box 1.

75. Brochure, 20 April 1927, 164–79, Folder 31, *Alain Locke Papers*, Howard University.

76. White, *The Tastemaker*, 249.

77. Eslanda Robeson to Carl Van Vechten, 14 June 1928, Box RJ-RZ, *Carl Van Vechten Papers*, Yale University, New Haven, Connecticut.

78. *New York Times*, 18 November 1928.

79. Eslanda Goode Robeson, *Paul Robeson*, 136.

80. Countee Cullen to "My Dear Paul,": 5 September 1928, Box 2.

81. Comment, *Rutgers Alumni Monthly*, 7 (February 1928), Box 22. See also *New York Sun*, 5 November 1927.

82. Diary of Paul Robeson, 12 November 1929, Box 1.

83. Robeson Diary, 10 November 1929.

84. Carl Van Vechten to Gertrude Stein, 27 November 1928, in Bruce Kellner, ed., *Letters of Carl Van Vechten*, New Haven: Yale University Press, 1987, 106.

85. Evelyn Waugh, *Decline and Fall*, London: Chapman & Hall, 1928.

86. Eslanda Goode Robeson, *Paul Robeson*, 168.

87. *Philadelphia Tribune*, 13 September 1928.

88. BBC Transcript, 22 June 1960, Box 35.

89. Robeson Diary, 8 November 1929.

90. Philip Cox to "My Dear Paul and Essie," 8 November 1929, Box 2.

91. Article attached to Philip Cox to Essie and Paul Robeson, 22 October 1929, Box BS-DO Correspondence.

92. Herbert Murray to Paul Robeson, circa 1929, Box SF-WAL Correspondence.

Chapter 3

1. Ramdin, *Paul Robeson*, 67.

2. *New York World*, 15 June 1930.

3. *Hartford Courant*, 7 June 1930.

4. Durylin, *Ira Aldridge*, 15–17.

5. Gerald Horne, *Powell v. Alabama: The Scottsboro Boys and American Justice*, New York: Watts, 1997.

6. Horne, *Black Revolutionary*, passim.

7. NAACP Press Release, 1930, Box 22.

8. Alexander Woolcott on Robeson in *Nash's Pall Mall Magazine*, London, September 1933, Box 22.
9. *New Statesman*, 24 September 1955, Box 23.
10. Stephen R. Fox, "The Development of Paul Robeson's Thought," 25 April 1964, Box 19.
11. *New York Times*, 22 May 1930.
12. Robeson, Autobiographical Writings, 1950, Box 20.
13. Herbert Marshall, "Reminiscences of Paul Robeson," 1957, Box 23.
14. *Daily Express*, 4 June 1930.
15. Eslanda Robeson to Victor Gollacz, 21 February 1930.
16. Anita Reynolds, *American Cocktail: A 'Colored Girl' in the World*, Cambridge: Harvard University Press, 2014, 174.
17. Letter to Victor Gollancz, 9 May 1930, Box S-Z, *Eslanda Robeson Papers*.
18. Emma Goldman to Eslanda Robeson, 7 March 1930, Box DJ-HS, *Eslanda Robeson Papers*.
19. Frederick Messiah to Philadelphia Record, 28 May 1930 and attached editorial, Box MB-PE Correspondence.
20. Lois G. Gordon, *Nancy Cunard: Heiress, Muse, Political Idealist*, New York: Columbia University Press, 2007, 167–8.
21. Paul Robeson to "Dear Sirs," 2 November 1932, *Nancy Cunard Papers*, University of Texas-Austin.
22. Eslanda Robeson to "Mama Dear," 20 January 1935, Box 6, *Eslanda Robeson Papers*.
23. Diary, 15 August 1924, Box 16, *Eslanda Robeson Papers*.
24. Diary, 30 and 31 October 1931, Box 16.
25. Remarks of Ms. Robeson, circa 1932, Box 11, *Eslanda Robeson Papers*.
26. Eslanda Robeson to George.Horace Lorimar, 6 May 1932, Box 4HT-MH, *Eslanda Robeson Papers*.
27. Eslanda Robeson to Etta Moten, 3 March 1935, Box 199, Folder 2, *Claude Barnett Papers*, Chicago History Museum.
28. Ibid.; White, *The Tastemaker*, 187.
29. Paul Robeson to Eslanda Robeson, 2 August 1932, Box 13.
30. Paul Robeson to Eslanda Robeson, 27 August 1931, Box 6, *Eslanda Robeson Papers*.
31. Carl Van Vechten to Eslanda Robeson, 12 January 1931, Box 5S-Z, *Eslanda Robeson Papers*.
32. Diary, 18 April 1931, Box 16.
33. Noel Coward to "My Dear Essie," 20 December 1930, Box 3, *Eslanda Robeson Papers*.

34. Noel Coward to Eslanda Robeson, 13 December 1930, Box 3.

35. See file on the pending divorce, 1932, Box 28.

36. Letter from Ms. Robeson, 10 November 1931, *James Weldon Johnson Miscellany Files*, Yale University.

37. Eslanda Robeson to "Carlo Darling," 13 July 1932, *Johnson Miscellany*.

38. Letter from Ms. Robeson, 19 December 1930, *Johnson Miscellany*.

39. Eslanda Robeson to Bess and Frank, 17 September 1933, Box HT-MH, *Eslanda Robeson Papers*.

40. *Daily Express*, 4 June 1930.

41. Eslanda Robeson to Bess and Frank, 17 September 1933, Box HT-MH.

42. Horne, *Black Revolutionary*.

43. Eslanda Robeson to Carl Van Vechten and Fania Marinoff, circa 1930, Group 41, *Johnson Miscellany*.

44. Eslanda Robeson to Carl Van Vechten and Fania Marinoff, 25 March 1930, Group 41, *Johnson Miscellany*. See also Leaflet, "The Emperor Jones (Kaiser Jones)," 31 March and 1 April 1930, Box 37.

45. Eslanda Robeson to Carl Van Vechten and Fania Marinoff, 22 April 1930, Group 41, *Johnson Miscellany*.

46. Thomas Cripps, "Paul Robeson and Black Identity in American Movies," 475.

47. Eslanda Robeson to Carl Van Vechten and Fania Marinoff, 2 September 1930, Group 41, *Johnson Miscellany*.

48. Leaflet, 19 April 1931, "African Peoples Freedom Day", St. Pancras Town Hall, London, Box 36. See e.g. Sterling Stuckey, "'I Want to Be African': Paul Robeson and the Ends of Nationalist Theory and Practice, 1914–1945," *Massachusetts Review*, 17 (Number 1, Spring 1976): 81–138.

49. Leaflet, 12 December 1934, Robeson on "The Negro in the Modern World," Memorial Hall, Farrington Street near Ludgate Circus, Box 36.

50. Lindsay Swindall, *Paul Robeson: A Life of Activism and Art*, Lanham, Maryland: Rowman & Littlefield, 2013, 67.

51. Remarks of Paul Robeson, 1953, Box 20.

52. *West Africa*, 7 November 1936, Box 29.

53. *Empire News* [Manchester], 16 December 1934, Box 28.

54. *Cape Argus*, 29 January 1935, Box 29.

55. Remarks of Paul Robeson, 1935, Box 2.

56. Gerald Horne, *Race Woman: The Lives of Shirley Graham Du Bois*, New York: New York University Press, 2001.

57. Gerald Horne, *Black and Red: W.E.B. Du Bois and the Afro-American Response to the Cold War, 1944–1963*, Albany: State University of New York Press, 1986.

58. Shirley Graham McCanns, "A Day at Hampstead," *Opportunity*, 9 (Number 1, January 1931): 14–15, 14.

59. Woolcott on Robeson in *Nash's Pall Mall Magazine*.

60. Robeson, Autobiographical Writings, 1950, Box 20.

61. Paul Robeson to Eslanda Robeson, 2 August 1932, Box 13.

62. *Picturegoer Weekly*, 26 October 1935, Box 29.

63. Du Bose Heyward to "Dear Paul," 21 June 1934, Box H-KA Correspondence.

64. Dorothy Heyward to Eslanda Robeson, 1934, Box H-KA.

65. Dorothy Heyward to Eslanda Robeson, 3 May 1939, Box H-KA.

66. Du Bose Heyward to Robeson, 19 August 1935, Box H-KA.

67. *Lancashire Gazette*, 13 December 1934, Box 28.

68. Seton, *Paul Robeson*, 79, 57.

69. Robeson, Autobiographical Writings, 1950, Box 20.

70. Seton, *Paul Robeson*, 81.

71. Diary, 7 August 1931, Box 16, *Eslanda Robeson Papers*.

72. Diary, 3 November 1931, Box 16, *Eslanda Robeson Papers*.

73. Robeson, Autobiographical Writings, 1950, Box 20.

74. Diary, 21 December 1935, Box 16, *Eslanda Robeson Papers*.

75. *New York Herald Tribune*, 16 November 1943, Reel 7, *Paul Robeson Collection*, Schomburg Center-New York Public Library.

76. Marie Seton to "Dear Sir," 1951, Box 23.

77. Stephen R. Fox to Paul Robeson, 9 June 1964 and attached paper, Box 24.

Chapter 4

1. Robeson, Autobiographical Writings, 1950, Box 20. See e.g. Stephen F. Cohen, *Bukharin and the Bolshevik Revolution; A Political Biography, 1888–1938*, New York: Knopf, 1973.

2. Diary, 20 January 1932, Box 16, *Eslanda Robeson Papers*.

3. Eslanda Robeson to Ann Buckman, 3 January 1935, Box 3, *Eslanda Robeson Papers*. On the school attended by Paul Robeson, Jr. in Moscow, see Larry E. Holmes, *Stalin's School: Moscow's Model School No. 25, 1931–1937*, Pittsburgh: University of Pittsburgh Press, 1999. On African-Americans and the U.S. Communist Party, see e.g. Gerald Horne, *Black Liberation/ Red Scare: Ben Davis and the Communist Party*, Newark: University of

Delaware Press, 1994; Gerald Horne, *Red Seas: Ferdinand Smith and Black Radical Black Sailors in the U.S. and Jamaica*, New York: New York University Press, 2005.

4. Eslanda Robeson to Carl Van Vechten and Fania Marinoff, 6 January 1936, Group 41, *Johnson Miscellany*.
5. Diary, 25–26 December 1934, Box 16, *Eslanda Robeson Papers*.
6. Eslanda Robeson to "Mama Dear," 1935, Box 6, *Eslanda Robeson Papers*.
7. Eslanda Robeson to "Mama Dear," 20 January 1935, Box 6.
8. Diary, 28 December 1934, Box 16.
9. Diary, 5 January 1935, Box 16.
10. Herbert Marshall, "Reminiscences of Paul Robeson," 1957, Box 23.
11. Seton, *Paul Robeson*, 96.
12. Invitation, 28 February 1935, Box KB-MA Correspondence.
13. *Northern Whig and Belfast Post*, 18 February 1935, Box 29.
14. *The Jewish Transcript*, 22 November 1935, Box 29.
15. *Courier and Advertiser* [Dundee], 27 March 1935, Box 29.
16. BBC Transcript, 17 June 1960, Box 35.
17. Eslanda Robeson to Carl Van Vechten, and Fania Marinoff, circa 1935, Group 41, *Johnson Miscellany*.
18. Stephen Gundle, *Glamour: A History*, New York: Oxford University Press, 2008.
19. Paul Robeson to Marcia De Sylva, circa 1935, Box BS-DO Correspondence.
20. *The Referee*, 7 April 1935, Box 29.
21. Leaflet, 1935, Box 37.
22. Transcription of cutting, May 1935, Box 22.
23. *New Statesman*, 18 May 1935.
24. Quoted in Christian Hogsbjerg, ed., *Toussaint Louverture: The Story of the Only Successful Slave Revolt in History: A Play in Three Acts by C.L.R. James*, Durham: Duke University Press, 2013, 18.
25. *Evening Standard* [London], 25 July 1938.
26. Program, 1938, *Plant in the Sun*, Box 37. See also Interview with Robeson by Sidney Cole, "The Cine-Technician," September–October 1938.
27. Herbert Marshall, "Reminiscences of Paul Robeson," 1957, Box 23.
28. Colin Chambers, *The Story of Unity Theatre*, London: Lawrence and Wishart, 1989, 152.
29. Marie Seton, "Let My People Go," June 1976, Box 25.
30. *New Statesman*, 21 March 1936.
31. *New York Times*, 16 March 1936.

32. Ibid.; Hogsbjerg, *Toussaint Louverture*, 26.
33. Alex Waugh to Paul Robeson, Jr., 12 January 1976, Box 11.
34. Rena Vale to the Robesons, 30 December 1935, Box SF-WAL Correspondence.
35. Maier Richard Harris to "Dear Paul," 2 February 1936, Box H-KA Correspondence.
36. Kathleen Ross to Robeson, 11 November 1960, Box PF-SE Correspondence.
37. James Whale to Paul Robeson, 28 August 1936, Box WAM-Z Correspondence.
38. *California Eagle*, no date, circa 1937, Box 29.
39. BBC Transcript, 8 June 1960, Box 35.
40. Eslanda to Miss Strassman, 6 June 1938, Box S-Z, *Eslanda Robeson Papers*.
41. A.H. Belmont to L.V. Boardman, 18 April 1957, Reel 2, *FBI File on Paul Robeson*, University of Texas, San Antonio: "allegation of an affair between Mountbatten's wife and [Robeson] . . . Lord Mountbatten was known in British circles to be a homosexual with a perversion for young boys; and, further, that his wife . . . took Paul Robeson on a 6 week caravan into the Sahara desert a few years before the war began and they were unchaperoned . . . [she] has a huge naked statue of [Robeson] in her home . . . ." *Jet* [U.S.], 18 September 1980: Here this story is confirmed.
42. Article, circa 1937, Box 29.
43. Paul Tabori, *Alexander Korda: A Biography*, New York: Living Books, 1968, 157, 156.
44. Interview with Robeson by Sidney Cole in "The Cine-Technician," September-October 1938, Box 22.
45. Letter from Marie Seton, 30 November 1957, Box 32.
46. Ibid., Thomas W. Cripps, "Paul Robeson and Black Identity in American Movies," 470,
47. For a typical excoriation, see e.g. *Baltimore Afro-American*, 6 July 1935.
48. Publicity Manager of London Film Productions to Eslanda Robeson, 11 April 1915, Box KB-MA Correspondence. Contrary to the statement above, this writer thanked Robeson for speaking at the premier.
49. *Daily Sketch* [U.K.], 3 April 1935, Box 29.
50. *Daily Express*, 20 January 1936, Box 29.
51. *Daily Worker*, 10 May 1936.
52. *Baltimore Afro-American*, 6 July 1935.
53. Comment, *The Black Man*, January 1937, Box 29.
54. Letter from Marie Seton, 30 November 1957, Box 32.
55. Ibid.; Maier Richard Harris to "Dear Paul," 2 February 1936.

56. Remarks by Robeson, 27 September 1932, Box 14.
57. John Corfeld to Eslanda Robeson, 14 November 1938, Box BS-DO Correspondence.
58. Sergei Eisenstein to "Dear Essie and Paul," 9 April 1938, Box DP-G Correspondence.
59. Louis Marx, General Sales Manager for Continental Europe of Universal Pictures to Paul Robeson, 1937, Box KB-MA Correspondence.
60. See e.g. Gerald Horne, *Class Struggle in Hollywood, 1930–1950: Moguls, Mobsters, Stars, Reds and Trade Unionists*, Austin: University of Texas Press, 2001. Robeson on quote from Cole interview below.
61. Interview with Robeson by Sidney Cole, "The Cine-Technician," September–October 1938, Box 22.
62. See e.g. Gerald Horne, *The Final Victim of the Blacklist: John Howard Lawson, Dean of the Hollywood Ten*, Berkeley: University of California Press, 2006.
63. Marie Seton to "Dear Sir," 1951, Box 23.
64. Waldo Frank to Eslanda Robeson, 4 December circa 1930s, Box DP-G Correspondence.
65. Remarks by Robeson, 1 November 1938, Box 30.
66. *Daily Worker*, 10 May 1936.
67. Cutting, 3 November 1936, Box 39.
68. "West Africa," 7 November 1936, Box 29.
69. Ralph Bunche to Paul Robeson, 11 January 1938, Box 2. Similar letter in Box BS-DO Correspondence.
70. Max Yergan to Paul Robeson, 25 May 1937, Box WAM-Z Correspondence.
71. *Baltimore Afro-American*, 22 May 1937.
72. Eslanda Robeson to Mr. Taylor, 16 June circa 1935, Box 40.
73. *Aberdeen Press and Journal*, 13 January 1939.
74. *News Chronicle*, 5 November circa 1937, Box 22.
75. While in Spain, Juan Plaza made a musical Spanish folklore film of about 20 minutes with Robeson, who sang: see William Pickens to "Dear Paul," 22 October 1940, Box PF-SE Correspondence.
76. Article, "The American," May 1944, Box 22.
77. *Daily Worker*, 15 February 1938.
78. *Daily Worker* [U.K.], 14 November 1937. These words can also be found in Ibid., Philip S. Foner, 118–119.
79. Robeson, Autobiographical Writings, 1950, Box 20.
80. Hakim Adi, *Pan-Africanism and Communism: The Communist International, Africa and the Diaspora, 1919–1939*, Trenton: Africa World Press, 2013, 289.

81. Leaflet, "Great Youth Rally," 12 June 1938, Box 37.

82. "Negro Committee to Aid Spain," circa 1938, Box 39.

83. "Report of the Tour of the Negro People's Ambulance for Loyalist Spain," circa 1938, Box 39.

84. Stephen R. Fox to Robeson and attached, 9 June 1964, Box 19.

85. Eslanda Robeson to Carl Van Vechten and Fania Marinoff, Group 41, *Johnson Miscellany.*

86. Interview with Robeson by Sidney Cole, "The Cine-Technician," September-October 1938, Box 22.

87. Cutting, 22 August 1938, Box 30.

88. *Picturegoer Weekly*, 20 November 1937, Box 29.

89. Eslanda Robeson to Carl Van Vechten and Fania Marinoff, 4 April 1938, Group 41, *James Weldon Johnson Miscellany.*

90. Richmond Barthe to Eslanda Robeson, 27 September 1938, Box 3, *Eslanda Robeson Papers.*

91. Letter from Eslanda Robeson, 6 September 1939, Box 3, A-DIA, *Eslanda Robeson Papers.*

Chapter 5

1. Marie Seton, "Let My People Go," June 1976, Box 25.

2. *Picturegoer & Film Weekly*, 18 May 1940, Box 30.

3. Robeson typescript remarks, 1940s, Box 22.

4. Article, "The American," 137 (Number 5, May 1944): 28–9, 142–4, Box 22.

5. *PM* [New York], 12 September 1943.

6. Interview with Robeson, 1965, Box 21.

7. Eslanda Robeson to Carl Van Vechten and Fania Marinoff, 18 July 1939, Group 41, *Johnson Miscellany.*

8. *New York Times*, 23 September 1942.

9. *New York Amsterdam News*, 5 August 1942.

10. *Pittsburgh Courier*, 26 September 1942.

11. Cutting, 10 September 1942, Box 30.

12. *New York Amsterdam News*, 3 October 1942.

13. *Pittsburgh Courier*, 13 August 1949.

14. Marie Seton, *Paul Robeson*, 122, 166, 194.

15. Gerald Horne, *Race War! White Supremacy and the Japanese Attack on the British Empire*, New York: New York University Press, 2003. See also Gerald Horne, "Tokyo Bound: African-Americans and Japan Confront

White Supremacy," *Souls: A Critical Journal of Black Politics, Culture and Society*, 3 (Number 3, Summer 2001): 16–28; Gerald Horne, "The Revenge of the Black Pacific?" *Callaloo: A Journal of African Diaspora Arts and Letters*, 24 (Number 1, 2000): 94–96; Gerald Horne, *Facing the Rising Sun: African-Americans and Japan Confront White Supremacy*, forthcoming. See also Gerald Horne, *The End of Empires: African-Americans and India*, Philadelphia: Temple University Press, 2009.

16. Ambrose Caliver, Senior Specialist in the Education of Negroes, Federal Security Agency, U.S. Office of Education, to Robeson, 14 October 1941, Box 2.
17. Eleanor Roosevelt to Paul Robeson, 6 November 1944, Box MI-R, *Eslanda Robeson Papers*.
18. *Daily Worker*, 24 January 1942.
19. D. Richard Baren, U.S. Treasury Department to Robeson, 15 February 1944, Box A-BR Correspondence.
20. Paul Levitan to Paul Robeson, no date, Box 7.
21. Mr. and Mrs. Francis Biddle to Robeson, 21 June 1941, Box A-BR.
22. Congressman William Dawson to "My Dear Paul," 23 November 1943, Box BS-DO Correspondence.
23. Hew Patterson, Department of National Defense, Canada, to Robeson, 13 November 1941, Box BS-DO.
24. Jawaharlal Nehru to Eslanda Robeson, 21 June 1939, Box MB-PE Correspondence.
25. W.A. Domingo of West Indies National Emergency Committee to Robeson, 29 July 1940, Box 39.
26. Seton, *Paul Robeson*, 122.
27. *New Haven Register*, 24 August 1941, Box 30.
28. Eslanda Robeson to Carl Van Vechten and Fania Marinoff, 17 November 1941, Group 41, *Johnson Miscellany*.
29. Eslanda Robeson to Carl Van Vechten and Fania Marinoff, 26 April 1944, Group 41.
30. Cutting, 29 July 1940, Box 30.
31. *Daily Worker*, 15 September 1940.
32. *New York Amsterdam News*, 12 October 1940.
33. *Daily Worker*, 17 December 1940.
34. *Norfolk Journal & Guide*, 19 July 1941.
35. *Pittsburgh Courier*, 12 July 1941.

36. "Fred" of Metropolitan Music Bureau to Robeson, 18 February 1942, Box PF-SE Correspondence. See also *New York World-Telegram*, 18 February 1942.
37. Lucile Bluford to Paul Robeson, 21 February 1943, Box 30.
38. Robeson Remarks, December 1963, Box 21.
39. Ron Ramdin, *Paul Robeson*, 102.
40. *PM* [New York], 30 April 1941.
41. John H. Johnson to Robeson, 31 August 1944, Box H-KA Correspondence. See also John H. Johnson, *Succeeding Against the Odds*, New York: Warner, 1989.
42. *Daily Worker*, 17 November 1940.
43. "Official Program Fifth All Southern Negro Youth Conference" at Tuskegee Institute, 17–19 April 1942, Box 38.
44. J. Edgar Hoover to Special Agent, Los Angeles, 27 May 1943, Reel 1, *FBI File on Paul Robeson*, University of Texas-San Antonio.
45. Carl Van Vechten to Walter White, 14 December 1939, in Bruce Kellner, ed., *Letters of Carl Van Vechten*, New Haven: Yale University Press, 1987, 171.
46. Letter from Lord Beaverbrook, circa 1930s, Box A-BR Correspondence.
47. FBI Memorandum, 8 December 1942, in David Gallen, ed., *Black Americans: The FBI Files*, New York: Carroll & Graf, 1994, 342–6.
48. Memorandum, 28 November 1942 in Ibid., Gallen, 347.
49. Harry Haywood, *Black Bolshevik: Autobiography of an Afro-American Communist*, Chicago: Liberation Press, 1978, 564–5; Lawrence Lamphere, "Paul Robeson: 'Freedom' Newspaper and the Black Press," Ph.d. dissertation, Boston College, 2003, 58.
50. FBI Memorandum, 18 December 1943, Reel 1, *FBI Files on Paul Robeson*.
51. Eslanda Robeson to Mr. and Mrs. Litvinov, 28 January 1942, Box 4, *Eslanda Robeson Papers*.
52. Ben Davis to Eslanda Robeson, 27 April 1943, Box 3.
53. Robeson Eulogy for Ben Davis, 27 August 1964, Box 21.
54. Countee Cullen to "Dear Paul," 30 October 1943, Box 2: "to ask that you will look with a kindly and considerate eye on a musical setting of my poem 'Incident'...."
55. Countee Cullen to "Dear Essie," 5 February 1940, Box 2.
56. *Daily Worker*, 3 October 1941. On Hughes, see Ms. Robeson letter, 25 June 1939, Box 6, *Eslanda Robeson Papers*.
57. *People's Voice*, 20 December 1947.
58. Helen Dreiser to Paul Robeson, 14 May 1940, Box DP-G Correspondence.

59. Program re: "Dorothy Parker," 23 March 1942, Box 40.
60. Pearl Buck to Paul Robeson, 28 August 1942, Box BS-DO Correspondence.
61. Jawaharlal Nehru to Paul Robeson, 4 April 1942, Box MB-PE Correspondence.
62. Nehru to Eslanda Robeson, 2 August 1942, Box 0 (this box had no number, thus I am listing it arbitrarily as Box 0).
63. Gerald Horne, *The End of Empires: African-Americans and India*, Philadelphia: Temple University Press, 2008, 169.
64. *Times of Ceylon*, 16 April 1944, Box 3.
65. Article, "Ceylon Men," August 1944, Box 22.
66. Edgar De Silva and Kurana Negombo to Ms. Robeson, 4 January 1946, Box 3.
67. Nehru to Robeson, 16 May 1946, Box MB-PE.
68. P.L. Prattis in "Horizon," 18 November 1944, Box 22.
69. Benjamin Mays, President of Morehouse College to Paul Robeson, 25 January 1943, Box KB-MA Correspondence.
70. Benjamin Mays to Eslanda Robeson, 4 June 1943, Box KB-MA.
71. James Nabrit, Secretary of Board of Trustees to Paul Robeson, 20 April 1945, Box MB-PE Correspondence.
72. Program from Princeton Playgoers, 17–22 August 1942, Box 38.
73. *New York Amsterdam News*, 10 July 1943.
74. *TIME*, 1 November 1943, Box 31.
75. BBC Transcript, 17 June 1960, Box 35.
76. *TIME*, 1 November 1943.
77. Eslanda Robeson to Paul Robeson, 25 June 1939, Box 6, *Eslanda Robeson Papers*.
78. Raymond Pace Alexander to Robeson, 14 March 1973, Box 8.
79. Walter Wanger to Paul Robeson, 23 April 1944, Box 7.
80. Sherwin Cody to Robeson, 17 January 1944, Box 2.
81. Margaret Webster, "Paul Robeson and Othello," June 1944, Box 22.
82. Article, "The American," May 1944, Box 22.
83. See for example Florence Colombani, *Marlon Brando: Anatomy of an Actor*, London: Phaidon Press, 2013.
84. 1942 Itinerary, Box 39.
85. Ben Davis to Ms. Robeson, 27 April 1943, Box 3.
86. *Daily Worker*, 16 April 1944.
87. Article, "The American," May 1944, Box 22.

88. Eslanda Robeson to Carl Van Vechten and Faina Marinoff, 18 July 1939, Group 41, *Johnson Miscellany*.

89. *Daily Worker*, 16 April 1944.

90. *New York Post*, 10 December 1943.

91. *Daily Worker*, 16 April 1944.

92. Robeson, "Trends in Modern Music," circa 1950s, Box 20.

93. BBC Transcript, 15 June 1960, Box 35.

94. *People's Voice*, 29 November 1947, Box 10, *Henry Foner Papers, New York University*.

95. Program "For a New Africa," 14 April 1944, Box 39.

96. "New Africa," April 1944, Box 39.

97. Memorandum, 7 April 1944, Box 7.

98. George "Babe" Ruth to Robeson, 11 April 1944, Box 0. Also sending greetings were the boxers Barney Ross and Benny Leonard and the football coach, Lou Little.

99. Kwame Nkrumah to Robeson, 26 March 1944, Box MB-PE Correspondence.

100. "New Africa," May 1944, Box 39. See also *Daily Worker*, 19 April 1944: Among the artists performing were Count Basie and Teddy Wilson, also known as the "Marxist Mozart." *New York Post*, 11 April 1944: The dancer Pearl Primus and the singer Josh White were also present. See also the *Minneapolis Times*, 17 April 1944: according to this source, 8,000 were in attendance.

101. Program, 23 January 1945, Box 39.

102. Lawrence Brown to Ms. Robeson, 8 August 1945, Box 3, *Eslanda Robeson Papers*.

103. Robeson, "Genocide Stalks the USA", *New World Review*, 20 (Number 2, February 1952): 26–29, 27.

104. Robeson Remarks, 29 September 1945, Box 31.

105. E.E. Conroy, FBI-New York to J. Edgar Hoover, 2 July 1946, Reel 1, *FBI File on Paul Robeson*.

106. Major General Frank A. Keating to Robeson, 20 August 1945, Box KB-MA Correspondence.

107. *Daily Worker*, 13 February 1945.

108. Ibid., Gallen, FBI Memo, 9 May 1947, 350.

Chapter 6

1. Ms. Robeson to "Sergei", 3 December 1945, Box S-Z, *Eslanda Robeson Papers*.

2. Gerald Horne, *Class Struggle in Hollywood, 1930–1950*, passim: Robeson's role as a screen actor of global proportions cannot be discounted in explicating the postwar persecution of him.

3. *People's Voice*, 8 November 1947. Gerald Horne, *The Final Victim of the Blacklist: John Howard Lawson, Dean of the Hollywood Ten*, Berkeley: University of California Press, 2006.

4. *People's Voice*, 22 November 1947.

5. Ms. Robeson to Paul Robeson, 1 December 1946, Box 6, *Eslanda Robeson Papers*: Here she complains about his attorney and manager, Robert Rockmore and how he parceled out their funds, notably to her: "He'd never have dared to do that to a white woman. Never. But I'm colored" which explains his "patronage, the scolding, the high-handedness." Whereas in "Chicago . . . your white lawyer and his wife were elegantly housed [,] your colored wife was put in first one dump, and then another . . . ." She desired to be a "wife" and not "merely a paid housekeeper", forcing her to ask: "am I to continue to be Mrs. Robeson? Yes or no." Earlier, she had asserted, "Bob [Rockmore] is Paul's friend, not mine . . . I have never liked him, nor he me . . . .": Ms. Robeson to "Mama Dear," 20 January 1935, Box 6. See also Robert Rockmore to Harold Davison, 14 January 1959, Box 15: At a time when the Robeson's tax matters became more tangled, he said dismissively in regard to Ms. Robeson, "I doubt she has any personal income"; she is not her spouse's manager "nor has she had anything to do with his professional activities for the past 20 years"—an exaggeration at best.

6. *Springfield Republican*, 20 May 1946.

7. Article, "The American," May 1944, Box 22.

8. Gerald Horne, *Black Liberation/Red Scare*, 137–46.

9. Report on Ben Davis, 3 June 1945, Reel 1, *FBI File on Paul Robeson*.

10. *Daily Worker*, 11 October 1946.

11. Report, 25 July 1945, in ibid., Gallen, 347–9.

12. *Pittsburgh Courier*, 27 October 1945.

13. Ben Burns of "Negro Digest" to Ms. Robeson, 14 June 1945, Box 3, *Eslanda Robeson Papers*.

14. John H. Johnson to Ms. Robeson, 11 March 1945, Box 4, *Esland Robeson Papers*.

15. Ben Davis to Ms. Robeson, 7 August 1947, Box 3, *Eslanda Robeson Papers*.

16. "The Easterner," May 1946, Box 22.

17. Article, "The American," May 1944, Box 22.

18. "New Africa," 5 (Number 1, January 1946), Box 39.

19. *PM*, 4 June 1946.
20. "New Africa," 5 (Number 7, July–August 1946), Box 39.
21. Nehru to Ms. Robeson, 26 June 1947, Box HT-MH, *Eslanda Robeson Papers*.
22. Norman Manley to Robeson, 5 July 1946, Box KB-MA Correspondence.
23. Robeson Speech, 7 June 1946, Reel 7, *Paul Robeson Collection*.
24. "New Africa," 5 (Number 11, December 1946), Box 39.
25. *New York Times*, 29 September 1946.
26. *New York Times*, 28 October 1979.
27. Cutting, circa 1946, Box 31.
28. Raymond Pace Alexander to Robeson, 17 February 1947, Box A-BR Correspondence.
29. *New York World Telegram*, 23 September 1946.
30. Ibid., Leonard Lamphere, 59.
31. See e.g. Gerald Horne, *The Counter-Revolution of 1776*, passim. See also *New York Times*, 24 September 1946; *Boston Chronicle*, 28 September 1946; *People's Voice*, 28 September 1946, *Philadelphia Tribune*, 24 September 1946.
32. Gerald Horne, *Black Revolutionary*, passim.
33. *People's Voice*, 6 December 1947, Box 10, *Foner Papers*.
34. Remarks by Robeson, 12 September 1946, Reel 7, *Paul Robeson Collection*.
35. Interview with Leonard Boudin, circa 1982, Box 33, *Rabinowitz and Boudin Legal Files*, New York University.
36. Wilbur C. Rich, *Coleman Young and Detroit Politics: From Social Activist to Power Broker*, Detroit: Wayne State University Press, 1989.
37. Cutting, 18 June 1946, Box 22.
38. *St. Louis Argus*, 31 January 1947; Ibid., Lawrence Lamphere, 67.
39. *Pittsburgh Courier*, 1 February 1947.
40. Transcript of Robeson Testimony, 31 May 1948, Box 0.
41. Cutting, no date, circa 1949, Box 31.
42. Speech by Robeson, 4 July 1952, Box 20.
43. *People's Voice*, 1 February 1947.
44. *People's Voice*, 1 November 1947.
45. *People's Voice*, 3, 10, 17 May 1947.
46. Gil Green, *Cold War Fugitive: A Personal Story of the McCarthy Years*, New York: International, 1984, 121–3.
47. *People's Voice*, 6 September 1947, Box 10, *Foner Papers*.
48. Robeson Remarks, 25 April 1947, Reel 7, *Robeson Collection*.
49. *The Nation*, 27 May 1947, RG 59, Box 5943, 811F.5043/5–1947, *NARA-CP*.

50. *People's Voice*, 4 October 1947, Box 10.
51. Earl Robinson to Alphaeus Hunton, 18 November 1949, Box PE-SE Correspondence.
52. Ben Davis to Robeson, 20 March 1955, Box 2.
53. *People's Voice*, 11 October 1947.
54. *People's Voice*, 18 October 1947.
55. *People's Voice*, 30 August 1947.
56. *Daily Gleaner*, 16 November 1948.
57. Michael Manley to Robeson, 22 March 1973, Box 8.
58. *National Guardian* [New York], 20 December 1948.
59. Nelson Park, U.S. Counsel General to Secretary of State, 7 December 1948, RG59, Box 15, 032robeson, paul/12–748, *NARA-CP*.
60. U.S. Legation-Panama to State Department, 19 May 1947, RG 59, Box 5943, 811F.5043/5–1947, *NARA-CP*.
61. U.S. Legation-Panama to State Department, 6 June 1947, RG 59, Box 5943.
62. Victor Navasky, *Naming Names*, New York: Viking, 1980, 187.
63. Mary Church Terrell to W. Alphaeus Hunton, 5 June 1949, Box 23.
64. Donald R. McCoy and Richard T. Reutten, *Quest and Response: Minority Rights and the Truman Administration*, Lawrence: University Press of Kansas, 1973, 263–6.
65. Samuel Rosen, *Autobiography*, 73.
66. Harry Keelan to Robeson, 4 May 1958, Box KB-MA Correspondence.
67. *New York Post*, 5 April 1948.
68. "Spotlight on Africa," 11 June 1953, Box 39.
69. Ms. Robeson to CAA, 17 April 1948, Box 39.
70. Penny M. Von Eschen, *Race Against Empire: Black Americans and Anticolonialism, 1937–1957*, Ithaca: Cornell University Press, 1997, 115.
71. CAA Press Release, 13 April 1949, Box 39.
72. "Emergency Appeal," circa 1949, Box 38.
73. Transcript of Robeson Testimony, 31 May 1948, Box 0.
74. *PM*, 31 May 1948.
75. Junius Scales and Richard Nickson, *Cause at Hand: A Former Communist Remembers*, Athens: University of Georgia Press, 1987, 167.
76. *Daily Worker*, 3 June 1948.
77. Eslanda Robeson to Carl Van Vechten and Fania Marinoff, 10 July 1948, Group 41, *Johnson Miscellany*.
78. *People's Voice*, 9 August 1947.
79. *Daily Worker*, 11 October 1948.

80. John J. A Abt, *Advocate and Activist: Memoirs of an American Communist Lawyer*, Urbana: University of Illinois Press, 1993, 164.

81. There remains contestation as to what Robeson actually said in his unrecorded remarks: See e.g. Paul Robeson, Jr., *The Undiscovered Paul Robeson: Quest for Freedom, 1939–1976*, New York: Wiley, 2010, 142–3. Cf. Speech by Ms. Robeson citing her spouse's words, 27 April 1949, Box 12, *Eslanda Robeson Papers*: "to quote him exactly: 'it is unthinkable that American Negroes will go to war on behalf of those who oppressed us for generations, against a country, which in one generation has raised Our People (people like us) to the full dignity of mankind…'" See also *New York Amsterdam News*, 25 July 1949: Robeson is cited as saying: "At the Paris conference I said it was unthinkable that the Negro people of America or elsewhere in the world could be drawn into a war with the Soviet Union." *New York Herald Tribune*, 20 June 1949: Robeson in Harlem: "Unthinkable that the Negro people of America or elsewhere in the world could be drawn into a war with the Soviet Union. I repeat it with hundred-folk emphasis."

82. W.E.B. Du Bois, "Paul Robeson," *Negro Digest*, 8 (Number 5, March 1950): 8, 10–14, Box 23.

83. *Philadelphia Tribune*, 24 July 1949.

84. *New York Times*, 15 July 1949. See Testimony of Manning Johnson, 14 July 1949, Reel 7, *Robeson Collection*: "During the time I was a member of the Communist Party, Paul Robeson was a member . . . he has delusions of grandeur. He wants to be the Black Stalin among Negroes . . . the Communist Party can very effectively use Robeson to further their penetration among Negroes . . . he can attract to him large amounts of people."

85. *New York Daily News*, 15 July 1949.

86. *Pittsburgh Courier*, 7 May 1949.

87. *New York Herald Tribune*, 23 April 1949.

88. NAACP Press Release, 21 April 1949, Box 23.

89. *New York Sun*, 28 September 1949.

90. *Pittsburgh Courier*, 7 May 1949.

91. Lawrence Brown to Ms. Robeson, 4 March 1949, Box 3, *Eslanda Robeson Papers*.

92. Cutting, 12 July 1949, Box 31.

93. Remarks by Ulf Christensen, 6 June 1949, Box 22.

94. Testimony of Robeson, 12 June 1956, Box 21.

95. Interview with Robeson, April 1949, Box 23.

96. Press Release of Council on African Affairs, 11 May 1949, Box 39.

97. Paul Robeson to Carl Murphy, 14 July 1949, Box MB-PE Correspondence.

98. Clifford Odets to "Dear Friends," 19 June 1949, Box MB-PE.

99. Gerald Horne, *Black Liberation/Red Scare*, 215.

100. Ben Davis to Robeson, no date, Box BS-DO Correspondence.

101. *New York Herald Tribune*, 21 September 1949.

102. Ben Davis to Ms. Robeson, 25 May 1949, Box 23.

103. Lawrence Brown to Eslanda Robeson, 4 March 1949, Box 3.

104. Ronald A. Smith, "The Paul Robeson–Jackie Robinson Saga and a Political Collision," *Journal of Sport History*, 6 (Number 2, Summer 1979): 5–27.

105. Text of Robinson remarks, *New York Times*, 19 July 1949.

106. *Congressional Record*, 3 August 1949.

107. Robeson to Jackie Robinson, 11 July 1949, Box PF-SE Correspondence.

108. Attorney Charles Howard to Ms. Robeson, 21 July 1949, Box DJ-HS, *Eslanda Robeson Papers*.

109. Gerald Horne, *Race Woman: The Lives of Shirley Graham Du Bois*, New York: New York University Press, 2001.

110. Fang Ying Yang to Ms. Robeson, 11 December 1949, Box DJ-HS, *Eslanda Robeson Papers*.

111. Chiao Kwan-Hua to Ms. Robeson, 8 December 1949, Box 4, *Eslanda Robeson Papers*.

112. *New York Daily News*, 17 June 1949.

113. *New York Herald Tribune*, 20 June 1949.

114. *Baltimore Afro-American*, 11 March 1950.

115. Ibid.

Chapter 7

1. For detail, see Gerald Horne, *Communist Front?* and Gerald Horne, *Black Revolutionary*.

2. Ms. Robeson to "Emily Dear," 25 December 1950, Box S-Z, *Eslanda Robeson Papers*.

3. *Daily Worker*, 1 May 1952.

4. Robeson Speech, 4 July 1952, Chicago, Box 20.

5. *The Violence in Peekskill: A Report on the Violations of Civil Liberties at Two Paul Robeson Concerts Near Peekskill, New York, August 27th and September 4th, 1949*, New York: ACLU, 1949, University of Texas-Austin.

6. Report by Ms. Robeson, 1949, Box 12, *Eslanda Robeson Papers*.

7. *Peekskill Evening Star*, 6 September 1949; Ibid., ACLU Report; *Christian Science Monitor*, 6 September 1949; *New York Herald Tribune*, 6 September 1949; *New York Sun*, 29 August 1949; *New York Post*, 6 September 1949.

8. Howard Fast, *Peekskill USA*, New York: Civil Rights Congress, 1951.

9. Jordan Goodman, *Paul Robeson: A Watched Man*, New York: Verso, 2013, 122.

10. *New York Amsterdam News*, 10 and 17 September 1949.

11. Report, 26 July 1950, RG 59, Box 3071, 711.001/7–2650, *NARA-CP*.

12. Grand Jury Investigation, October 1949, Box 17.

13. *Los Angeles Times*, 1 October 1949; *California Eagle*, 8, 15, 22 September and 6 , 13 October 1949. See also Press Release, circa 1949, Box 22.

14. Release, Circa 1949, Box 23.

15. Release, circa 1949, Box 23.

16. *Daily Worker*, 5 June 1952.

17. Cutting, circa 1950, Box 23.

18. Release, 1 August 1951, Box 23.

19. *Daily Worker*, 21 October 1949.

20. Robeson Testimony, 12 June 1956, Box 21.

21. *Observer* [U.K.], 10 May 1951.

22. *Washington News*, 26 April 1951.

23. Robeson, "The Negro People and the Soviet Union," 1950, Box 20.

24. Robeson Speech, December 1952 in Ibid., Philip S. Foner, ed., *Paul Robeson Speaks*, 328–9.

25. *Springfield Republican*, 4 August 1950.

26. Nathan Witt to Dean Acheson, 1 August 1950, Box 17.

27. *Freedom*, April 1952.

28. *Baltimore Afro-American*, 12, 26 August 1950.

29. Ibid., Lawrence Lamphere, 237.

30. Louis Burnham to Ms. Robeson, 22 November 1950, Box 3.

31. *Sydney Morning Herald*, 13 October 1960.

32. *Baltimore Afro-American*, 4 March 1950.

33. *Springfield Republican*, 21 September 1950.

34. Release, 16 November 1952, Reel 8, *Robeson Collection*.

35. Ms. Robeson to Emily, 6 February 1952, Box S-Z.

36. W.E.B. Du Bois, "Paul Robeson," *Negro Digest*, 8 (Number 5, March 1950): 8, 10–14, Box 23.

37. Gerald Horne, *Black Revolutionary*, 125–9, passim.

38. *Baltimore Afro-American*, 3 November 1951.

39. Walter White, "The Strange Case of Paul Robeson," *Ebony*, February 1951, Box 4, *Eslanda Robeson Papers*.

40. Charles Howard to Roy Wilkins, 26 May 1949, Box 23.
41. Robert Alan Arthur, "Paul Robeson: The Lost Shepherd," *The Crisis*, 59 (Number 9, November 1951): 569–74.
42. Cutting, no date, Reel 7, *Robeson Collection*.
43. Remarks by Peter Blackman, 1949, Box 19/26. (This box is listed thusly since it was denoted as Box 19 but I deduced that it was actually Box 26.)
44. Ms. Robeson to John H. Johnson, 1 February 1951, Box 4, *Eslanda Robeson Papers*.
45. *Daily Worker*, 13 August 1950.
46. *Baltimore Afro-American*, 1 December 1951.
47. U.S. Embassy-Delhi to Secretary of State, 19 March 1949, RG 59, Box 15, 032robeson, paul/3–11849, *NARA-CP*.
48. U.S. Embassy-India to Secretary of State, 4 November 1949, RG 59, Box 6082, 845.111/11–11–449, *NARA-CP*.
49. Vijaya Lakshmi Pandit to "Essie Darling," 26 September 1949, Box HT-MH Correspondence, *Eslanda Robeson Papers*.
50. *Freedom*, September 1951.
51. *Freedom*, August 14, 1951.
52. Report, 16–22 November 1950, Reel 8, *Robeson Collection*.
53. Report, 20 November 1950, Reel 9, *Robeson Collection*.
54. Louis Burnham to "Dear John," circa early 1950s, Reel 9, *Robeson Collection*.
55. *Daily Worker*, 23 May 1953.
56. Script for "Concert at the Peace Arch," 18 May 1952, Box 35. See also *Vancouver Sun Province*, 17 August 1953.
57. *Freedom*, March 1952.
58. Robeson, Jr. to Editor, 29 June 1971, Box 40.
59. Charles Ringrose of WMA to Louise Patterson, 2 January 1951, Box 17.
60. Collet's Holdings, London to Othello Recording, Harlem, 12 January 1953, Box 17: Maurice Dobb, the British economist, sat on the Board of Directors of Collet's.
61. Robeson Remarks, 26 October 1951, Reel 8, *Robeson Collection*.
62. *Boston Chronicle*, 6 October 1951.
63. William Pearson to Robeson, 28 September 1951, Box 6.
64. U.S. Consul General-Vancouver to Julian Harrington, 17 February 1947, RG 59, Box 5997, 842.00b/2–2747, *NARA-CP*.
65. Robeson Appeal to Free Hikmet, circa 1950, Box 20.
66. Nazim Hikmet to Robeson, circa 1950, Box H-KA Correspondence.
67. Nazim Hikmet to Robeson, 1949, Box H-KA Correspondence.

68. Robeson Testimony, 29 May 1957, Box 17.

69. *New York Herald Tribune*, 8 November 1951.

70. Lawrence Lamphere, "Paul Robeson: 'Freedom' Newspaper and the Black Press," 2, 6,136, 206: According to the author, a "high percentage of New Yorkers (about half the total)," comprised subscribers and, similarly, there was a "very high percentage of Jewish surnames [sic]" among those.

71. Report, 29 March 1950, RG 59, Box 3583, 745N.001/3–2950, *NARA-CP*.

72. Ethiopian Legation to State Department, 18 September 1949, RG 59, Box 3001, 701.8411/9-1948, *NARA-CP*.

73. Robeson to Secretary of State George Marshall, 19 September 1948, RG 59, Box 3001, 701.8411/9-1948.

74. Stanley Woodward to Robeson, 27 September 1948, RG 59, Box 3001, 701.8411/9-1948.

75. Ethiopian Legation to State Department, 20 September 1948, RG 59, Box 3001.

76. U.S. Legation/Moscow to State Department, 21 September 1948, RG 59, Box 3001.

77. U.S. Consul General-Bombay to State Department, 21 September 1948, RG 59, Box 3001.

78. Ibid.

79. *New York Compass*, 12 June 1950.

80. "The Record of the Council on African Affairs: The Testimony of Africa's Own Progressive Leaders," 29 January 1950, Box 39.

81. *Freedom*, October 1952; Ibid., Lawrence Lamphere, 202.

82. Letters from Walter Sisulu and Ahmad Kathrada, 1954, Box 6.

83. Ruth First to Maude Greene, 14 May 1954, Box 6.

84. *Daily Worker*, 3 and 7 April 1952.

85. "Spotlight on Africa," 14 April 1952, Box 39.

86. *Freedom*, April 1953.

87. Robeson Speech, 21 November 1952, in Ibid., Philip S. Foner, ed., *Paul Robeson Speaks*, 330–3.

88. CAA Release, 13 April 1953, Box 39.

89. Robeson Remarks, 13 April 1953, Box 20.

90. Ms. Robeson to "Emily Dear," 25 December 1950, Box S-Z.

91. Ms. Robeson to Emily, 6 February 1952, Box S-Z.

92. "Minutes of Meeting of National Committee" of PP, 24–25 June 1950, Box 39.

93. Robeson Remarks, 27 October 1952, Reel 8, *Robeson Collection*.

94. Statement by Robeson, 1950, Box 20.

95. Progressive Party Release, 19 August 1950, Reel 8, *Robeson Collection.*
96. Release, 14 March 1950, Box 23.
97. Badge for Founding of National Negro Labor Council, 27–28 October 1951, Box 39.
98. Minutes of "United Freedom Fund," 12 February 1952, Reel 8, *Robeson Collection.*
99. "Spotlight on Africa," 21–23 November 1952, Box 39.
100. *Daily Worker*, 15 April 1951.
101. Stefan Kanfer, *A Journal of the Plague Years*, New York: Atheneum, 1973, 178–81; *Daily Worker*, 23 May 1952.
102. *Daily Worker*, 1 March 1952. On the tie between Robeson and Childress, see Alice Childress to Robeson, 17 March 1952, Box BS-DO Correspondence.
103. *Freedom*, April 1952.
104. Robeson, Address at "Conference for Equal Rights for Negroes in the Arts, Sciences and Professions," 10 November 1951, Box 20.
105. Transcript of Interview with Poitier, 1978, Box 25.
106. Robeson Remarks, circa 1950s, Box 20.
107. Ms. Robeson to James Hicks, 29 January 1952, Box 32.
108. Robeson, "Open Letter to Jackie Robinson," April 1953, Box 20.
109. Testimony of Robeson, 12 June 1956, Box 21.
110. *Freedom*, December 1952.
111. Samuel Walker, *In Defense of American Liberties: A History of the ACLU*, Carbondale: Southern Illinois University Press, 1999, 199–200; I.F. Stone, *The Truman Era*, New York: Monthly Review Press, 1953, 103–104.
112. *Baltimore Afro-American*, 24 May 1952; *Freedom*, June 1952; *Daily Worker*, 21 May 1952.
113. Gerald Horne, *Red Seas*, passim.
114. Ibid., Lawrence Lamphere, 214.
115. Robeson Remarks, 9 July 1954, Box 21.
116. *Freedom*, May 1952.
117. Robeson Remarks, 9 July 1954.
118. CAA Pamphlet, 1952, Box 20.
119. Robeson to "Dear Friends," December 1952, Box 6.
120. Ibid., Lawrence Lamphere, 241.

Chapter 8

1. *Freedom*, March 1954.
2. Remarks by Robeson, 9 July 1954, Box 21.

3. *Baltimore Afro-American*, 12 March 1955.
4. *Baltimore Afro-American*, 8 January 1955.
5. Leonard Boudin to Frances Knight of State Department, 3 October 1955, Box SF-WAL Correspondence.
6. Robeson to Chu Tu-Nan, 1 October 1955, Box SF-WAL Correspondence.
7. *Freedom*, April 1955. See also Robeson message on Bandung, April 1955, Box 21.
8. Brochure, 30 April 1957, Box 38.
9. Robeson to Editor, 11 September 1954, Box PF-SE Correspondence.
10. Robeson Remarks, 1955, Box 21.
11. D. Buckle to "My Dear Paul," 26 May 1957, Box 2.
12. Pablo Neruda to Robeson, 2 July 1955, Box MB-PE Correspondence.
13. Letter from Neruda, 7 July 1958, Box MB-PE.
14. Bulletin of the World Council of Peace, 1 October 1954, Reel 9, *Robeson Collection*.
15. Yusuf Cachalia to Howard Fast, Box 6.
16. Leaflet, circa May 1954, Reel 7, *Robeson Collection*.
17. Letter, 24 May 1954, Box 6.
18. Article, *New Frontiers*, 4 (Number 4, Winter 1955): 16, Box 32.
19. Ms. Robeson to 300th anniversary of Jewish People, New York City, 16 October 1954, Box 3, *Eslanda Robeson Papers*.
20. Paul Robeson, Jr., "How My Father Last Met Itzik Feffer," *Jewish Currents* [New York], (November 1981): 216–21. See also Adam Clayton Powell, Jr., "What Negroes think of Jews," *New Currents*, circa 1947, Box 22.
21. Letter from Maurice Dobb, 14 May 1954, Box 6.
22. Letter from Charles Chaplin, 18 May 1954, Box 6.
23. Robeson to Charles Chaplin, 23 June 1954, Box 2.
24. Letter from Ivor Montagu, 22 May 1954, Box 6.
25. John Williamson, *Dangerous Scot: The Life and Work of an American 'Undesirable'*, New York: International, 213.
26. Robeson to Earl of Harewood, 4 January 1956.
27. "Bert" of Aldridge Society, 6 January 1956, Box BS-DO Correspondence.
28. Robeson to the "Ukrainian People," 15 December 1957, Box 21.
29. Robeson statement, 18 July 1955, Box 21.
30. Bulletin of the World Council of Peace, 15 April 1955, Reel 9, *Robeson Collection*.
31. *Daily Worker*, August 1955, Box 32.
32. *National Guardian*, April 1958, Box 33.
33. Ferdinand Smith to Robeson, 26 July 1958, Box SF-WAL Correspondence.

34. Material on Robeson concert, 1957, Box 23.
35. Robeson Testimony, 29 May 1957, Box 17.
36. *New Statesman*, 24 September 1955, Box 23.
37. Cedric Belfrage to Robeson, 6 October 1956, Box 6.
38. Program, 1956, Box 21.
39. Report on Manchester Conference, 2 December 1956, Box 39.
40. *Manchester Guardian*, 4 May 1957.
41. Letter from Earl Baldwin, 1957, Box 39.
42. Article, *New Frontiers*, 4 (Number 4, Winter 1955): 16.
43. Release, 31 October 1955, Box 23.
44. William Patterson to "Dear Sir," 14 November 1955, Box 23.
45. *New York Times*, 13 June 1956.
46. Interview with Leonard Boudin, circa 1982, Box 33, *Rabinowitz and Boudin Legal Files*, New York University.
47. Cliff Macky to Robeson, 10 May 1956, Box KB-MA Correspondence.
48. Robeson Testimony, 12 June 1956, Box 21.
49. *Milwaukee Journal*, 13 June 1956.
50. Robeson to Leonard Boudin, 17 July 1956, Box 33, *Rabinowitz Boudin Legal Files*.
51. U.S. vs. CAA, 7 October 1954, Reel 7, *Robeson Collection*.
52. Attorney General Herbert Brownell vs. CAA, 20 April 1953, Box 17.
53. Robeson to "Transvaal Peace Congress," 17 April 1951, *Robeson Collection*. See also Editor of "New Age" of Cape Town to Robeson, 14 March 1956, Box DP-G Correspondence.
54. *New York Amsterdam News*, 12 September 1955.
55. William Patterson to John Gray, 25 February 1954, Reel 7, *Robeson Collection*.
56. *New Statesman*, 24 September 1955, Box 23.
57. Report on Radio Broadcast of Hubert Kregeloh on Robeson and "Bricker Amendment," 20 July 1956, Box 23.
58. Robeson to "Dear Friends in Britain," 18 May 1956, Box KB-MA Correspondence.
59. Alice Childress to Robeson, 21 June 1956, Box BS-DO Correspondence.
60. William Z. Foster to Robeson, 27 March circa 1957, Box DP-G Correspondence.
61. William Z. Foster to Robeson, 25 April 1958, Box DP-G.
62. FBI Agent to J. Edgar Hoover, 20 March 1958, Reel 2, *FBI File on Paul Robeson*.
63. *Baltimore Afro-American*, 13 November 1956.

64. George Murphy to the Robesons, 17 November 1956, Box MB-PE Correspondence.
65. *New York World-Telegram*, 14 November 1956.
66. *Sydney Morning Herald*, 13 October 1960.
67. Cedric Belfrage to Robeson, 19 November 1956, Box 4, *Cedric Belfrage Papers*, New York University.
68. John Takman to Cedric Belfrage, 26 September 1957, Box 4, *Belfrage Papers*.
69. *New York Herald Tribune*, 17 August 1955.
70. *New York Herald Tribune*, 8 June 1956.
71. "Motion for Leave to File Brief and Brief 'Amici Curiae'" in U.S. Court of Appeals, "Robeson vs. John Foster Dulles," 27 February 1956, Box 17.
72. Letter to IRS, 1 June 1954, Box 15.
73. Ms. Robeson to "Mr. [Glen Byam] Shaw," 22 February 1958, Box SF-WAL Correspondence.
74. Robeson law firm to Herbert Hagan, 8 November 1956, Box 15.
75. See Tax Returns, 1955–58, Box 15.
76. Bill from Rabinowitz, Boudin firm, 31 January 1957, Box 17.
77. Ben Davis to Robeson, 20 March 1955, Box 2.
78. George Crockett to "Dear Paul," 23 November 1955, Box 2.
79. Richard Arens of HUAC to Milton Friedman, 31 May 1956, Box A-BR Correspondence.
80. Report by Dr. V. McKinley Wiles, 25 May 1956, Box A-BR Correspondence.
81. *New York Amsterdam News*, October 1955, Box 32.
82. Report by Dr. Aaron Wells, 26 May 1956, Box A-BR Correspondence.
83. *Birmingham Post* [U.K.], 7 May 1959.
84. Ms. Robeson to William Longridge, Secretary-Treasurer of Mine, Mill, Smelter Workers, Box KB-MA Correspondence.
85. Cutting, 25 March 1955, Box 32.
86. Howard Fast to Robeson, 16 November 1955, Box DP-G Correspondence.
87. Tribute to Robeson by Lorraine Hansberry, circa 1950s, Box 19–26.
88. *Los Angeles Herald Dispatch*, 25 August 1955.
89. FBI Report, 25 April 1958, Box 9, *Amiri Baraka Papers*, Howard University.
90. Mary Helen Washington, *The Other Blacklist: The African American Literary and Cultural Left of the 1950s*, New York: Columbia University Press, 2014, 256–7.
91. Interview with Carl Rowan, 1957, Box 19–26.
92. Kenzo Nishikawa to Robeson, 23 July 1959, Box MB-PE Correspondence.

93. Frederick Seabrook to *Ebony*, 20 September 1957, Box DP-G Correspondence.

94. Mary Cygan, "Paul Robeson and the Press," 1 June 1973, "Senior Seminar" Paper at Northwestern University, Box 1926.

95. Remarks of Dr. A. Chester Clark, 3 May 1958, Box 33.

96. Mrs. L.C. Bates to Robeson, 24 January 1958, Box A-BR Correspondence.

97. Ms. Robeson to Daisy Bates, 22 February 1958, Box A-BR.

98. Robeson to A. Philip Randolph, 24 September 1955, Box PF-SE Correspondence.

99. Ralph Bunche to "Dear Paul," 14 February 1958, Box BS-DO Correspondence.

100. Archie Moore to Robeson, 26 January 1958, Box MB-PE Correspondence.

101. Ms. Robeson Remarks, October 1957, Box 9, *Eslanda Robeson Papers*.

102. Transcript of Testimony of Ms. Robeson, 7 July 1953, Box 13, *Eslanda Robeson Papers*.

103. Noah Griffin to Robeson, 25 October 1957, Box DP-G Correspondence.

104. *Daily Worker*, 15 August 1957.

105. Ms. Robeson to Helen Riley, 27 May 1958, Box PF-SE Correspondence.

106. Ms. Robeson to Adam Holender, 14 February 1957, Box H-KA Correspondence.

107. FBI Agent to J. Edgar Hoover, 28 June 1958, Reel 2, *FBI File on Paul Robeson*.

108. W.C. Sullivan to A.H. Belmont, 21 June 1958, Reel 2, *FBI File on Paul Robeson*.

109. Robeson Testimony, 29 May 1957, Box 17.

110. Robeson Remarks, 12 September 1957, Box 21.

111. *New Zealand Herald*, 18 October 1960.

112. Memorandum, 6 March 1958, Box 13.

113. Ms. Robeson to Mr. Krishnaswami, 26 March 1958, Box KB-MA Correspondence.

114. Robeson Testimony, 29 May 1957, Box 17.

115. Ms. Robeson to Indira Gandhi, 31 March 1958, Box DJ-HS, *Eslanda Robeson Papers*.

116. Report from New Delhi to Secretary of State, 19 March 1958, RG 59, Box 3896, 791.001/3–1958, *NARA-CP*.

117. *New York Times*, 22 March 1958.

118. *Pittsburgh Courier*, 26 January 1956.

119. Ms. Robeson to Prime Minister Nehru, 31 March 1958, Box MI-R Correspondence, *Eslanda Robeson Papers*.

120. Ms. Robeson to Harry Francis, 1 April 1958, Box DP-G Correspondence.
121. Ms. Robeson to Robeson, 6 March 1958, Box 6, *Eslanda Robeson Papers*.
122. Ms. Robeson to Paul Endicott, 19 June 1958, Box DP-G.
123. Ms. Robeson to Paul Endicott, 15 January 1957, Box DP-G.

Chapter 9

1. Louis Burnham, "Paul Robeson-Where He Stands," *New World Review*, 26 (Number 5, May 1958): 22–24, Box 23.
2. BBC Transcript, 15 June 1960, Box 35.
3. Ms. Robeson, "Paul Robeson: The 'Dear Guest'," 1958–59, Box 14, *Eslanda Robeson Papers*.
4. *Edinburgh Evening Dispatch*, 14 November 1958.
5. Rudolph Dunbar to Robeson, 31 January 1958, Box DP-G Correspondence.
6. Report on Robeson arrival in London, 1958, Box 23.
7. Peggy Middleton to Ms. Robeson, 16 January 1958, Box MI-R Correspondence, *Eslanda Robeson Papers*.
8. Herbert Marshall, "Reminiscences of Paul Robeson," 1957, Box 23.
9. Ms. Robeson to Lloyd Brown, 6 August 1958, Box 3, *Eslanda Robeson Papers*.
10. S. Wales Miners to Robeson, October 1958, Box 40.
11. BBC Transcript, 20 May 1960, Box 35.
12. "Branch News" of "Waterside Workers' Federation" of Sydney, 1960, Box 23.
13. R.R. Roberts to Robeson, 10 April 1973, Box PF-SE Correspondence.
14. *The Star* [U.K.], 16 August 1958.
15. Report, 23 November 1958, Reel 2, *FBI File on Paul Robeson*.
16. *The Witness*, 13 November 1958, Box 23.
17. The Robesons were in Britain for a month beginning in July 1958, then it was on to the Soviet Union for a month, then back to Britain for three and a half months. He was in the Soviet Union from late December 1958 to the first week of March in 1959, when he was hospitalized. Then it was back to Britain for three months, then to Prague for two days and to Britain for almost two months; then it was to Austria for three days and Britain for 16, Romania for four, Britain for ten days. There followed a day in France, then to Britain again for three and a half months and the Soviet Union for three weeks. From early February 1960 to the middle of that year he was in Britain; then he spent two days in Germany, before returning to Britain once more for two weeks. Then it was four days in France, three months in Britain, a week in Budapest. Three weeks in Britain followed,

then two more days in Germany. The end of 1960 found him in Australia and New Zealand for two months. Then there were three more months in Britain. He was hospitalized again in the Soviet Union for three months in 1960. Then there were two more weeks in Britain and then further hospitalization in the Soviet Union for three weeks. He then returned to Britain by September 1961 where he was to be found ill in a nursing home. See Ms. Robeson report on travel, no date, Box 6.

18. Nnamdi Azikiwe to Robeson, 23 August 1958, Box A-BR Correspondence.
19. Nnamdi Azikiwe to Ms. Robeson, 26 October 1960, Box A-BR.
20. U.S. Consul General-Lagos to State Department, 30 July 1958,RG 59, Box 121, 032robeson, paul, *NARA-CP*.
21. *West Indian Gazette*, July 1959, Box 40.
22. FBI Agent to J. Edgar Hoover, 26 October 1958, Reel 2.
23. Ms. Robeson to Mikhail Kotov, 15 December 1960, Box 4, *Eslanda Robeson Papers*.
24. *Baltimore Afro-American*, 22 February 1958.
25. *Pittsburgh Courier*, 22 February 1958 and 29 March 1958.
26. *The Crisis*, March 1958.
27. FBI Agent, New York to J. Edgar Hoover, 15 January 1958, Reel 2, *FBI File on Paul Robeson*.
28. London *Times*, 14 August 1958.
29. Lloyd Brown, Review of "Here I Stand," circa 1968, Box 22. The Gillespie quote can be found here.
30. Akira Iwasaki to Mrs. Middleton, 26 August 1958, Box 4, *Eslanda Robeson Papers*.
31. Financial Report, 31 May 1958, Box 17.
32. Ms. Robeson to George Bernard Shaw, 15 November 1957, Box SF-WAL Correspondence.
33. Newsletter, July 1959, Box 23.
34. Press Release, 1959, Box 23.
35. Laurence Olivier to Peggy Middleton, 2 August 1957, Box 4, *Cedric Belfrage Papers*.
36. Itinerary, July 1959, Box 39.
37. Ms. Robeson to George Bernard Shaw, 20 January 1959, Box SF-WAL Correspondence.
38. *San Francisco Chronicle*, 5 February 1958.
39. U.S. Consul General-Edinburgh to State Department, 18 November 1958, RG 59, Box 121, 032 robeson, paul, *NARA-CP*.
40. *Melbourne Age*, 16 November 1960.
41. *Edinburgh Evening Dispatch*, 14 November 1958.

42. *Lancashire Evening Post*, 20 April 1960.
43. *The Scotsman*, 23 September 1958.
44. Herman T. Skofield to State Department, 9 December 1958, RG 59, Box 121, 032 robeson, paul. *NARA-CP*.
45. Parker Hart to Acting Secretary, 11 December 1958, RG 59, Box 121, 032 robeson, paul.
46. "Memorandum of Conversation," 24 December 1958, RG 59, Box 121.
47. Harold Davison to Robert Rockmore, 10 November 1958, Box 15.
48. Robert Rockmore to Ms. Robeson, 5 December 1958, Box 15.
49. Robert Rockmore to Harold Davison, 16 December 1958, Box 15.
50. Harold Davison to Robert Rockmore, 22 January 1959, Box 15.
51. "Motion for Decision" in U.S. Tax Court on "no deficiency in income tax due from or overpayment due," 4 February 1959 plus Tax Return of 1959, Box 15.
52. Ms. Robeson to "Fredie Dear," 8 February 1959, Box 3, *Eslanda Robeson Papers*.
53. Robert Rockmore to Robeson, 5 January 1960, Box 15.
54. Letter to Robeson, 26 November 1961, Box A-BR Correspondence.
55. *Melbourne Guardian*, 1960, Box 34.
56. Rockmore to Robeson, 6 December 1960, Box 15.
57. Ms. Robeson to "Bobby Dear," 8 January 1960, Box 15.
58. Paul Hoylen, U.S. Consul-London to Robeson, 8 January 1960, Box 15.
59. Robert Rockmore to Robeson, 17 March 1960, Box 15.
60. Rockmore to Robeson, 8 April 1960, Box 15.
61. Harold Davison to Robert Rockmore, 31 March 1960, Box 15.
62. Rockmore to Robeson, 29 April 1960, Box 15.
63. Rockmore to Harold Davison, 4 May 1960, Box 15.
64. Harold Davison to Rockmore, 10 May 1960, Box 15.
65. Harold Davison to Rockmore, 28 June 1960, Box 15.
66. Cutting, 17 September 1959, Box 23.
67. Rockmore to Davison, 20 September 1960, Box 15.
68. Ben Davis to Rockmore, 28 February 1960, Box 15.
69. Marilyn Robeson to Rockmore, 29 September 1960, Box 15.
70. Rockmore to Davison, 28 September 1960, Box 15.
71. Rockmore to Robeson, 11 January 1961, Box 15.
72. Rockmore to Robeson, 6 December 1960, Box 15.
73. Report, 25 November 1960, Reel 2, *FBI File on Paul Robeson*.
74. Cheddi Jagan to Robeson, 14 June 1961, Box H-KA Correspondence.
75. Report to J. Edgar Hoover, 17 May 1961, Reel 2, *FBI File on Paul Robeson*.
76. Report, May 1958, Reel 1, *FBI File on Paul Robeson*.

77. Letter from Elizabeth Catlett, circa 1960, Box MB-PE Correspondence.

78. Gavin Greenlee to Robeson, 11 April 1963, Box DP-G Correspondence.

79. Card from Nehru, circa 1961, Box MB-PE Correspondence. See also Ms. Robeson to "Dear Jawaharlal," 19 September 1962, Box HT-MH Correspondence.

80. FBI Agent to J. Edgar Hoover, 24 March 1958; attached editorial from *New York Mirror,* 22 March 1958; Reel 2, *FBI File on Paul Robeson.*

81. K.P. S. Menon to Ms. Robeson, 12 January 1959, Box HT-MH, *Eslanda Robeson Papers.*

82. E. Tomlin Baley to J. Edgar Hoover, 27 March 1958, Reel 2, *FBI File on Paul Robeson.*

83. Robeson, "The Negro People and the Soviet Union," 1950, Box 20.

84. Peggy Middleton to Ms. Robeson, 19 January 1958, Box MI-R, *Eslanda Robeson Papers.*

85. Colin Sweet to Ms. Robeson, 23 September 1963, Box S-Z, *Eslanda Robeson Papers.*

86. Ms. Robeson to "Bobby Dear," 16 January 1960, Box 15.

87. Ms. Robeson to "Dear Bobby and Beautiful," 5 August 1960, Box 15.

88. Ms. Robeson to Rockmore, 9 September 1960, Box 15.

89. See www.bbc.co.uk/programmes/p009y8oh for his choice of discs. Accessed 10 October 2015.

90. BBC Transcript, 15 June 1960, Box 35.

91. BBC Transcript, 13 August 1960, Box 35.

92. BBC Transcript, 20 May 1960, Box 35.

93. Ms. Robeson to Betty Bateman, 7 November 1961, Box 3, *Eslanda Robeson Papers.*

94. Ms. Robeson to Mikhail Kotov, 15 December 1960, Box 4. See also Itinerary, October–November 1960, Box 39.

95. J.E. Anderson, Secretary of Operative Painters and Decorators Union of Australia-Sydney to Robeson, 19 November 1960, Box A-BR Correspondence. See also Gordon Bryant, MP-Australia, to Robeson, 27 November 1960, Box A-BR: "I have concerned myself with the plight of the Australian aborigine ....you may be able to help us..."

96. *Sydney Sunday Mirror,* 13 November 1960. Box 46.

97. *Brisbane Sunday Truth,* 16 October 1960, Box 46.

98. Ms. Robeson to "Fredie Dear," 13 November 1960, Box 3, *Eslanda Robeson Papers.*

99. Ms. Robeson to Rockmore, 17 February 1961, Box 15.

100. Cutting, 14 October 1960, Box 46.

101. Kwame Nkrumah to the Robesons, 29 July 1960, Box MB-PE Correspondence.

102. Ms. Robeson to Fredie Dear, 25 March 1961, Box 3, *Eslanda Robeson Papers.*

103. Harry Francis to "New Statesman," 2 September 1963, Box DP-G Correspondence.

104. Robeson, Jr., "The Paul Robeson Files," *The Nation*, 20 December 1999, Box 10, *Henry Foner Papers*. For an elaboration of this provocative thesis, see e.g. Paul Robeson, Jr., *The Undiscovered Paul Robeson: Quest for Freedom, 1939–1976*, New York: Wiley, 2010, 308–29. As suggested by the preceding volume, Paul Robeson, Jr. had a complicated relationship with both of his parents and seemed to be unnecessarily critical of his mother: see also Paul Robeson, Jr., *The Undiscovered Paul Robeson: An Artist's Journey, 1898–1939*, New York: Wiley, 2001. See also *Daily Worker*, 25 October 1979: "Was FBI Involved in Plot to kill Robeson?" See Dr. Brian Ackner, London to Dr. Morris Pearlmutter, New York City, "confidential," 9 January 1964, Box 0: "I have always taken the view that Mr. Robeson was suffering from one of those somewhat rare chronic depressions which fail to respond to any therapy or continue to relapse but which in the long run have a good prognosis." After sifting through the evidence presenting opposing viewpoints on Robeson's health, my own view is close to that of Dr. Ackner.

105. Interview with Boudin, 1982, Box 33, *Rabinowitz and Boudin Legal Files.*

106. Ms. Robeson to "Peggy Dear," 17 August 1961, Box MB-PE Correspondence.

107. Ms. Robeson to Rockmore, 17 February 1961, Box 15.

108. Article by Lloyd Brown, 1976, Box 19–26.

109. Ms. Robeson to Freda Diamond, 9 May 1961, Box 3, *Eslanda Robeson Papers.*

110. Ms. Robeson to Freda Diamond, 26 October 1962, Box 3.

111. Ms. Robeson to Rockmore, 5 May 1961, Box 15.

112. W.A. Hunton to Robesons, 23 May 1960, Box H-KA Correspondence.

113. W.A. Hunton to Robesons, 7 August 1960, Box H-KA Correspondence.

114. W.A. Hunton to Robesons, 14 May 1962.

115. John Abt to Robesons, 26 November 1961, Box 2.

116. W.E.B. Du Bois to Robeson, 25 July 1961, Box DP-G Correspondence.

117. Ms. Robeson to "Pauli and Marilyn," 7 October 1961, Box 6.

118. Ms. Robeson to "Hi Dolls!," 30 October 1961, Box 6, *Eslanda Robeson Papers.*

119. Nkrumah to Ms. Robeson, 7 June 1960, Box MB-PE Correspondence.
120. Nkrumah to Ms. Robeson, 10 May 1961, Box MB-PE Correspondence.
121. Ms. Robeson to Kwame Nkrumah, 24 May 1962, Box MB-PE Correspondence.
122. Ms. Robeson to Ralph Bunche, 25 August 1962, Box 2.
123. Ms. Robeson to Ben Davis and John Abt, 13 July 1962, Box A-BR Correspondence.
124. Cutting, 16 September 1960, Box 23.
125. Ms. Robeson to Janet Jagan, 13 April 1962, Box H-KA Correspondence.
126. Anna Louise Strong to Robeson, 7 April 1962, Box SF-WAL Correspondence.
127. Letter from Nkrumah, 10 August 1960, Box HT-MH, *Eslanda Robeson Papers*.
128. Ms. Robeson to Thomas Hodgkin, 17 February 1963, Box H-KA Correspondence.

Chapter 10

1. Certificate of Death, 1965, Box 7.
2. Ms. Robeson to Harold Davison, 2 October 1965, Box 16.
3. Ms. Robeson to Alan Rinzler, 18 June 1965, Box 15.
4. Funeral Program of Lorraine Hansberry, 16 January 1965, Box 38: Honorary pallbearers included Ossie Davis, Sammy Davis, Jr., Dick Gregory, Clarence Jones, John Oliver Killens, Rita Moreno, Diana Sands and Dore Schary.
5. Interview with Robeson, 1964, Box 19–26. (Comment on Robeson in preceding paragraph from Interviewer.)
6. Jordan Goodman, *Paul Robeson: A Watched Man*, 112.
7. Earl Robinson to Robeson, 9 October 1966, Box PF-SE Correspondence.
8. James Forman to Robeson, 4 April 1966, Box DP-G Correspondence.
9. Joan Baez to James Herndon, 25 May 1965, Box 40.
10. Joan Baez to Harry Belafonte, 9 April 1973.
11. New York Urban League News, 5 September 1972, Box 40.
12. Congressman Charles Rangel, et.al. to Robeson, September 1975, Box 40.
13. Chief Justice Warren Burger to Robeson, 18 April 1973, Box 8. Earlier Assistant Attorney General Burger stressed the "security aspects" of the Robeson passport denial: See Warren Burger to J.Edgar Hoover, 2 April 1956, Reel 2, *FBI File on Paul Robeson*.
14. Arthur Ashe to "Brother Robeson," 1973, Box 8.
15. Cesar Chavez to Harry Belafonte, 13 April 1973, Box 8.

16. Andrew Young to Robeson, 17 April 1973, Box WAM-Z.
17. Coleman Young to Ossie Davis, 6 April 1965, Box WAM-Z.
18. *Washington Post*, January 1964, Box 34.
19. David Susskind to Freedomways, 2 April 1965, Box WAM-Z and others.
20. Article, 29 April 1965, Box 19–26.
21. Michael Eric Dyson, *Making Malcolm: The Myth and Meaning of Malcolm X*, New York: Oxford University Press, 1995, 34.
22. Lloyd L. Brown, *The Young Paul Robeson: 'On My Journey Now'*, Boulder: Westview, 1997, 143.
23. Barbara Ransby, *Ella Baker & the Black Freedom Movement: A Radical Democratic Vision*, Chapel Hill: University of North Carolina Press, 2003, 57.
24. W.J. Weathersby, *James Baldwin: Artist on Fire*, New York: Donald Fine, 1989, 328.
25. Ibid., Mary Cygan, "Paul Robeson and the Press," 1 June 1973, "Senior Seminar" paper, Northwestern University, Box 19–26.
26. Julius Silverman to 'Freedomways,' 3 April 1965, Box SF-WAL Correspondence.
27. Message from W.A. Hunton, April 1965, Box H-KA Correspondence.
28. Letter from Kenneth Kaunda, 15 April 1973, Box 8.
29. Letter from Julius K. Nyerere, 21 March 1973, Box 8.
30. Letter from Anatoly Dobrynin, 12 April 1973, Box 8.
31. P.M. Gandhi to Robeson, Jr., 12 March 1973, Box 8.
32. 70th Birthday Celebration, 8 April 1968, Box 40.
33. Errol Barrow to Robeson, 1973, Box 8.
34. Letter from Michael Manley, 22 March 1973, Box 8.
35. Tax Returns, 1960s, Box 16.
36. Marian Forsythe to Lee Laurie, 7 November 1966, Box 16.
37. Lloyd Brown to Lee Laurie, 25 September 1969, Box 16.
38. Robeson, Jr. to Alan Walker, 6 June 1974, Box SF-WAL Correspondence.
39. *Jet*, 11 April 1974, Box 1.
40. Paul Robeson, Jr., *The Undiscovered Paul Robeson: Quest for Freedom, 1939–1976*, 370.
41. *New York Times*, 4 February 1976.
42. Carl Lawrence to Robeson, Jr., 27 January 1976, Box 11.
43. Wallace Muhammad to Robeson, Jr., 26 January 1976, Box 11.

Index

Robeson, Paul Jr. (son)
  birth of 36
  learns of PR's death 145
  PR relocates near to 190, 191
  on PR's suicide attempt 186
  in Soviet Union 59–60
Robeson, William D. (father) 10–11,
  15
Robinson, Earl 108
Robinson, Jackie 117, 140, 191–2
Rockmore, Robert 177–80
Rogers, Alex 22
Rogers, J.A. 23, 34, 115, 127
Roosevelt, Eleanor 81–2, 103, 137
Rosen, Samuel 15, 109
Rowan, Carl 160
Russia. *See* Soviet Union
Russian language 53, 54–5, 59, 60,
  61, 62, 125
Rutgers University 13–16, 17, 36

Sanders of the River 65–6, 68, 81
Saturday Review 25
Savoy Hotel 38, 40
Schevchenko, Taras 148
School of Oriental and African
  Studies (SOAS) 51
schools and colleges
  honorary degrees 90, 195
  PR at
    Columbia Law School 16–18,
      19, 22
    elementary and high school 11,
      12–13
    Rutgers University 13–16, 17
    SOAS 51
  segregation in 11, 13, 15, 161
  violence in 14–15, 161
Schuyler, George 115
Scotland 8, 9, 63, 77, 132–3, 175
Scottsboro case 41–2, 49, 64

Seeger, Pete 5, 193
segregation
  at concerts and plays 38, 84–5,
    107
  foreign diplomats subjected to
    134–5
  in hotels and restaurants 21–2, 30,
    38, 40
  repeal of Jim Crow laws 142–3
  in schools and colleges 11, 13, 15,
    161
Seton, Marie 56, 57, 58, 64, 71
Shakespeare, William 12, 16
Showboat 33–5, 66, 69
Sisulu, Walter 135, 136, 146
Smith, Ferdinand 76, 103, 109, 141,
  149
socialism 4–5, 7, 62
Song of the Rivers 145
South Africa
  PR's anti-apartheid stance 108–9,
    136, 142, 170
  support for PR in 135–6, 146
South America, popularity in 2, 146,
  180–1
Southern Negro Youth Congress 85
Soviet Union
  affection for 59, 62, 72, 174
  concerts in 28–9, 169
  Hungarian invasion 154–6
  popularity in 61, 62, 170, 180, 194
  racism, purported lack of in 4, 60,
    105, 112, 125
  Russian language skills 53, 54–5,
    59, 60, 61, 62, 125
  visits to 59–64, 71, 170, 178,
    186–8
Spain 4, 74–6
Spanish, fluency in 14, 54
speeches
  on Africa (1952) 136

Wales 33, 79–80, 164, 169–70
  film on Welsh miners (*Proud Valley*) 9, 67, 79
Wallace, Henry A. 96–7, 114, 133, 152
Walls, William 141
wars (anti-Communist), rejects Negro support for 114–15, 116, 126, 143–4, 155, 220–1n81
Washington and Lee University 15
Waugh, Alex 65–6
Waugh, Evelyn 37
West African Student Union 51, 72
West Indian Gazette 171
Whale, James 66
White, Walter 29–30, 87, 115, 129, 159

Williamson, John 147
Wilson, Woodrow 11
Winston, Henry 119
Woollcott, Alexander 53–4
Wright, Richard 71, 84, 88, 96
writing and publishing 108–9, 125, 133–4, 172
  Freedom newspaper 131, 134, 135, 138, 142, 190

Yakuts people 7
Yergan, Max 73, 110–11, 115
Yiddish language 54, 93–4
Young, Andrew 193
Young, Coleman 106, 137, 193
Young Communist League 85